MW01707586

Structure and Form

Elementary Science Activity Series

High/Scope Elementary Curriculum Materials

Elementary Curriculum Guides

Foundations in Elementary Education: Movement
Foundations in Elementary Education: Music
Foundations in Elementary Education: Overview
Language & Literacy
Learning Environment
Mathematics
Science

Elementary Curriculum Videotapes

Active Learning
Classroom Environment
Language & Literacy
Mathematics

Related Movement and Music Materials

Teaching Movement & Dance: A Sequential Approach to Rhythmic Movement, Third Edition
Round the Circle: Key Experiences in Movement for Children
Movement Plus Music: Activities for Children Ages 3 to 7, Second Edition
Movement Plus Rhymes, Songs, & Singing Games
Movement in Steady Beat
Rhythmically Moving 1–9 (records, cassettes, CDs)
Changing Directions 1–6 (records, cassettes, CDs)
Foundations in Elementary Education: Music Recordings (cassettes, CDs)
Rhythmically Walking (cassettes)
Guide to Rhythmically Moving 1
Guide to Rhythmically Moving 2

Related High/Scope Press Publications

A School Administrator's Guide to Early Childhood Programs
High/Scope Buyer's Guide to Children's Software, Eleventh Edition
Young Children & Computers
Learning Through Construction
Learning Through Sewing and Pattern Design

Available from
HIGH/SCOPE PRESS
600 North River Street, Ypsilanti, Michigan 48198-2898
ORDERS: Phone (800) 40-PRESS Fax (800) 442-4FAX

FRANK F. BLACKWELL

Structure and Form

Elementary Science Activity Series

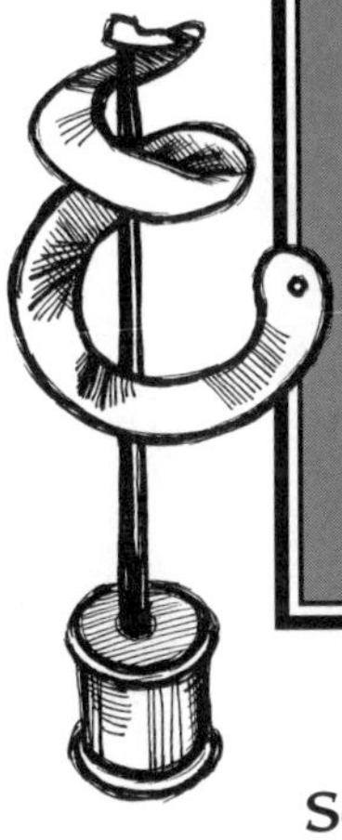

Series Consultant: ANN S. EPSTEIN

HIGH/SCOPE PRESS
YPSILANTI, MICHIGAN

Published by
HIGH/SCOPE® PRESS

A division of
High/Scope Educational Research Foundation
600 North River Street
Ypsilanti, Michigan 48198-2898
313/485-2000, Fax 313/485-0704

Editor: Marcia LaBrenz
Cover and Text Design: Linda Eckel
Illustrations: Lily Taylor

Library of Congress Cataloging-in-Publication Data

Blackwell, Frank.
Elementary science activity series / by Frank Blackwell.
p. cm.
Includes index.
Contents: 2. Structure and form.
ISBN 1-57379-010-9 (v. 2)
1. Science—Study and teaching (Elementary)—United States—Activity programs. I. Title.
LB 1585.3.B53 1996
372.3'5—dc20 96-6806
CIP

Printed in the United States of America

10 9 8 7 6 5 4 3 2 1

TO MARY

In memory of her constant encouragement and support

Contents

List of Illustrations

Appendix I: Teaching Aids

Acknowledgments

The author would like to thank Mr. Charles Wallgren, Executive Vice President, High/Scope Educational Research Foundation, for his encouragement and support, and Dr. Ann Epstein, Senior Research Associate, for her insightful help throughout the production of the manuscripts. Thanks also to the High/Scope Press editorial staff for their work in seeing the books through the production process.

► *Overview of the* Elementary Science Activity Series

The Process of Science in Elementary Education

Science, in the context of education, is a way of thinking and working in the pursuit of answers to problems about the world in which we live. For children, this pursuit is most often about their immediate concerns, either in material or experiential terms, or both. In fact, hands-on experience is the vehicle for science education in the elementary stage. Throughout their daily lives, children have experiences—often first-time experiences—that reflect their environment and their contacts with it. Children's experiences can, and frequently do, bring into sharp focus even the smallest components of the world around them. This revelation process is as random as it is fortuitous. In addition to these relatively unpredictable sources of children's insights, there also will be opportunities for learning that the teacher deliberately creates for children. These opportunities can be loosely structured, as on a field trip, or more precisely arranged, as in a planned classroom activity.

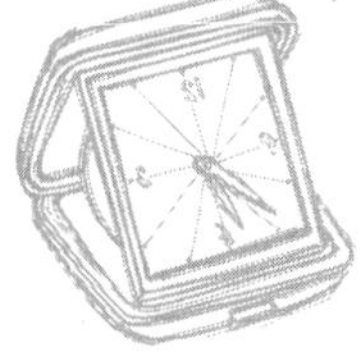

Whatever the source of these experiences, however, the insights gained will remain as diffuse and unrelated items of knowledge unless the teacher helps children to see the patterns in these fragments. This process—building knowledge from individual observations and insights—is what defines science. With proper guidance and encouragement from the teacher, children in the elementary grades will see how different elements can be fitted together to illuminate their knowledge of, and understanding about, the world in which they live.

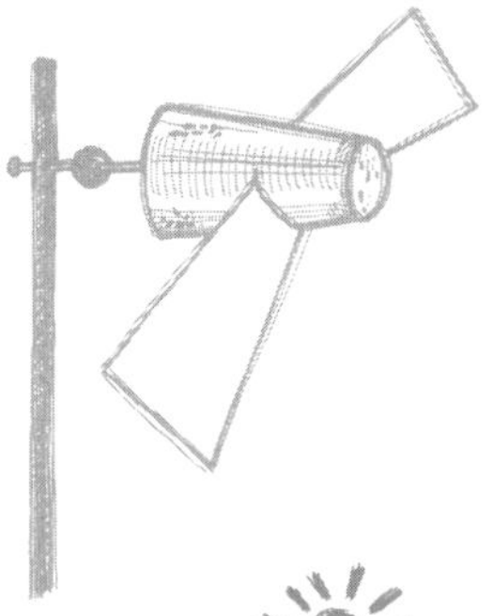

Developing a Contemporary Approach to Science Education

Science in education first appeared as a body of knowledge about certain phenomena, or as studies of the structure and form of materials. Using this base, the early science curriculum emphasized the teaching of three general content areas: *physics* was associated with heat, light and sound, and electricity and magnetism; *chemistry* focused on the analysis of substances and on transformations and changes; and *biology* was mainly a descriptive science, concerned with dissection, classification, and identification. This view of science continued until the middle 1950s and early 1960s, when it was largely put aside in favor of a new view of science as a process. Instead of being built around content, science education now began to emphasize learning through an active discovery process, in which children gained firsthand experiences of many aspects of the world. The tidy content boxes of the past were set aside.

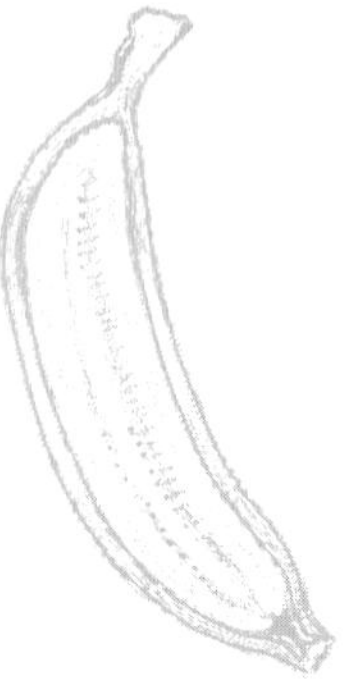

One consequence of these changes for the nonspecialist, however, was a growing sense of bewilderment concerning science. The subject seemed to have little pattern or coherence and rapidly became a fragmented set of experiences. Educators felt they had lost their basis for planning and structuring the science component of the classroom curriculum. On the one hand, they were able to recognize that this new process approach to science was appropriate; children worked on a discovery basis quite naturally. On the other hand, teachers needed some new headings under which the vast array of science knowledge could be organized and made meaningful. Furthermore, the entire discovery process required a broader framework that would relate all elementary learning experiences to the development of thinking skills. In other words, as children developed their observational and analytical skills, teachers needed a sense of when children were in fact acting as true scientists intent on discovering the complexities of their environment.

The High/Scope approach to education is especially suited to giving reality to the teacher's function of "putting children's work into a meaningful relationship with science activities." Posing questions, providing materials and activities, and encouraging a discover-for-yourself approach are essential attributes of the High/Scope classroom, of science education in general, and of the scientific method itself. The High/Scope curriculum for elementary education provides teachers with both a general framework for understanding how children learn and with a specific framework for understanding the role of science education in children's development. With the High/Scope Elementary Curriculum as a reference point, teachers can see how each specific activity contributes to the overall goals of science education and to the general development of children's thinking skills. To be most useful, the High/Scope elementary science curriculum should be

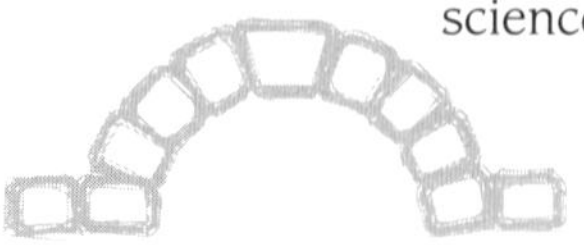

1. Generic in content—exploring broad areas of investigation rather than isolated topics
2. Open in its interpretation—allowing students to observe and analyze what they see instead of internalizing the teacher's explanation
3. Nonprescriptive in its age-related demands—relating activities to children's developmental levels rather than to their specific age

This series of elementary science books presents a wealth of ideas for science activities for the elementary school teacher. Each book in the series serves as a detailed starting point for various classroom activities. Eventually, drawing on their basic understanding of the High/Scope approach and the lessons they have learned from implementing the activities in these books, teachers will be able to develop their own ideas and to enrich the course of science education for their students and themselves.

The High/Scope Approach to Science Education

A guiding principle of the High/Scope Curriculum is the belief that young children are capable of making decisions and solving problems about activities that are interesting to them. Teachers use these individual interests as the springboard for teaching the social and academic concepts that children need to be successful in our society. Another central tenet of the High/Scope approach is the idea of "developmental validity"—the belief that children develop in predictable sequences, that there are

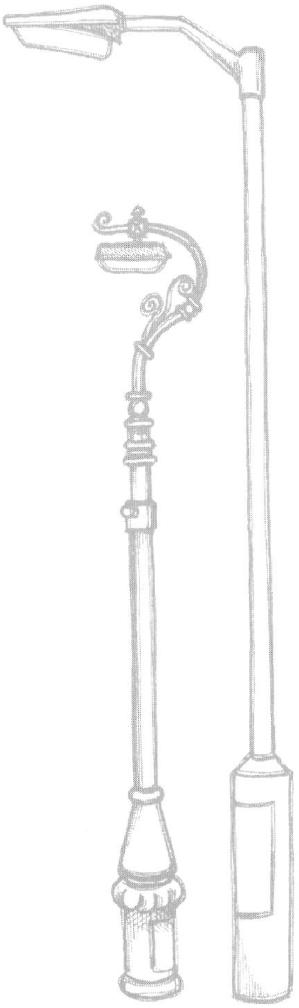

optimal times for particular kinds of learning, and that there are teaching methods that are more appropriate at certain times in the developmental sequence than others.

High/Scope's developmental perspective on science learning means that the emphasis is on **stages, not ages.** Children in any one grade level will be at various stages of development; additionally, some children will be at more than one stage in different aspects of science work. Although children progress through the stages in the same general sequence, the rate of progress varies from child to child. Some children will remain at the early stages longer than others; some may never achieve the later stages.

Based on research and knowledge of the developmental patterns typical of how children learn, the High/Scope educational approach has made **active learning** its cornerstone. "Active learning" is learning initiated by the child rather than information handed down or transmitted by the teacher. An activity involves active learning if it includes the following five ingredients:

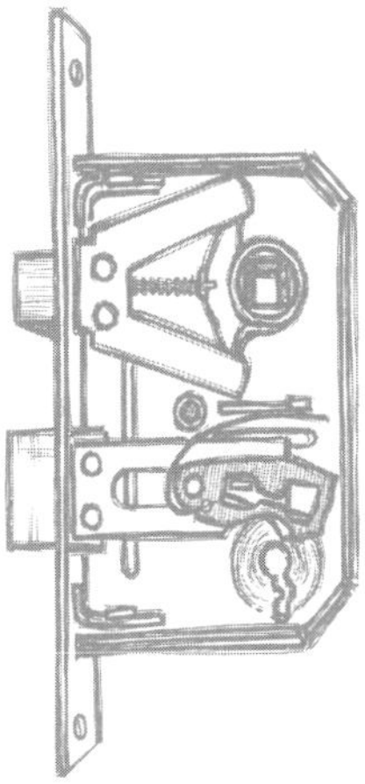

- *Materials.* A variety of interesting materials are readily accessible to children.
- *Manipulation.* Children are free to handle, explore, and work with the materials.
- *Choice.* Children have opportunities to set their own goals and to select materials and activities.
- *Language from the children.* Children talk about what they are doing and what they have done.
- *Support from adults.* Adults encourage children's efforts and help them extend or build upon their work by talking with them about what they are doing, by asking open-ended questions, by joining them in their activities, and by helping them solve problems that arise.

The High/Scope Curriculum therefore advocates an activity-based science curriculum that stresses active-learning experiences—experiences such as making collections; conducting surveys; building and modifying structures; and representing such experiences in pictures, graphs, and writing. In the High/Scope Elementary Curriculum, teachers are encouraged to provide a **classroom environment that is rich in materials for children's hands-on activities.** The classroom environment and teaching approach are designed to stimulate exploring, discovering, comparing, combining, constructing, and representing activities that are the external reflections of the child's inward construction of knowledge.

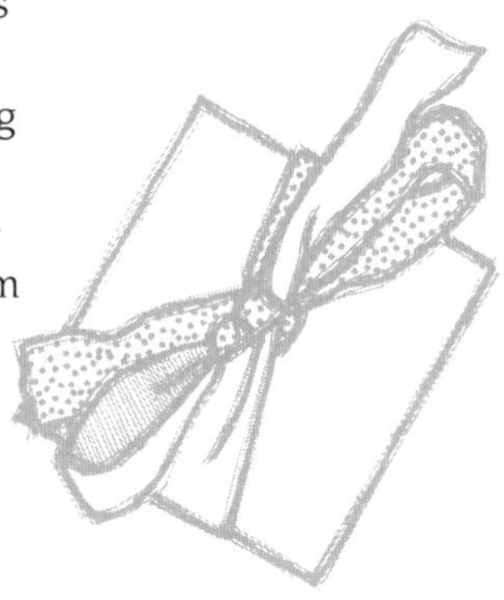

Science starts with careful observations and with the use of logical thinking skills to organize and interpret these observations. Science is both a spontaneous and a planned activity, one that depends not only on careful measurement and systematic experimentation but also on the readiness to learn from trial and error, from guesswork, and from serendipity. As emphasized throughout this overview, these basic science processes are simply extensions of children's natural inclination to learn about the world through direct observation and manipulation of materials.

While children engage in this active process, the role of the teacher is to help focus the child's efforts to answer questions and solve problems. In order to make science an active process, the teacher uses **six groups of key experiences for science learning.** "Key experiences" are broadly defined activities and processes that use the important intellectual, social, and physical abilities emerging in children throughout the elementary school years. The six science key experiences describe scientific activity as it is experienced by the children themselves as they observe, experiment, and create explanations for what they see and do.

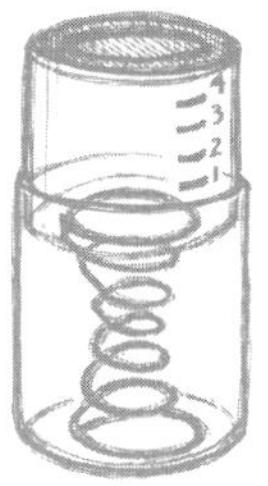

The six groups of key experiences in the High/Scope Elementary Curriculum are as follows:

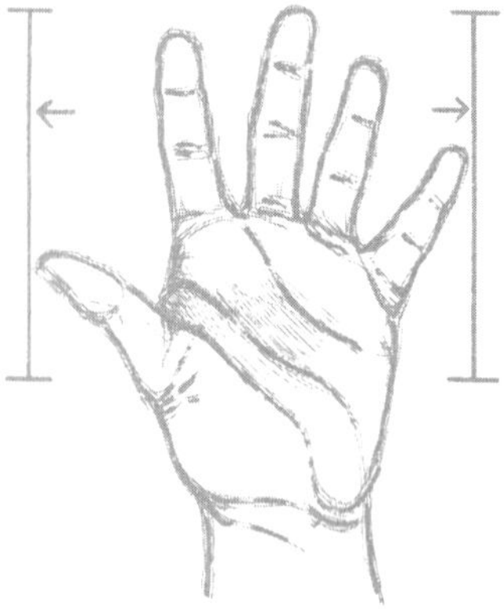

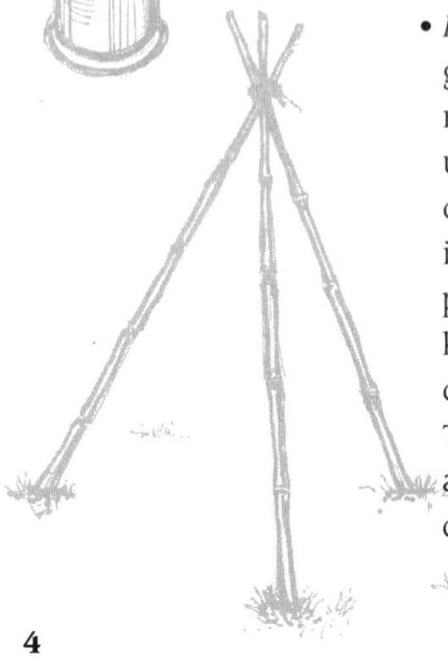

- *Looking with a purpose: observing and collecting data.* This group of key experiences includes the activity most basic to science: looking with a purpose or a plan in mind. All other science activity is an elaboration on this basic theme. When children observe, they are not passively recording their impressions as a camera or tape recorder does. Rather, their observing is a process of reconstruction and interpretation guided by their active minds—they literally see, hear, feel, smell, and taste what they are looking for. Because observation is such an active process, the capacity to observe develops as the thinking abilities of children mature and develop. Thus, although looking with a purpose is a key experience appropriate to all ages, developing capacities in this area will change the nature and extent of knowledge gained and created in this process.

- *Classifying and ordering materials according to their attributes and properties.* This group of key experiences describes children's use of logical thinking skills to organize observations and findings into meaningful groups. The processes of classifying and ordering are fundamental to science. When children notice attributes or structural patterns in living and nonliving materials and then group or order these materials accordingly, they are developing a better understanding of the relationships among materials, organisms, and events in their environment.

- *Measuring, testing, and analyzing: assessing the properties and composition of materials.* In this group of key experiences, children use systematic procedures to make their senses more acute and their observations more precise. These related procedures enable children to quantify the properties and attributes of objects and materials, to express similarities and differences in numeric terms, and to describe cause-effect relationships quantitatively. As they use these basic techniques, children gain a deeper understanding not only of the materials they are examining, but also of the importance of careful assessment.

- *Observing, predicting, and controlling change: understanding causality.* While the previous groups of key experiences mainly involve ways of measuring materials systematically, this group focuses on causes. Here again, children are organizing and interpreting their observations, but the focus is on interaction and change rather than fixed attributes. As children notice and describe sequences of events in the world, they begin to notice regular patterns of change. This leads them to the heart of scientific inquiry: the effort to explain the causes behind the phenomena of nature.

- *Designing, building, fabricating, and modifying structures or materials.* In this group of key experiences, children apply scientific knowledge as they solve real-life problems. Working in this practical vein, children develop their understanding of fundamental physicai causes. The building projects that children undertake can range from the simple to the complex, and can include projects of the teacher's design as well as inventions that are completely child-initiated. As they work through the processes in this group of key experiences, children begin to learn the reasons for observable changes in the position, motion, shape, and size of objects and materials. They begin to understand how objects interact by pushing, pulling, holding, and bumping one another, and they begin to see how they can exert some control over these events by manipulating the factors involved.

- *Reporting and interpreting data and results.* In this group of key experiences, children use language, pictures, and mathematical symbols to represent, and thus communicate, their observations and findings. Representation serves the practical and essential scientific function of sharing results with others. Engaging in this recording process also helps children sharpen their observations and clarify their thinking.

Taken together with the content themes and activities in this series of elementary science books, the key experiences provide a process-oriented framework that teachers can use to focus children's science learning. Keeping the key experiences in mind helps the teacher recognize and build on the valuable scientific activity children engage in spontaneously as they explore the world.

Three Major Curriculum Areas in Science Education

The following three curriculum areas contain the principal elements needed to develop an approach to science education: **life and environment, structure and form,** and **energy and change.** These three areas, which correspond to the three books in the High/Scope elementary science series, provide a framework for embracing all of the major themes of science. They also provide a framework for organizing the diverse opportunities for science work that will arise in any classroom. With an insight into some of the ideas associated with these generic headings, teachers can determine what science is about in the context of their own work in the classroom. Furthermore, this broad framework should help teachers put children's science work into a more meaningful relationship with other educational activities throughout the curriculum.

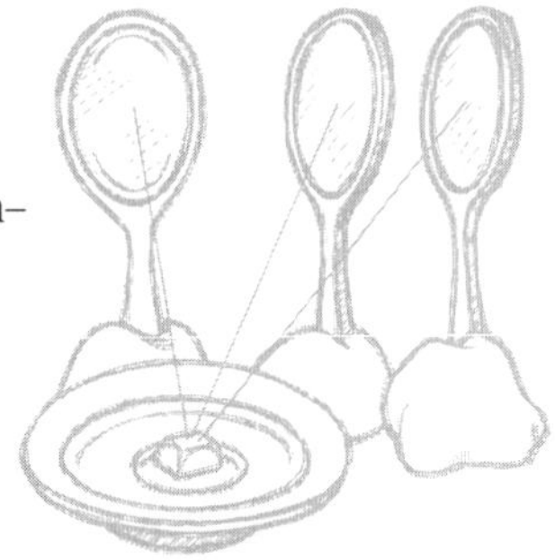

The lists that follow describe the specific subthemes included within each of the three main curriculum areas in the High/Scope elementary science books. These should not be viewed as definitive lists but rather as working ones that can be changed by teachers to suit their specific circumstances and the children's emerging interests. An advantage of using a broad, thematically based list is its compatibility with a wide range of other currently available print and audiovisual science education material. These additional resources can be used to supplement and enrich the activities described in the High/Scope elementary science series. As these themes and activities are used in the elementary school classroom, however, teachers should always keep in mind the High/Scope emphasis on active learning and developmental stages rather than passive and age-defined instruction.

Major Curriculum Areas and Subthemes in High/Scope Elementary Science Education

Life and Environment

The Environment Is Where You Are
Moving in an Environment
Communication Between Environments
Your Environment: Beneath Your Feet
Your Environment: On the Walls
Your Environment: Above Your Head
Taking Care of Our Environment
Basic Materials for Supporting the Study of Living Things in the Environment

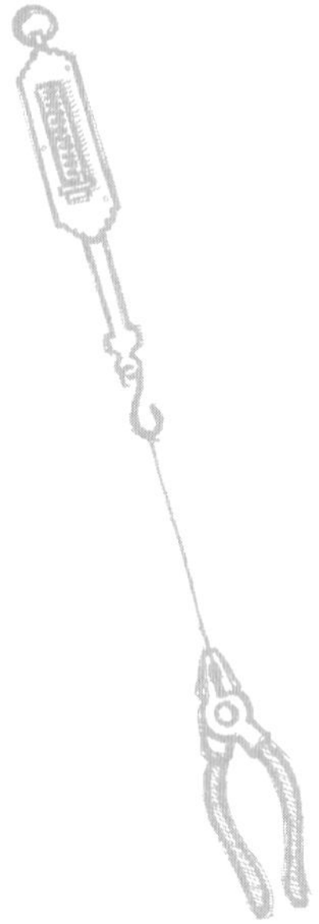

Collecting, Collections, and the Environment
Looking at Living Forms in the Environment
Food for Life From Living Forms
Animals in the Environment: Invertebrates and Vertebrates

Structure and Form

Triangles
Structures Around Us
Structures for Fastening
Natural Structures and Forms
Structure, Size, Symmetry, and Shape
Structure and Patterns
The Structural Properties of Materials
Skin: A Living Structure
The Structure of Everyday Items in the Science Context
Common Textbook Topics on Structure From a New Perspective

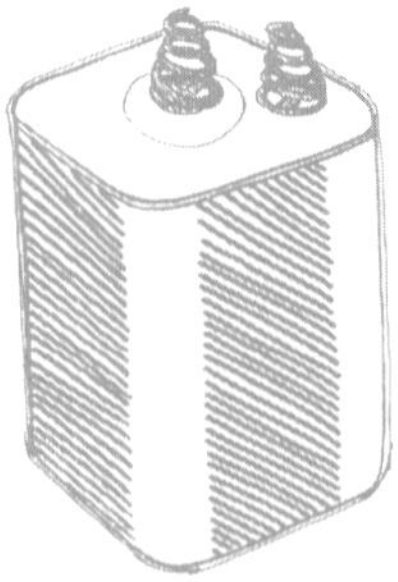

Energy and Change

Using Gravity
Energy From the Air: Wind Energy
Human Energy
Sound Energy
Heat Energy
Weather
Change in the Garden
Diversity in Change
Electrical Energy
Magnets and Magnetism

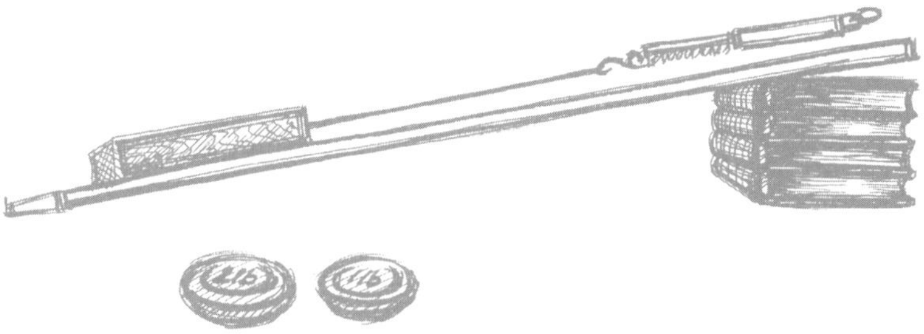

How the Books Are Organized

The High/Scope Elementary Curriculum science books are organized into three volumes, one for each of the major content areas: **life and environment, structure and form,** and **energy and change.** Within each volume, various activities are described for each of the subthemes listed above. Included with each activity is a standard set of information designed to help teachers determine the activity's appropriateness for their students, plan its implementation, and help children focus on a range of exciting and relevant learning experiences. The following information accompanies each activity:

- *Developmental level.* For each activity, the appropriate developmental level is suggested. As noted above, these levels are based on stages rather than ages. Because there is wide variation within and across any group of children, developmental levels are given according to a three-grade span: K–2, 1–3, 2–4, 3–5, and 4–6. Some activities are complex and allow variations that span more than one developmental level; these increasing levels of developmental complexity are also indicated in the text.

- *Group size.* Each activity specifies whether it is suitable for a large or a small group. Although traditional classrooms generally involve all of the students in the same activity at the same time, the High/Scope approach advocates a balance of large- and small-group activity. Some activities are suitable for the entire class, such as a field trip to observe the plant and animal wildlife around the school building. Other activities allow for more intense interaction and varied approaches to the same problem if they are carried out in small groups. In both situations, children may work independently, in pairs, or in a variety of other combinations. Teachers may circulate among individuals and groups to provide encouragement, ask open-ended questions, and observe the children's interests with an eye toward planning future activities. In both large and small groups, children should be given ample opportunity to share their observations, questions, hypotheses, and results with one another as well as with the teacher.

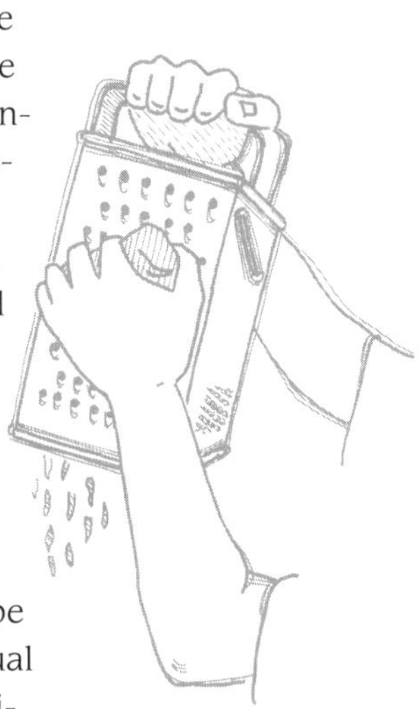

- *Key experiences.* Each activity lists the relevant key experience group or groups to help teachers focus children as they observe, explore, manipulate, and analyze materials. Most activities allow students to engage in more than one of the six science key experiences. Teachers should also be aware that unanticipated questions and spontaneous pursuits by individual students may provide an opportunity to draw out key experiences in addition to those listed here.
- *Notes to teachers.* Some activities include inset notes to teachers. These notes serve two purposes. First, they provide background information on topics about which teachers may have limited experience or knowledge themselves. Second, they provide additional information on topics that students may choose to explore in greater depth. Again, teachers are reminded that there is a wealth of science resource material available for classroom use. These notes are meant to illustrate that with some simple research and follow-through, teachers and students can pursue their interests and expand their science knowledge with confidence.

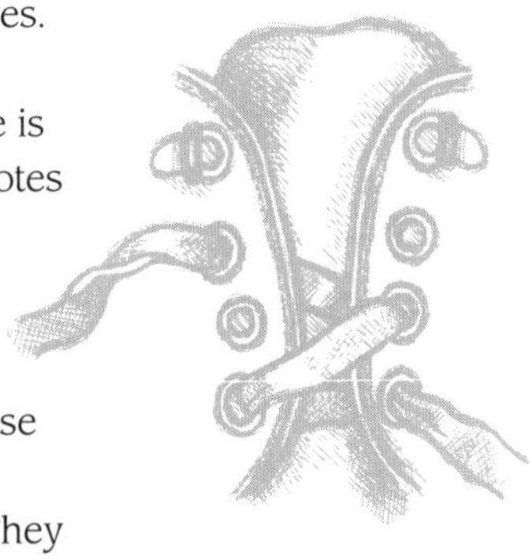

Following the specific activities within each volume is a section titled "Case Studies: Some Classroom Experiences." These case studies are drawn from the author's experiences in implementing science activities with groups of students. They are included to emphasize that science education is indeed a learning process, that what one has planned going into an activity may evolve in a series of other directions depending on the children's understanding and interest. For each classroom example, the author provides a lively discussion of general experiences the teacher had in mind, other experiences the teacher hoped to encourage, follow-up activities the teacher hoped to stimulate, and the activities that actually resulted. Reading these classroom experiences will help teachers gain an appreciation of active learning, the process children engage in as they shape their own activities and create their own knowledge. The case studies should also give teachers confidence to use the activities in these books as a starting point on which spontaneous happenings can build. Things may not go as planned, but a flexible teacher can ensure that learning will always occur.

Finally, each of the three volumes concludes with two appendixes:

- *Appendix I: Teaching Aids.* The first appendix provides teachers with some general ideas about how to carry out science education. It contains the following sections: (a) communication techniques for the classroom; (b) materials and equipment; (c) measurement in science (measurement techniques/simple devices and the metric system); (d) testing and analysis; and (e) safety and science.
- *Appendix II: The Development of Problem-Solving Skills.* Because science is a process of discovery and seeking answers to questions, this appendix explains the stages of development in children's problem-solving skills.

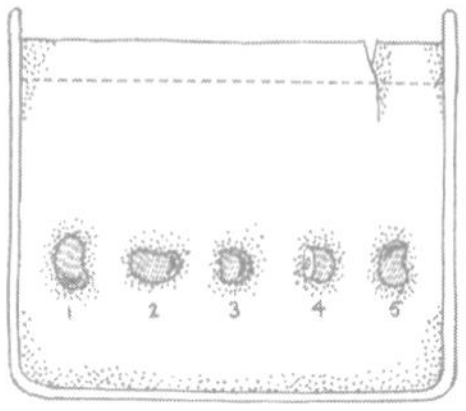

The information will be helpful to teachers as they select activities and adapt them to the developmental levels and skills of individuals and groups in the classroom.

As in all activities within the High/Scope Elementary Curriculum, science learning is seen as an active process of doing and experiencing, rather than a passive one of absorbing information presented by the teacher. Yet the fact that students are active by no means implies that teachers play a lesser role in children's learning. On the contrary, the more active the students, the more active and flexible teachers must be in creating the learning environment, in responding to children's observations and questions, and in building upon children's expanding interests. The High/Scope Elementary Curriculum allows teachers to learn and explore along with their students. Science education becomes a process of mutual discovery that can be as exciting for adults as it is for children.

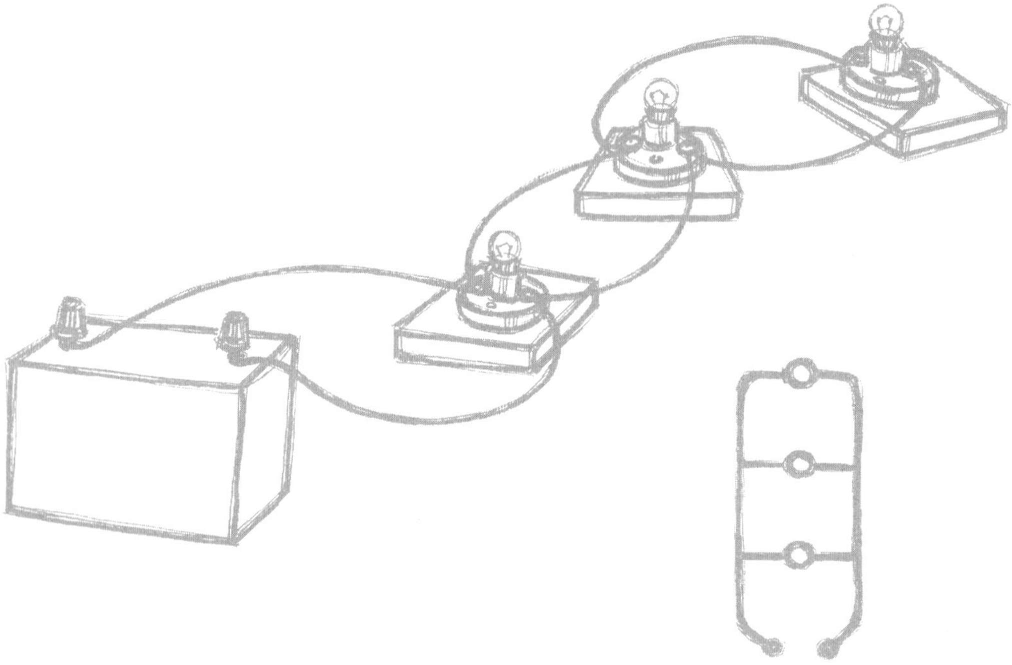

► *Introduction to Book 2*

Structure and Form

Structure and form are complicated concepts that involve the biological world as well as the physical world. This complexity, however, does not mean that these concepts cannot be incorporated into a curriculum for young children. From their earliest years, in fact, children actively explore simple elements of structure and form as they *create* and *construct* by putting objects together to form new wholes. Children love to build with blocks, model with clay, carve with snow, pile up sand, and engage in similar activities. Often these activities are accompanied by highly imaginative ideas that stimulate further inventiveness and meaningful conversation. It is through this active process that children begin to develop an early understanding of structure and form. By the time children are in elementary school, they can build on their already considerable experiences with elements of these concepts.

In today's world we can identify many, many structures—in the design and construction of our houses and towns, for example, and in the machines we see and use. Living things also have a characteristic structure by which we identify them as specific animals or plants. Young children have a general awareness of their surroundings, an awareness that can be increased as ideas, objects, patterns, and forms are brought more prominently into their view.

The consideration of structure leads children to make observations in new ways. Instead of becoming casually acquainted with things, children actively engaged in science will look more closely for likenesses and contrasts. They will look for differences, for example, between a spider and a bird, a cat and a fish. They will look for similarities among a bicycle, a truck, and a wheelbarrow. Thinking about structure through direct experience and careful activity also opens the way for children to appreciate the idea of *relationships.* For example, they can appreciate that the child is smaller than the adult, one building is narrower than another, one brick is linked to others to build a wall, and so on. Ideas of longer–shorter or heavier–lighter extend to more precise questioning about *how much* longer, *how much* heavier, and so on. Blocks in the correct relationship with one another can form a load-bearing column or an arch. Cords can be used to keep a tent stable or, in another structural form, to make a net.

Understanding the structure and form of an organism, a situation, an idea, an object, or a mechanism enlarges children's overall comprehension of the world in which they live. When children begin to comprehend structure and form, the world takes on a recognizable identity, and its interrelated parts and connections to other things or ideas can be established. Structure and form are fundamental concepts in the scientific study of the world.

► *Part One*

Triangles

The triangle is a strong shape. Builders view it as a perfect structure because when used as a unit in a building, it makes the perfect frame. It is a shape that does not collapse whichever way it is stressed, unlike many four-, five-, and six-sided shapes. This stability explains why the triangle is used in so many ways.

Triangles as Basic Structures

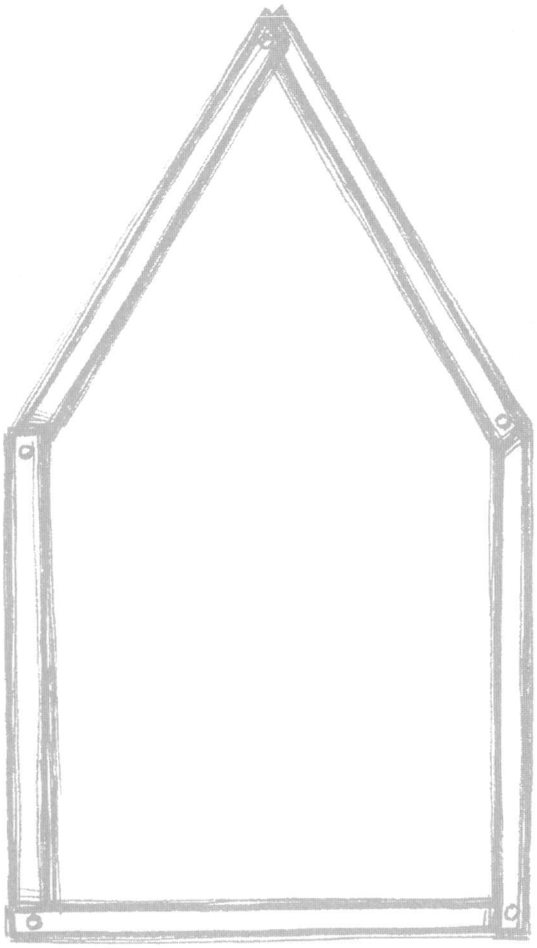

Triangles as Basic Structures ► *Activity 1*

DEVELOPMENTAL LEVEL
K–2

GROUP SIZE
Large

KEY EXPERIENCE
- *Designing, building, fabricating, and modifying structures or materials*

Creating Shapes

To begin this activity, provide students with strips of thin cardboard 6" (15 cm) long and ¾" (2 cm) wide. Punch holes in each end of the strips so brass paper fasteners can go through them to fasten the units together. Make a supply of half-length strips as well (see Illustration 1). Children will generally discover for themselves how to use the paper fasteners but if any children have trouble, demonstrate this process for them so they can proceed with the fun of creating shapes.

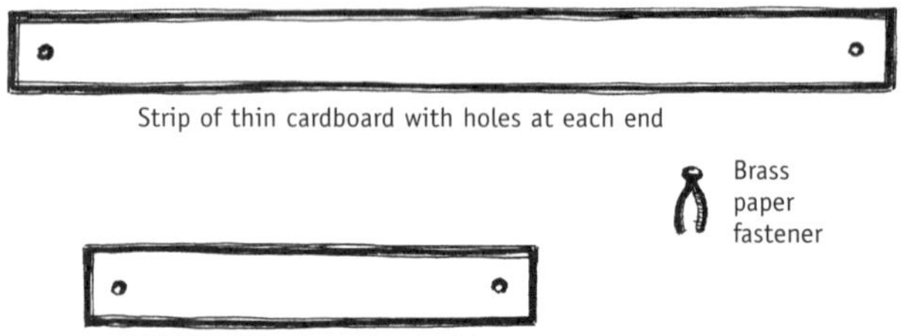

ILLUSTRATION 1

Making Shapes With Cardboard Strips

Making shapes with cardboard strips introduces children to simple elements of structure and form.

Let students choose which shapes to make. Many children will merely string together lengths of strips. Ask if they can fix them into different shapes; for example, can short and long strips be used? Encourage children to make a variety of shapes, such as those in Illustration 2.

At this stage, children will be most concerned with manipulating the strips and fasteners to see what they can make—a long line, a big outline, and so on. In this respect, their activity will be similar to that of preschool children building in the block area. Young children are generally not concerned about the names of the shapes they make, so avoid naming them unless the child asks.

ILLUSTRATION 2

Creating a Variety of Shapes

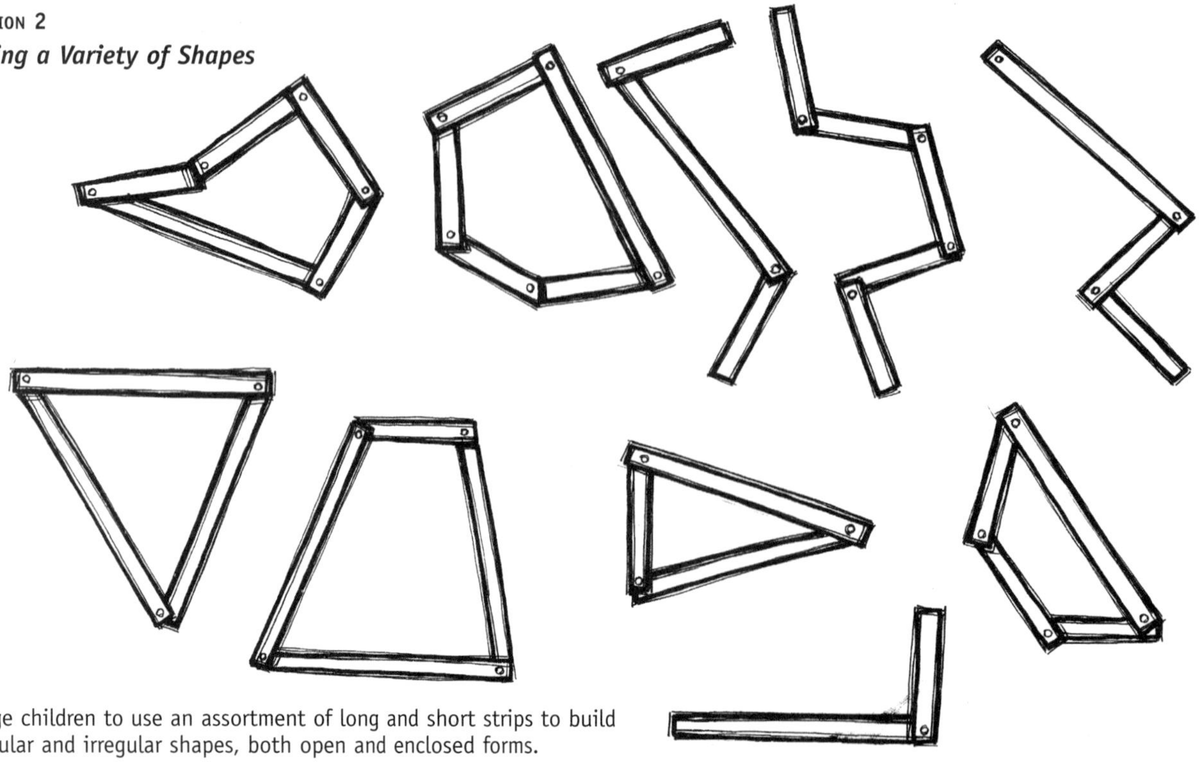

Encourage children to use an assortment of long and short strips to build both regular and irregular shapes, both open and enclosed forms.

The Idea of "Angle"

By working with shapes, children can begin to understand the concept of an angle. Two different types of experiences need to be combined before a child can develop a thorough grasp of this concept. The first set of experiences might be called "static": children need to understand the angle as a fixed corner shape. The right angle, or corner shape, provides a good beginning to this concept, but there will be examples of sharper or blunter angular shapes as well. The second set of experiences are "dynamic": children need to develop an understanding of an angle as the product of rotation.

A simple but revealing activity can be undertaken with a book. When a book is gradually opened its pages make an ever-increasing angle with each other. The growth of an angle also can be seen using two punched cardboard strips fastened at one end only. Holding one strip in place, the other can then be rotated through all the angles to make one complete revolution. There is no limit to the size of an angle when it is thought of as a measure of rotation. The movement of the hands on a clock face also provides a rich source of facts about angles that can be explored through dialogue between teacher and pupils and among the children themselves.

It is important that the static and dynamic aspects of angularity join together in the child's mind; then the angles formed by the sides of boundaries of shapes can be conceived as the parts of the circular movement. Children can understand the meanings of "right angle," "acute angle," "obtuse angle," "straight angle," or "half a complete turn" only after these concepts are firmly established through direct, active experiences.

Triangles as Basic Structures ► *Activity 2*

DEVELOPMENTAL LEVEL
1–3

GROUP SIZE
Small

KEY EXPERIENCE
- *Designing, building, fabricating, and modifying structures or materials*

Testing the Stability of Shapes

Older children generally master the fixing techniques of this activity more quickly than younger children. They often will build both regular and irregular shapes, both open and enclosed forms. When the enclosed forms begin to dominate a child's or group's constructions, the teacher may want to intervene to encourage additional creations. For example, the teacher might suggest that children make a "house shape" from five strips loosely fixed with the paper fasteners (see Illustration 3).

Once the children have made a five-sided house, have them hold up the shape by one of the bottom corners (corner A in Illustration 3). Let them give the opposite corner (B) a slight push and watch what happens. Have them restore the shape, hold by the other corners in turn, and repeat the test. Ask children the following types of questions:

- Does this five-sided shape always collapse?
- How well would this shape of frame work for a house?

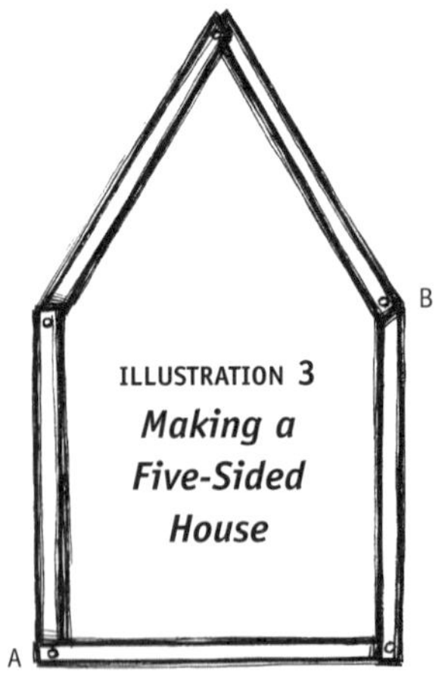

ILLUSTRATION 3
Making a Five-Sided House

Once children begin to construct enclosed forms, encourage additional creations such as this five-sided house, which is made from five strips loosely fixed with paper fasteners.

Let students experiment with another shape by removing one strip to make a four-sided shape, still loosely fixed. Have them test the four-sided by holding each corner and pushing the opposite one. Is it really as strong as it looks? Next, have the students take another strip away, leaving a shape with only three sides. See that the fasteners are just as loose as before. Students can now test this three-sided shape. Hold it at (A); push at (B). Does it collapse? Try pushing at (C). Does it collapse? Reverse the process; hold at (C) and push at (A), then (B) (see Illustration 4).

Once children have had this hands-on experience, you can tell them that this shape is called a **triangle.** At this point, they are ready to establish not only the *concept* of the triangle shape—enclosing three angles in three sides—but also the *name* of the shape. From now on it can become a real part of the child's vocabulary, and the teacher should encourage occasions for its use, especially when the review of work takes place.

Let children experiment by constructing triangles of many different sizes. Provide a supply of strips of at least four different lengths, such as 2" (5 cm), 4" (10 cm), 6" (15 cm), and 8" (20 cm). It is important for children to see for themselves that whatever the length of the sides, triangular shapes are always rigid. Let them repeat the test to see that triangles have this property.

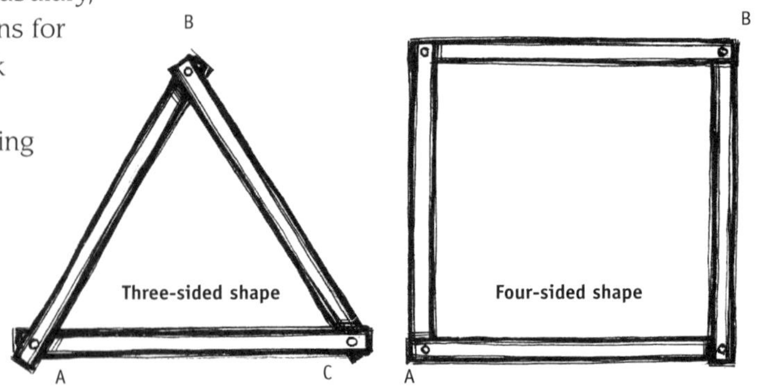

ILLUSTRATION 4
Testing the Strength of Various Shapes
Let students test the strength of four-sided and three-sided shapes. Which shape seems to be the strongest?

DEVELOPMENTAL LEVEL
1–3

GROUP SIZE
Small

KEY EXPERIENCE
- *Designing, building, fabricating, and modifying structures or materials*

Rotating Triangles

Turning, or moving around and around, is one of the earliest arm movements children make. By seeing others turn around and around or seeing objects rotate, children become used to these different views of the same object. However, some children do not see that the shape of the object itself is not changed by this rotation. Just as children need to establish the concept of the triangle *shape* by exploring it in as many ways as possible, they also need to observe the *conservation* of its shape as viewed from different positions. They need experience to see that the inherent shape stays the same even though the orientation may be changed by a particular rotation.

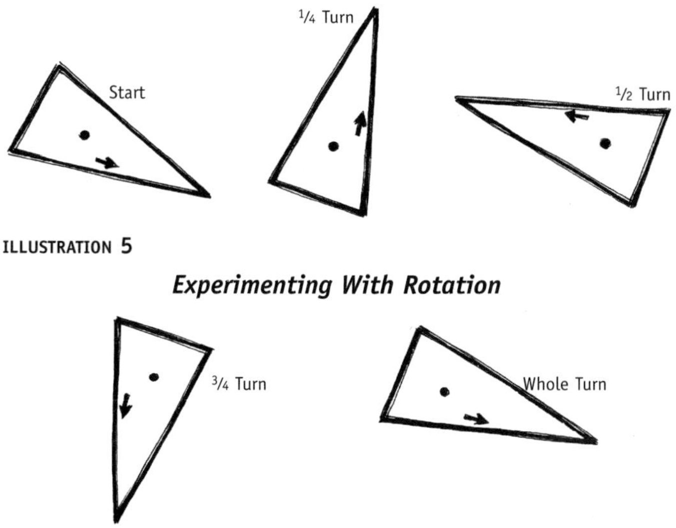

ILLUSTRATION 5

Experimenting With Rotation

By moving a triangle around in a complete circle—through the one-quarter, one-half, and three-quarter turns, students can begin to understand the concept of *rotation*.

When children have established the triangle shape using the strips, let them choose one of the shapes they have made, place it on thin cardboard, and draw around it. They can cut out this triangle for experiments in rotation. Have them put a large pin through the approximate center of the cardboard triangle and mark one side with an arrow (see Illustration 5).

Let the children rotate the triangle around in a complete circle, studying the views very closely each time a movement is made, such as at the one-quarter, one-half, and three-quarter turns. The teacher can ask students: Can the shape be brought back to its original position without rotating it in a *forward* motion? Understanding that the triangle can be rotated by moving it in a *backward* as well as a forward motion is an important concept for children to comprehend.

Rotation is a very important movement, not only in the turning movement of wheels but also in dials of all kinds. In mathematics it underlies the concept of finite number systems (as contrasted with infinite numbers, which can range without limit upwards or downwards from zero). The movement of rotation on a dial, such as a clock face, produces a finite number system; that is, it is limited to the numbers placed on the dial. When a second revolution takes place the numbers—always remaining the same—are repeated. Many measuring devices use dials. Children studying science will frequently encounter dials and the movement of rotation.

Triangles as Basic Structures ► *Activity 4*

DEVELOPMENTAL LEVEL
2–4

GROUP SIZE
Large

KEY EXPERIENCE
- *Designing, building, fabricating, and modifying structures or materials*

Building With Triangles

Teachers can sometimes stimulate children's interest in science by giving an account of a historical situation—how things used to be. Discussing how triangular structures have historically been used in building is one way that teachers can bring a new perspective to science. The following story and activities introduce history into the study of triangular structures.

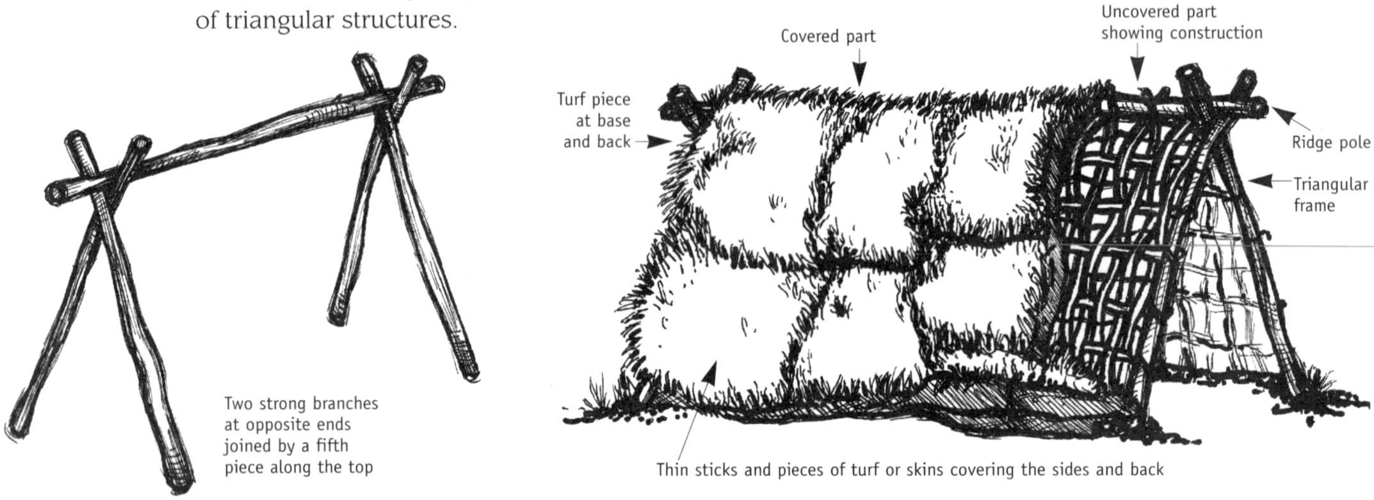

ILLUSTRATION 6

Simple Frame House

The simple frame house was made from two branches at either end and a fifth piece of wood along the top; the ends formed triangles with the ground as the base.

The first dwellings were caves. There were few people then. But when people wanted to live in other places or when there were too few caves, some form of shelter had to be devised. One of the earliest forms of shelter was a simple frame house made from two strong branches at either end and a fifth piece of wood along the top. The ends formed triangles with the ground as the base. The sides and back were woven with thin sticks and covered with pieces of turf or skins (see Illustration 6).

The finished frame house was not unlike a ridge tent, or double wigwam, in which the three sides of the triangles at either end are made of three branches (whereas the frame house has two branches and uses the ground as the third side of the triangle). In both cases, the triangles formed by the frame give the structure added strength. However, both have the same disadvantage—you can stand upright only in the middle.

If your school is in an area where the necessary raw materials are readily available, children can build a simple frame house for themselves. As a real challenge, have them use only natural materials—plant fibers rather than string, binding fastenings rather than nails, and so on.

Even when children are not able to build frame houses from raw materials, they can experiment with triangular structures using poles. Provide students with bamboo poles for these experiments because the poles are light, cheap, and strong. Fixing is best done with rough garden string, although adhesive tape will do. Pose the following questions and problems to encourage students to examine how triangles are used in various structures:

• Using poles, string, and old sheets, can you make tents for use outside on the school field or in the park? (See Illustration 7.)

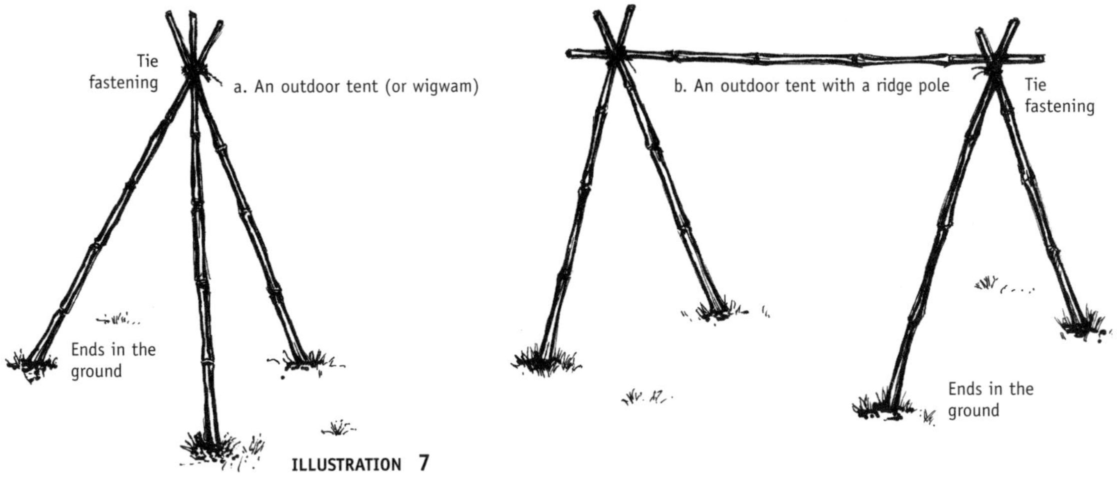

ILLUSTRATION 7

Making Tents for Outdoor Use

Using poles, strings, and old sheets, students can make tents for use outside on the school grounds or in the park.

• How are triangles used in these designs? How is a wigwam made? Does it use the triangle shape for its strength? Can you make a wigwam with the materials you have available?

• Can you make tents for inside use—in a classroom or hall where you cannot stick the ends of the poles in the ground? (See Illustration 8.)

• How are triangles used in these designs? How does each contribute to the rigidity of the tent?

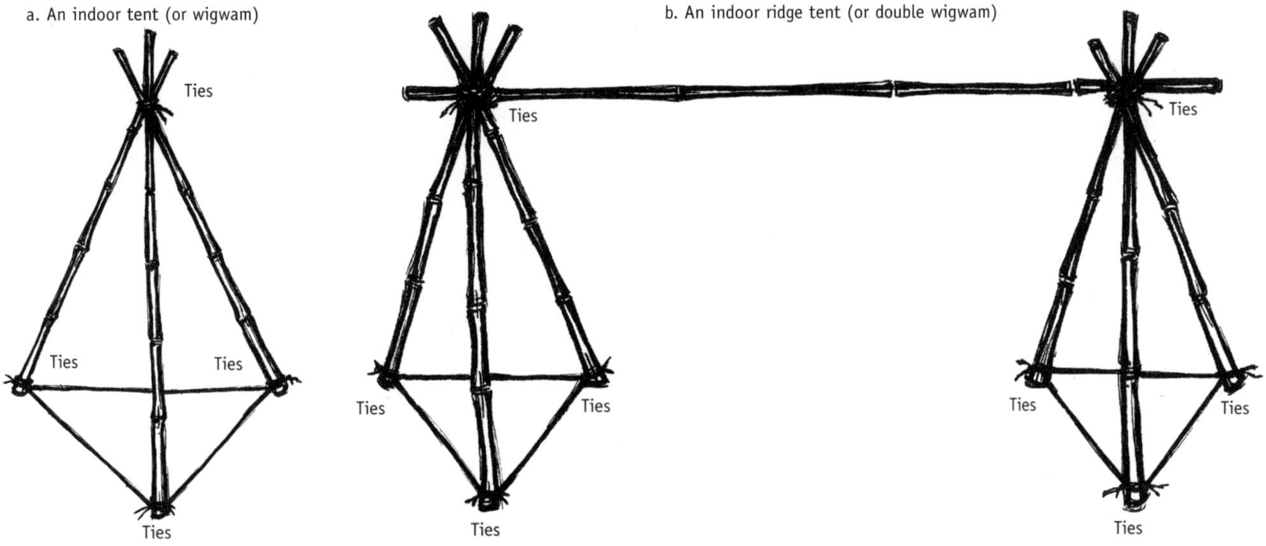

ILLUSTRATION 8

Making Tents for Indoor Use

How can tents be made for use inside—in a classroom or hallway where you cannot stick the ends of the poles in the ground?

► *Part Two*

Structures Around Us

In today's world, students can see many types of structures and buildings, such as towers, doorways and arches, and lattices and cranes. Young children have a natural curiosity about these everyday structures that they see in their surroundings, a curiosity that can be enhanced when these objects are brought more prominently into their view.

Tower Building ► *Activity 5*

DEVELOPMENTAL LEVEL
K–2

GROUP SIZE
Small

KEY EXPERIENCE
- *Measuring, testing, and analyzing: assessing the properties and composition of materials*

Building towers in the block area is a well-known and attractive activity for younger children, and one that teachers should encourage. It presents possibilities for trial-and-error reasoning, imaginative planning, and individual design. Introducing a few basic elements into the procedure will give block activity more purpose and help children to develop a critical awareness of structure. Teachers can introduce new elements by posing questions to children when they are using the block material.

As a simple beginning, have children see how high a tower of blocks they can build. Have them vary the size of the base as follows:

• Use a base of only one block unit. What is the tallest tower the students can build? It must remain upright for at least one minute.

• If the base is increased to two blocks, what is the highest tower that the students can build? Again, the tower should remain upright for at least one minute.

• Have students draw the pattern of blocks for the two towers and write the total number of blocks used. Graph paper will help with this recording activity.

• With a base of four blocks and using whatever building pattern they like, what is the tallest tower that students can make now? Have them draw the pattern of the tower that results and calculate the number of blocks that were used in this tower. Again, graph paper will help here. (See Illustration 9.)

• If the blocks were real bricks, the towers would each cost money. Which tower would cost the most? Would it be worth it? How much extra height did you get for the extra bricks used?

A. 1-block base: 10 units high and using 10 blocks

B. 2-block base: 14 units high and using 28 blocks

C. 4-block base: 19 units high and using 45 blocks

D. Different base patterns using four blocks

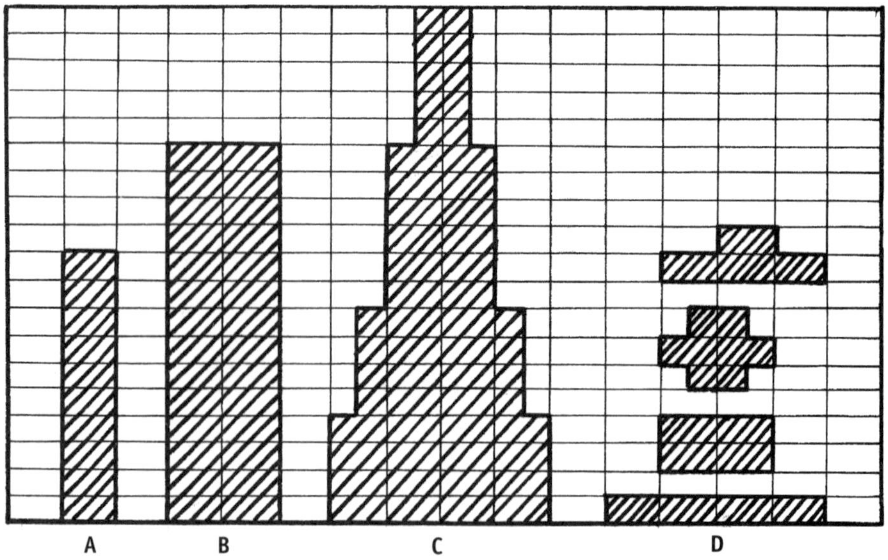

ILLUSTRATION 9

Recording Tower Building

Building towers with blocks presents opportunities for reasoning, imaginative planning, and individual design. In this activity, students build towers of various heights and sizes and record their results on graph paper.

The teacher can intervene at this point to encourage experiments with different base patterns if the children are fixed on linear thinking. Pose questions, for example, to encourage other design considerations, such as starting with a base in the shape of a cross. New towers can be built, and the students can record the results on graph paper.

Doorways and Arches ► *Activity 6*

DEVELOPMENTAL LEVEL
2–4

GROUP SIZE
Small

KEY EXPERIENCE

- *Measuring, testing, and analyzing: assessing the properties and composition of materials*

A NOTE FOR TEACHERS

Arches and Openings

The design and location of doors and windows is important in architectural design. Children can see examples of the problems, and their solutions, in the buildings around them. For example, the construction of doorways and window spaces presents few problems in single story buildings. In these low structures, there is only the weight of the roof to hold up. However, when the structure is built higher, the problem of spanning these gaps becomes greater. In many respects, it is the bridge-builder's problems on a smaller scale. In modern buildings where large windows are installed, the gaps requiring support become larger, and the building materials need to be stronger.

Young children's direct experience with building models can yield useful insights into the whole problem of construction. Many important learning situations can arise from construction activities with older children as well. For example, by building with blocks and cardboard strips, children can put their ideas to the test before accepting them. They can record the results of tests of situations so that they have the evidence to back up their conclusions. As children consider the overall design of structures they can acquire an awareness of symmetry and of shapes as features of structures. Through active experimentation they can appreciate the use of models for investigating problems, before large-scale work is done. They may be encouraged, through well-managed dialogue, to speculate on such mature concepts as how form and structure relate to the functions required in a building. By handling simple materials in a construction context, children will become aware of the need to visualize objects from different angles, and to see the shape of cross sections that result from construction work.

Extending the Building Possibilities

Introducing some simple cardboard strip units can greatly increase the designs children invent as they construct with blocks. Provide a supply of stiff cardboard strips as wide as the blocks in use and three times as long as a block. These new units of material will open up the design possibilities enormously. How children record their activities is another important component of this work. The plan-do-review sequence can be used in this context. In the *planning* stage, children both tell and sketch illustrations of their plans for constructions. In the *review* stage, children can draw finished constructions, as well as tell about the innovations and modifications introduced "en route" in the making and doing. The importance of "ad hoc" improvisations and innovations cannot be stressed too much; they represent children's creative abilities and inventiveness operating at an advanced level of educational activity. By encouraging dialogue and questioning, teachers can support and help to consolidate the developmental gains made during these creative processes.

Although solid block towers are the structures most common in kindergarten, teachers may want to introduce cardboard strips, which often encourage children to invent towers and buildings with doorways and window openings. Houses, not just towers, then become a building possibility, and linear constructions can incorporate new features. Children will also be more ready to respond to "what will happen if" types of questions and intervention.

Using the stiff cardboard strips, students can construct doorways and arches. Have students make each of the designs shown in Illustration 10. Pose the following questions and activities:

• Cut a strip of paper the same size as the firm cardboard strip. Rebuild the arches and test the paper strip on each one in turn using coins or large nails as weights and as loads. What are the results? Record them for each arch design.

• Try again using the single strip of cardboard. What are the results this time?

• Try again using two strips of cardboard stuck together to make a strong strip. What are the results this time? Use the same tests. Heavier loads may be needed.

• Why is a strong strip bridging the gap needed to support any building that takes place above it?

For children who are interested in numerical results, the strip of paper, the single cardboard strip, and the double (strong) cardboard strip could be tested with units of weight. Use a matchbox tray to carry the loading to do the tests. Thumbtacks and small nails are good test units for this investigation. Have students test each of the three arch forms shown in Illustration 10 and make a table for the results.

Some children may not be interested in such measuring experiments, but would rather get on with building activities using the new cardboard strips. The teacher can guide these children by posing questions such as the following:

• Could a two-story house be built now using the new cardboard strips? Can such a house be planned to include doors on the lower floor and windows on the lower and upper floors? Can larger door openings be made with smaller window openings above them? Have students make drawings showing views of the designs as looked at from different sides.

• How can students use the new cardboard strips to build towers containing windows and doors? Have them compare these towers using the thin single strips and the strong double strips. Keep to the same patterns of building so that comparisons are fair and produce valid results.

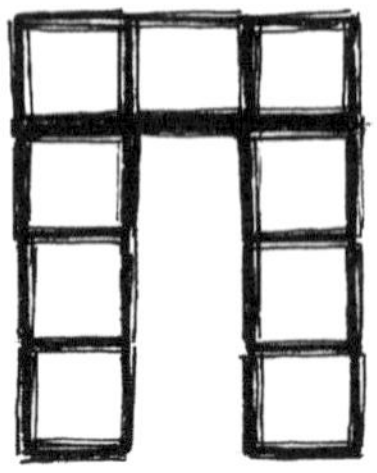

Arch 1
Plank fully over the supports

Arch 2
Plank halfway over each support

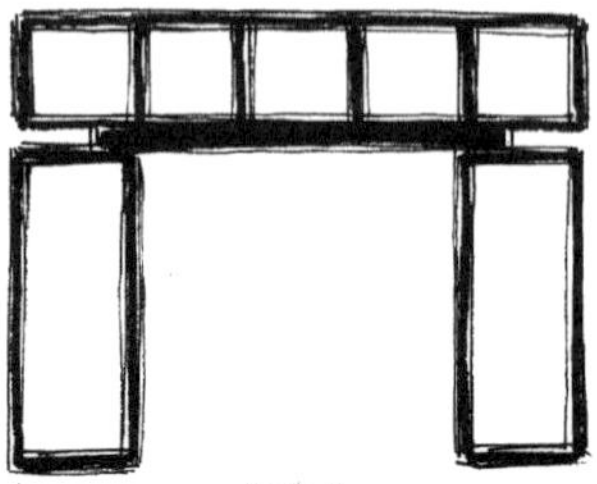

Arch 3
Plank one quarter over each support

ILLUSTRATION 10

Constructing an Arch

Students can create a variety of doorways and arches using stiff cardboard strips.

Making Another Building Material ► *Activity 7*

DEVELOPMENTAL LEVEL
K–2

GROUP SIZE
Large

KEY EXPERIENCE
- *Designing, building, fabricating, and modifying structures or materials*

In addition to building with wooden blocks, many children also enjoy using other materials to build larger structures, so it is important to carry supplies of different materials. Since actual full-sized building bricks are heavy and impractical, an excellent alternative building unit can be made out of stiff cardboard, such as that obtained from packaging boxes. Illustration 11 gives two possible template plans for producing cardboard building blocks. (Creating these blocks would be a good job for parent volunteers and classroom helpers.) There is no doubt that such materials are very popular; the main problem is often in getting enough blocks made to meet the ambitious structures that children plan and execute. Where permanence is desired, the unit blocks can be stuck together with water soluble paste similar to the way that bricklayers use mortar to hold bricks together. Children can try out many actual building practices with these materials.

Either small or large building blocks can be made using the templates in Illustration 11 (see pg. 25). To begin, make the template that will be used for marking all the cutouts. The template should have clean edges so that marking is easy. Mark the cardboard (or other material such as posterboard) and cut it out according to the pattern. Use a blunt knife to make notches (scores) on the cardboard in the places where it will be folded; take care not to cut through the cardboard. Fold along the notched or scored lines to make the box shape. Press the folds into position neatly and secure the open edges with strong adhesive tape. Do not tape until a flat well-shaped box block has been worked into position. You can make a supply of half blocks by cutting a new template as indicated by the dotted lines.

This template plan can be varied to produce blocks of any size—the limiting factor is the rigidity of the cardboard and the manipulation needed to tape it square and flat on all faces. To make blocks of a different thickness, increase the size of the three flaps and the centerfold section. Remember, however, that blocks thicker than 3" (8 cm) become more difficult for small hands to span and manipulate.

In addition to blocks of different sizes, you will also want a variety of weights. For example, heavier blocks are useful for the base of structures. Lighter blocks can easily be increased in weight by putting closed plastic bags of sand or gravel into them before sealing. Loose sand needs to be sealed with very tight tape to prevent it from leaking out.

To complete this set of structural building materials, obtain supplies of wooden boards (or other hard material) that are as wide as the block units chosen and four, six, eight, and ten times as long. The blocks and boards together will provide all that is needed for ambitious building plans to be carried out.

Children's enthusiasm for building, especially for building things with some degree of permanence, can be positively channeled into active planning. Building gives them the opportunity to plan ahead as well as to improvise as they meet problems. For example, the students could "contract" to build a house. This activity will call for much planning. How much space is there for building and how large can the house be? Where will they put the door? How many windows should the house have? What sizes will the window and door areas be? How will the spaces above be filled? Will the boards be strong enough for wide openings? The children can plan the decoration, apply the colors, and provide curtains for the windows. The greatest problem will undoubtedly be to supply sufficient blocks and half blocks to sustain the builders' ambitions! Once commenced, such a project can easily occupy a whole term as each decision raises new questions and gives rise to new possibilities.

As the student builders give their progress reports, teachers can participate by raising the following issues:

• How many bricks (full- and half-size) did we anticipate using? How many did we actually use? What areas of the construction required more (or fewer) bricks than we planned?

• How long will it take to build the house? Why did it take more (or less) time than anticipated?

• Which parts of the house were easy to build? Which were hard? Why?

• Where should the utilities go? Where would you put electric lights? Where would you put the plumbing? What about the telephone? Why would we locate each of these utilities in the place(s) you have chosen?

• How should the house be decorated? What are the best colors for the outside? For the inside? Will you have wallpaper or paint? How will the floors be decorated? What about window treatments? What kind of furniture do you want?

A project of this sort will call for good communication over a long period. It is a good source for mathematical work as well as illustrated records of all kinds. How far it goes will depend a great deal on the teacher's ability to organize and handle such a powerful educational stimulus and support the expanding interests of the students as they engage in the building process.

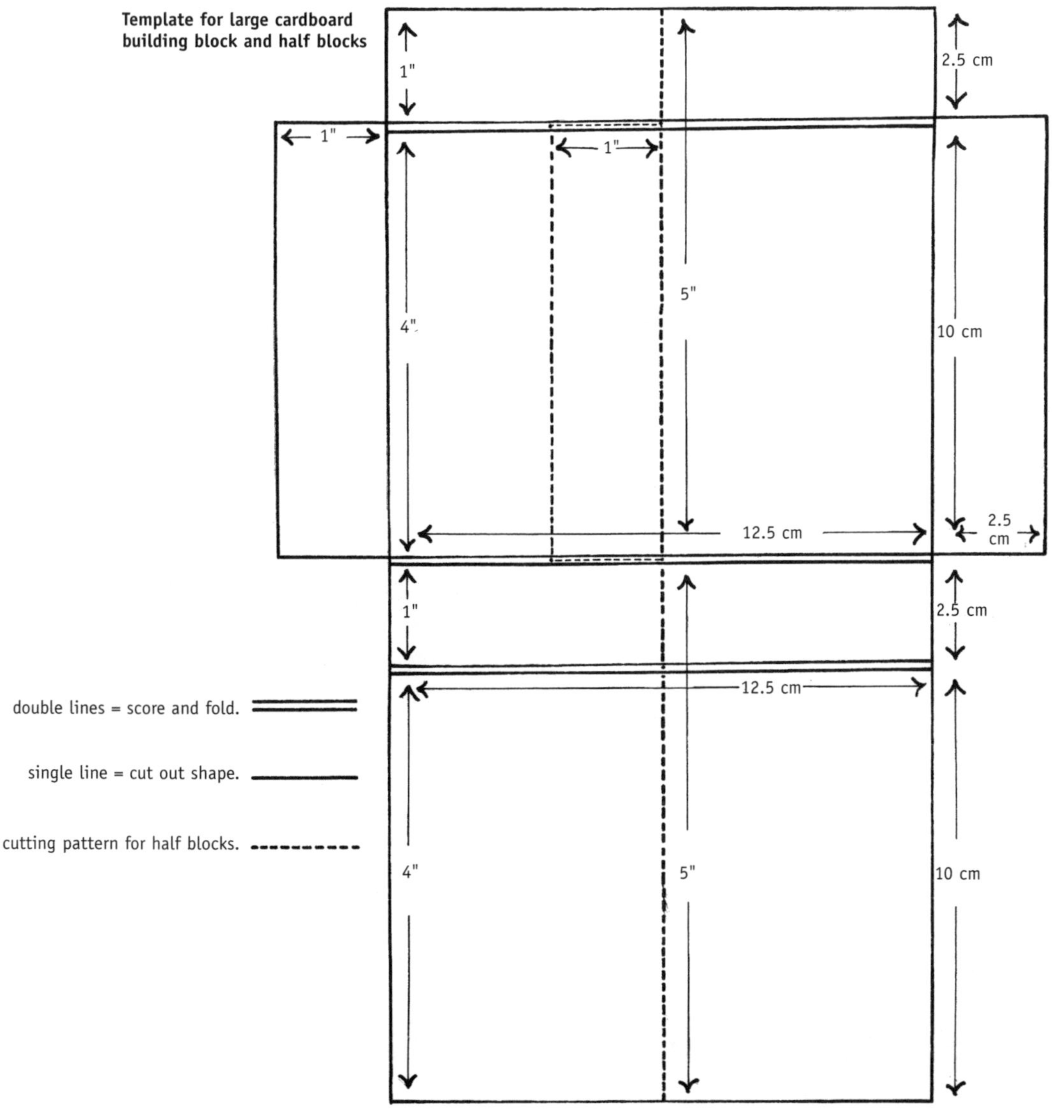

ILLUSTRATION 11

Templates for Creating Cardboard Building Blocks

By using small cardboard building blocks made from templates such as these, children can experiment with many actual building practices.

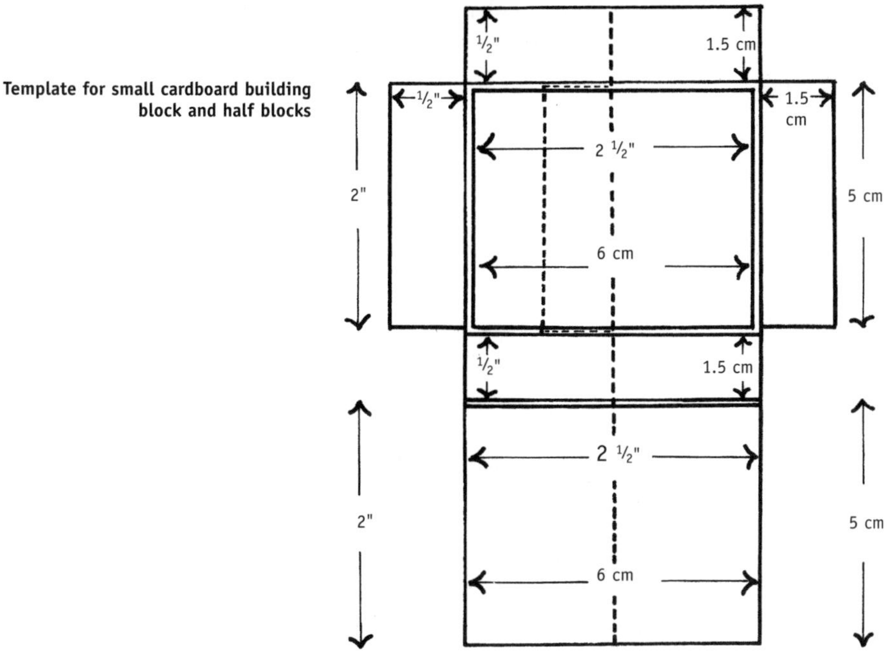

Lattices and Cranes ► *Activity 8*

DEVELOPMENTAL LEVEL
2–4

GROUP SIZE
Small

KEY EXPERIENCE
- *Looking with a purpose: observing and collecting data*

Most structures produce a pattern, or lattice. Students can observe many structural patterns in their surroundings—those created both by nature and by people. A good starting point is looking for triangles in buildings. Begin with the roof of the school or a nearby building. Does it form a triangle? If so, the roof is probably supported by lattice girders (see Illustration 12).

The lattice form is very strong. A collection of triangles forms a lattice. Triangles are the most rigid forms for structures, and they are especially useful when strength is needed. Lattices can be seen all around us. Have students make a collection of sketches of lattice patterns they see around them. There will be some in the school. There will be others in buildings they visit and in the equipment they see. Bicycles include a single lattice pattern, as well as other triangles. How many patterns can students find on their bicycles? If students live in a city, they will see this lattice design built into a crane (see Illustration 13).

ILLUSTRATION 12

Lattice Girder
Students can observe a collection of triangles in a lattice girder.

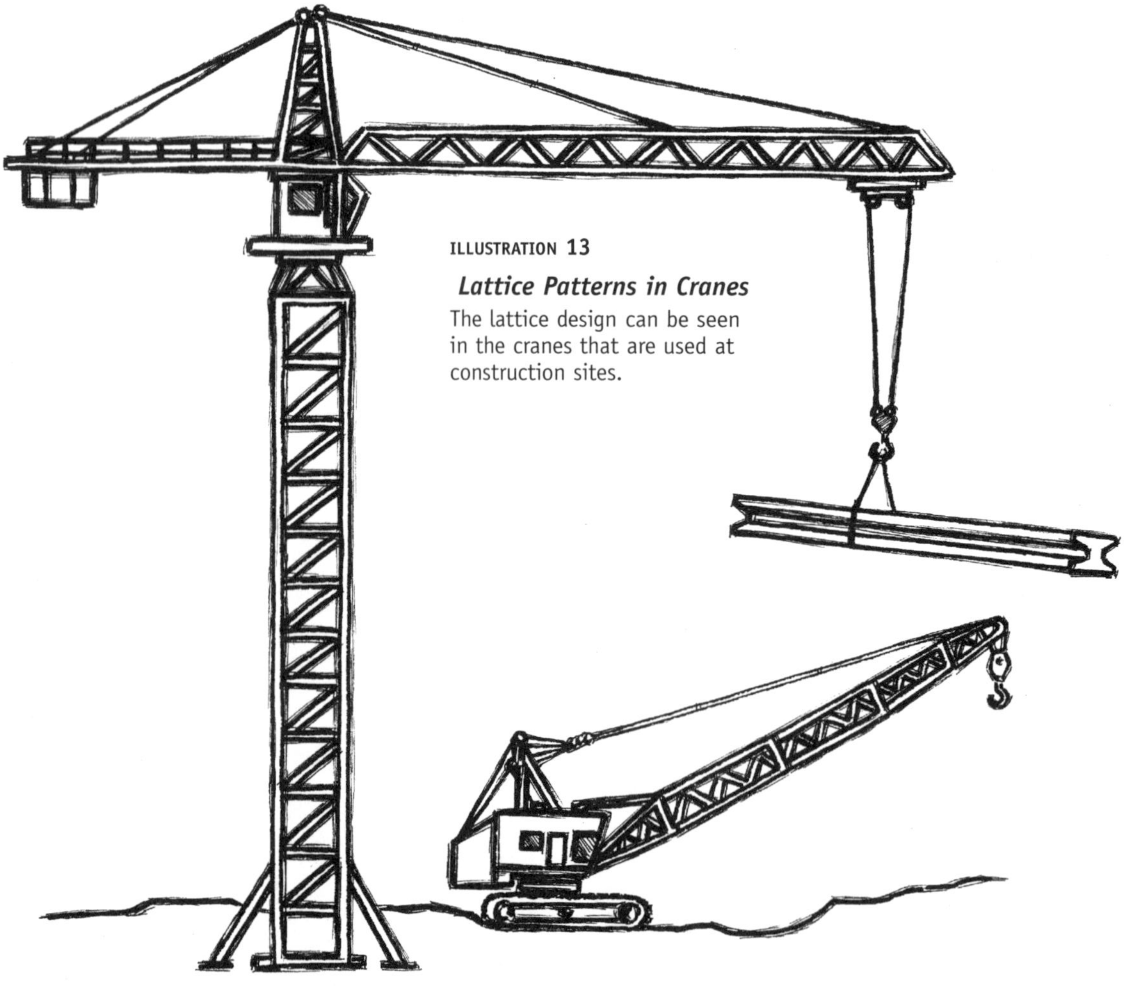

ILLUSTRATION 13

Lattice Patterns in Cranes
The lattice design can be seen in the cranes that are used at construction sites.

A crane can be thought of as an arm with a hand on the end of it. Have students try this experiment (see Illustration 14).

Step 1. Stand up straight with one arm by your side and the other straight up above your head.

Step 2. From the shoulders up you are like the jib of a crane; your extended arm is the jib. Now pick up a basket or a schoolbag filled with books and hold it straight above your head.

Step 3. You could hold it quite a time like that. But now lower your arm sideways until it is a quarter of the way to your body. Does the load feel heavier or lighter?

Step 4. Now lower your arm until it is halfway or perpendicular to your body, that is, horizontally sideways. How does the load feel now?

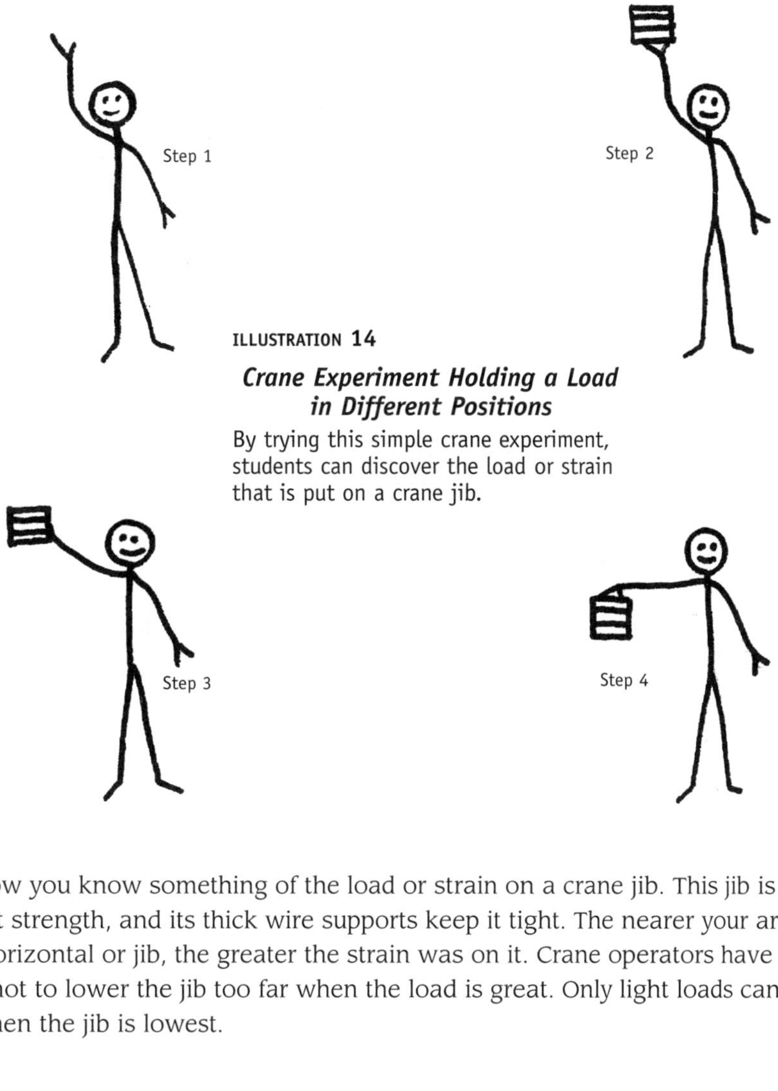

ILLUSTRATION **14**

Crane Experiment Holding a Load in Different Positions

By trying this simple crane experiment, students can discover the load or strain that is put on a crane jib.

Now you know something of the load or strain on a crane jib. This jib is latticed to give it strength, and its thick wire supports keep it tight. The nearer your arm got to the horizontal or jib, the greater the strain was on it. Crane operators have to be careful not to lower the jib too far when the load is great. Only light loads can be lifted when the jib is lowest.

Lattices and Cranes ► *Activity 9*

DEVELOPMENTAL LEVEL
3–5

GROUP SIZE
Small

KEY EXPERIENCE

- *Measuring, testing, and analyzing: assessing the properties and composition of materials*

A new kind of crane, the tower crane, was invented especially for high buildings. Tower cranes have made extensive building of tall structures possible in many places. Lattice construction means that a strong high tower can be built on which a crane arm turns. This arm is balanced by an equally long weighted arm to keep the crane stable as it turns around and around, lifting its loads. Sometimes, if there is no room for the crane outside a building, it is put inside.

Students can make and test a tower crane (see Illustration 15). First, test the single arm with loads consisting of large nails or marbles. See when the tower falls over and record the load. Next, put on the balanced arm and test this until the tower falls; record the results. Finally, make drawings and a chart to show the results of both experiments.

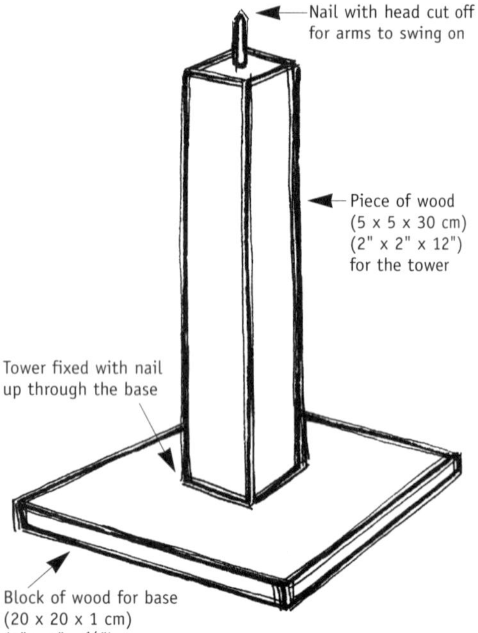

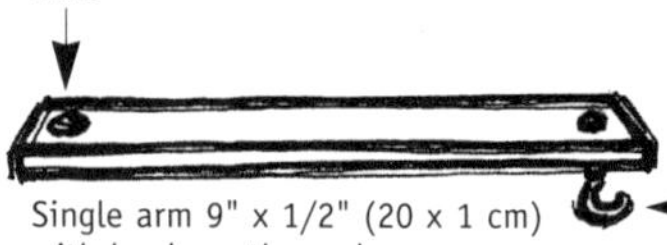

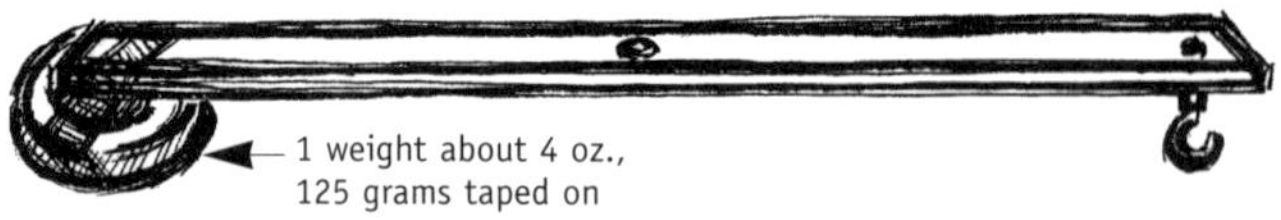

ILLUSTRATION 15

Making and Testing a Tower Crane

Students can make and test a tower crane. First, they load nails or marbles on the single arm to observe when the tower falls over. Next, they put on the balanced arm and repeat the test.

Students who live in the country may see a different type of lattice tower. The one shown in Illustration 16 (pg. 29) supports a well-drilling rig. The lattice structure allows it to be strong yet light. It can be bolted together in sections just like construction toys. It can be broken down into pieces and transported to another place, in the same way as the tower crane. If you are observant, you may see the whole thing in parts being transported by truck to the next place for its work.

As students become aware of triangles, encourage them to look for triangles in their environment. Some schools and many halls have roof patterns such as those in Illustration 17 (pg. 29). Can students see any in the schools or halls that they visit?

Triangles are all around us. Have students keep a record for one week of all the places they see triangles. The results will surprise them. Have them estimate the number of triangles in a building. There will probably be more than they want to count!

ILLUSTRATION **16**

Lattice Tower Used to Support a Well-Drilling Rig

This lattice tower is used to support a well-drilling rig. The lattice structure allows the rig to be strong yet light.

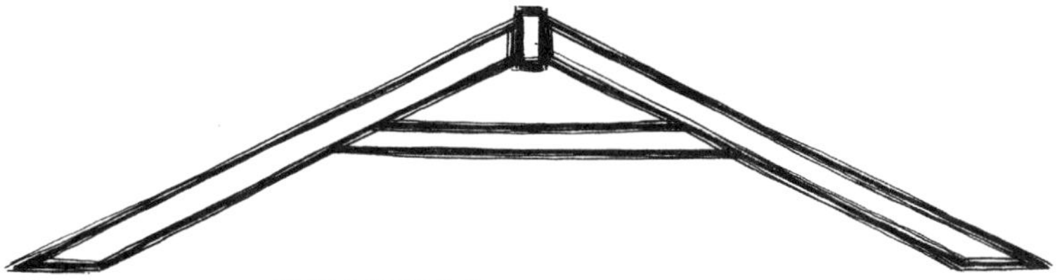

ILLUSTRATION **17**

Finding Triangles in Roofs

Encourage students to look for triangles in their everyday environments, such as in the roof patterns shown here.

► *Part Three*

Structures for Fastening

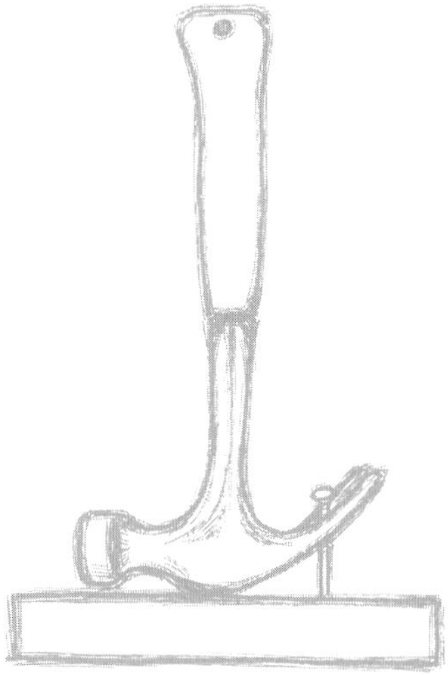

Many of the simple fastening devices we use each day have quite well-defined structures. Some of the most common have arisen as a response to everyday needs. Others have been developed by inventors with lively minds, who thought over problems that caught their imagination.

Keeping It On ► *Activity 10*

DEVELOPMENTAL LEVEL
K–2

GROUP SIZE
Small

KEY EXPERIENCE
- *Designing, building, fabricating, and modifying structures or materials*

Teachers may be familiar with the tactile equipment that was once presented to young children to help them practice fastening their clothes: buttons on tape strips, snaps, hooks and eyes, laces, ties, and so on. Children often failed to respond to these drill-like materials, however, mainly because their lack of realism and functional utility made the apparatus inappropriate. As one child commented, "Whoever thought of doing up buttons if they were not on a coat!"

However, the problem of fastening things together is a real one and the simple mechanisms developed for fastening clothing together are excellent examples of simple mechanisms worth investigating. Let children take a good look at them—not only for what they do but for how they work. Children can also consider which fasteners would be best for what circumstances and what the advantages are of one over the other.

Have the following fasteners available in sufficient quantities for all the children in each group to examine. (**Note:** Zippers are more complicated and are best left for children in grades 3 and up to examine.)

- Snaps—stud and bases separated and in various sizes
- Hooks and eyes—separated from each other and in various sizes
- Toggle and loop fastenings—separated from each other
- Laces and eyelets—large sizes and separated from each other
- Buttons of many shapes and colors
- Ribbons of different lengths, textures, and colors
- Lengths of Velcro with the press-on positive and negative strips separated

(**Note:** A magnifying glass is useful for examining the Velcro strips.)

Although children will know that these are all fastenings for garments, they now have a chance to closely examine them. Help them become aware that these fasteners are two-part structures; they work in pairs. Even the buttons work with buttonholes or loops. Children should sort the items to find the matching parts. They should match for mechanism and size, for positive to negative to make the pair. Then they can set about finding out exactly how each fastener works, being confident enough in the information to explain it at review time.

- Snaps (see Illustration 18)

The teacher can raise the question: Why do the top and bottom parts of the fastener have small holes around the edges?

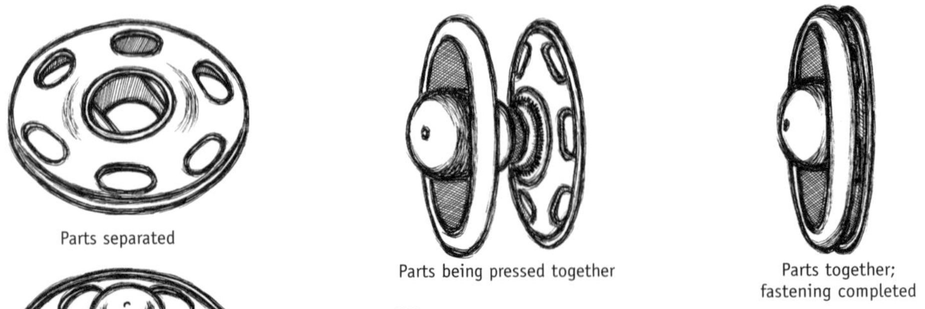

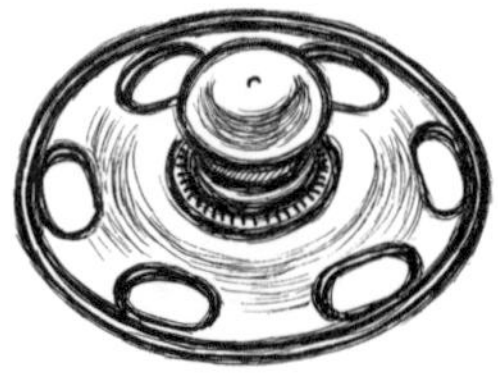

ILLUSTRATION 18

Snap Fasteners

Using ordinary snap fasteners, students can examine how a simple mechanism works by separating the parts and pressing them together to complete the fastening.

A NOTE FOR TEACHERS

Fastening Things

Fastening things together is so commonplace that the mechanisms for doing so are often overlooked as worthy of close study. However, fastenings of different sorts are all around us. Fasteners are used, for example, every time we put on clothes—buttons, zippers, snaps, hooks, buckles, and shoelaces are but a few types of fasteners. The front door, which uses one or more locking mechanisms, is fastened in a different way from clothes. The dog's leash fits on to its collar with its own special type of fastening. Plywood boards and covers are made by fastening thin sheets of wood together in layers. Some of this plywood is very strong and is used in boat building as well as in house construction. The trailer has a special fastening to the truck that pulls it. The seat belt has yet another sort of fastener and so has the parachute worn by fliers.

Living things also use fastening. Silkworms spin cocoons from a glue they produce, and spiders fix their webs with a glue-like substance. Bird claws have the power of fasteners, especially when birds are perching. In fact, the bird's way of life can be deduced from its claws. Compare the claws of the birds of prey, the duck, the finch, and the parrot. Trees also have fastenings in their roots that keep them stable in all but the worst storms. Another fastening mechanism is used by ivy plants and still others by climbing plants generally. It is difficult to miss seeing fastenings once an awareness of them is generated. Activities involving a study of fastenings will lead into many worthwhile studies in science—all from materials readily available.

- Hooks and eyes (see Illustration 19)

The teacher can raise questions such as the following: Why are there no sharp ends to the hooks? Why are the eyes smooth and rounded? When is it better to use hooks and eyes rather than snaps? Which are easier to undo? If you had to quickly change clothes, which would you use?

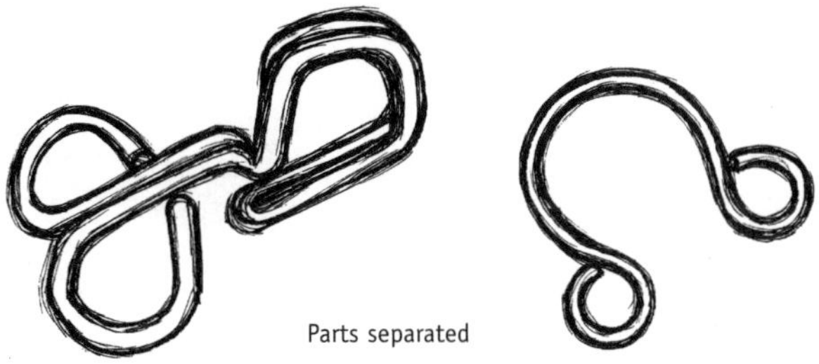

Parts separated

ILLUSTRATION 19

Hook-and-Eye Fasteners

As students examine hook-and-eye fasteners, encourage them to think about why the parts are shaped as they are.

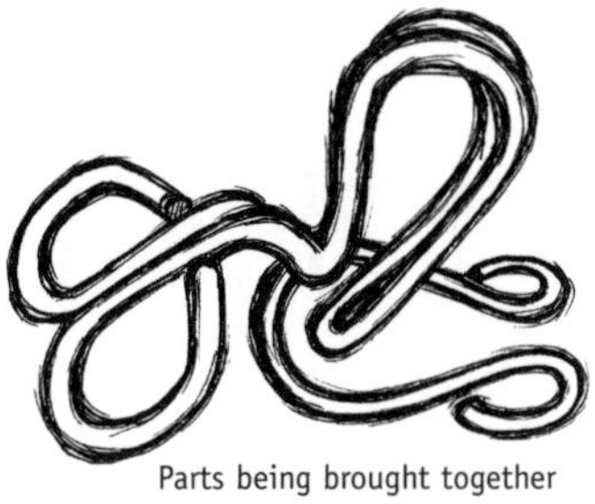

Parts being brought together

Fastening completed

• Toggle and loop (see Illustration 20)

Toggles and loops are used for fastening heavy clothes such as winter coats. Have the children discuss why certain types of clothing need such big fastenings (for example, to bear the weight of the clothing; so they can be done up when the wearer has gloves on). Let them think about what else could be fastened with toggles.

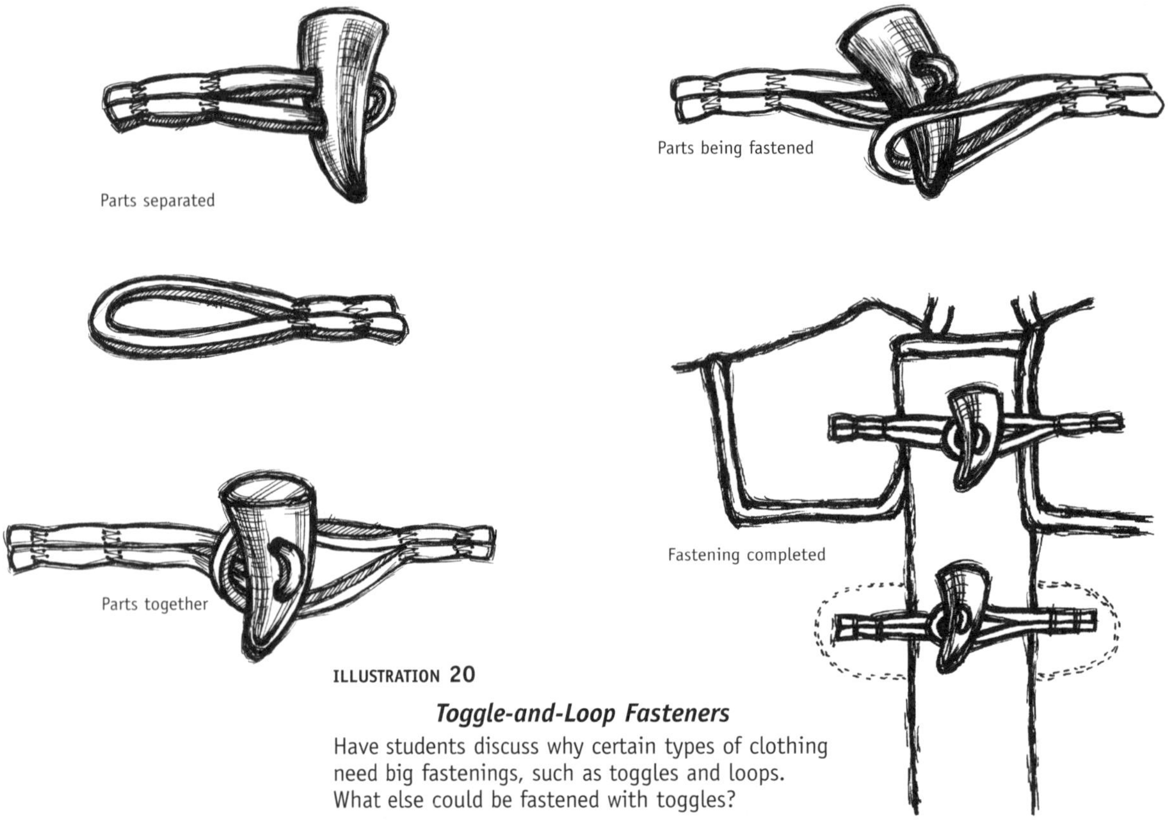

ILLUSTRATION 20

Toggle-and-Loop Fasteners

Have students discuss why certain types of clothing need big fastenings, such as toggles and loops. What else could be fastened with toggles?

• Laces and eyelets (see Illustration 21)

Here are some questions to ask about laces: Why are there laces on boots and shoes? Why are laces better than straps and buckles? What problems can you have with laces?

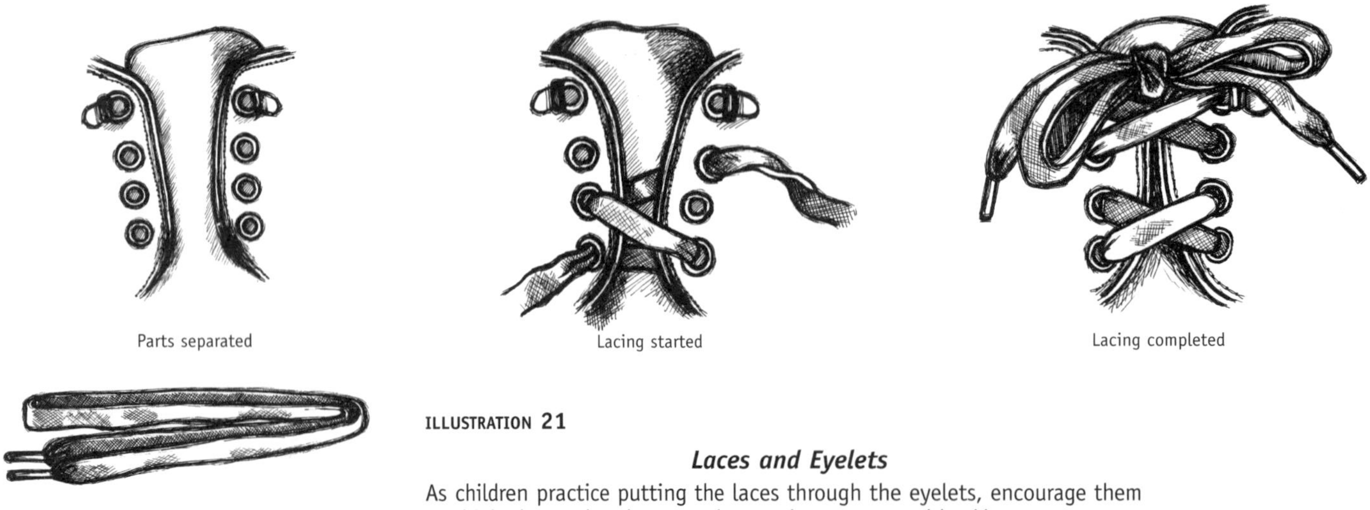

ILLUSTRATION 21

Laces and Eyelets

As children practice putting the laces through the eyelets, encourage them to think about when laces are better than straps and buckles.

• Buttons (see Illustration 22)

Here are some questions about buttons: When do we use buttons? Into what does a button fit to make a fastening? Why can't we find a button's "other half" in the collection?

Along with an extensive collection of buttons, have available swatches of cloth in solid colors and patterns. Have the students discuss: Which buttons would you choose for which patterns? On what did you base your decision (for example: color, lightweight or heavyweight fabric, indoor or outdoor use)?

ILLUSTRATION 22

Buttons

Along with an extensive collection of buttons, provide students with swatches of cloth in various colors and patterns. Ask students which buttons they would choose to put on the pieces of cloth.

• Ribbons (see Illustration 23)

Have students practice joining two pieces of ribbon, using any style of tying that they like (see Illustration 24). Which types of knots, ties, and bows pull apart easily? Which types join the ribbon so that the pieces do not pull apart? Why?

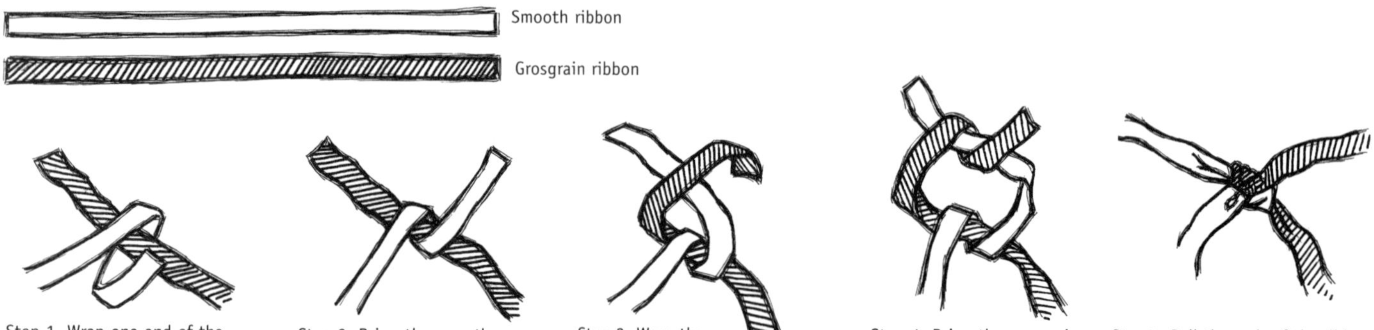

Step 1. Wrap one end of the smooth ribbon over and under the grosgrain ribbon.

Step 2. Bring the smooth ribbon up and over the grosgrain ribbon.

Step 3. Wrap the end of the grosgrain ribbon over the smooth ribbon.

Step 4. Bring the grosgrain ribbon under and over the smooth ribbon.

Step 5. Pull the ends of the ribbons in opposite directions to close up the hole and make a square knot.

ILLUSTRATION 23

Tying a Square Knot

Encourage students to practice tying two pieces of ribbon, using any style that they like.

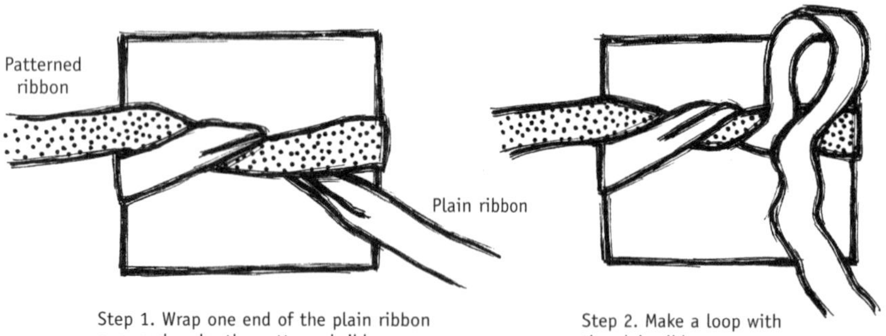

Step 1. Wrap one end of the plain ribbon over and under the patterned ribbon.

Step 2. Make a loop with the plain ribbon.

ILLUSTRATION 24

Tying a Bow

Tying a bow is not as easy as it looks. Which types of bows and knots pull apart easily? Which types do not?

Step 3. Wrap the end of the patterned ribbon over the loop of plain ribbon.

Step 4. Bring the patterned ribbon under the plain ribbon and pull it through the hole to make a loop.

Step 5. Pull the loops of the ribbons in opposite directions to close up the hole and make a bow.

- Velcro (see Illustration 25)

Have students get a magnifying glass to see just how this works. Here are some questions to ask about Velcro: How are the two strips alike? How are they different? How do they link together? Why is this such a useful fastening? What would you use it for?

These fastening activities provide excellent opportunities for oral reporting during review time, supported by the actual objects and demonstrations of their functioning. (Tying a knot or bow in public is not as easy as it sounds!) Often, children find many of these fastening devices being used as they examine the garments they wear.

ILLUSTRATION 25

Velcro

By using a magnifying glass, students can see just how a strip of Velcro works.

Keeping It Shut ► *Activity 11*

DEVELOPMENTAL LEVEL
K–2

GROUP SIZE
Large

KEY EXPERIENCE

- *Observing, predicting, and controlling change: understanding causality*

Ever since gates, doors, windows, and cupboards were invented, the problem of keeping them shut has been there too. Look at the fastening mechanisms in the school, around the surrounding grounds, at home, and in the area generally. How do some of these mechanisms work? Why do they use one way of fastening rather than another? Which are simple and easy to use? Which are inexpensive to make? Which are more complicated? Answering these questions demands on-site visits to see how these shutting mechanisms work and to discuss them as they are being examined. Here are some possible items to study and discuss:

- Outdoor gates (see Illustration 26)

Here are some questions to ask children about outdoor gates: What other shutting mechanisms can you find? How do they work? Why are they suitable for the job? What fastenings could you invent?

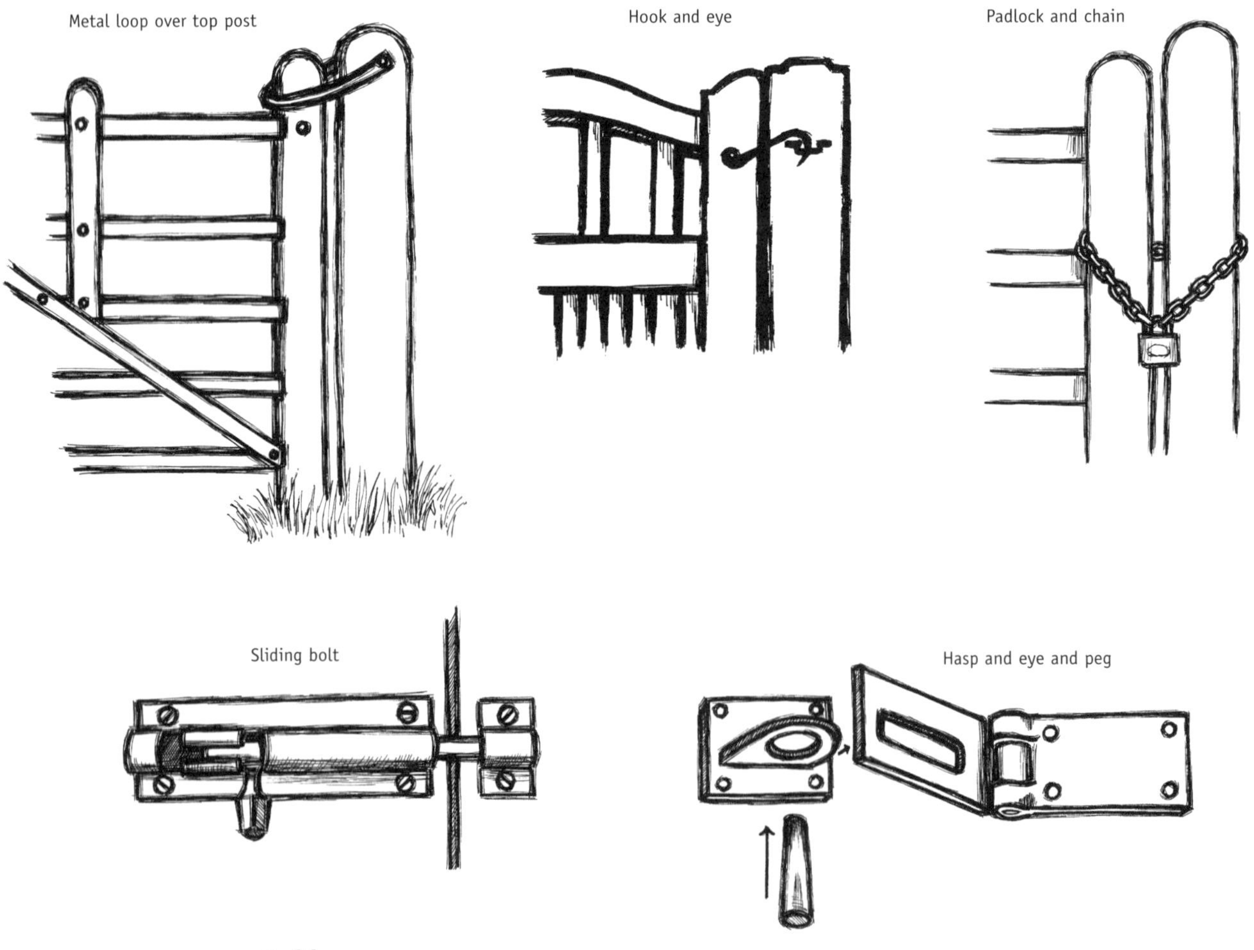

ILLUSTRATION 26

Ways to Fasten an Outdoor Gate

Outdoor gates may be fastened in a number of different ways. Encourage students to look in their school and home environments for examples of everyday shutting mechanisms such as these.

• Inside doors (see Illustration 27)

Here are some questions about inside doors: What other shutting mechanisms can you find? How do they work? Why are these fastenings good for their job? What fastenings can you invent?

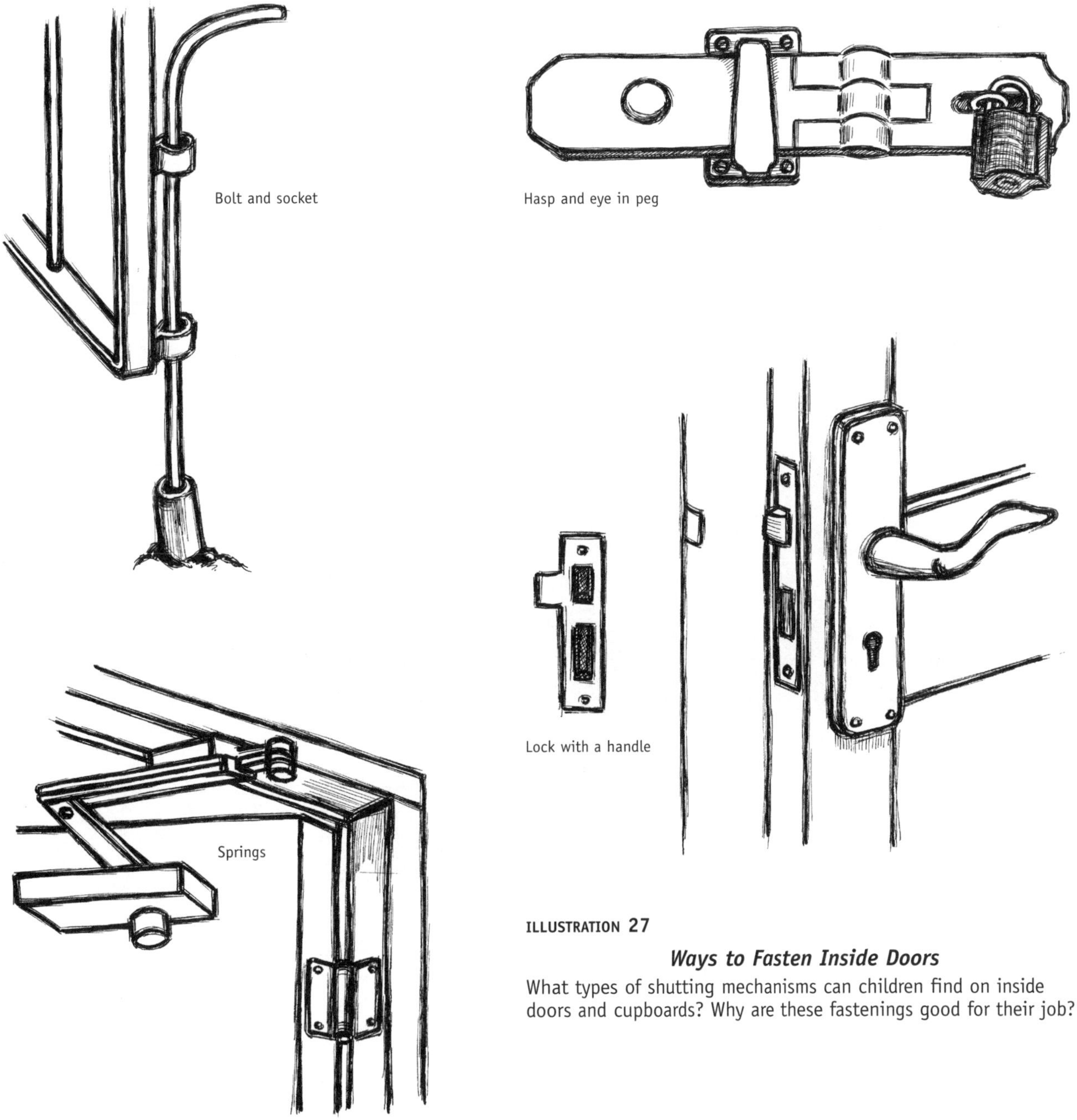

ILLUSTRATION 27

Ways to Fasten Inside Doors

What types of shutting mechanisms can children find on inside doors and cupboards? Why are these fastenings good for their job?

Looking at a Hidden Door Lock ► *Activity 12*

DEVELOPMENTAL LEVEL
1–3

GROUP SIZE
Small

KEY EXPERIENCES

- *Observing, predicting, and controlling change: understanding causality*

Some locks are hidden inside the door itself. These are called *mortise locks* (see Illustration 28).

Ask students the following types of questions: Why are they so safe? Why do they keep the door shut so well? Why are they better than locks that screw on to the door? Do you know what they look like inside?

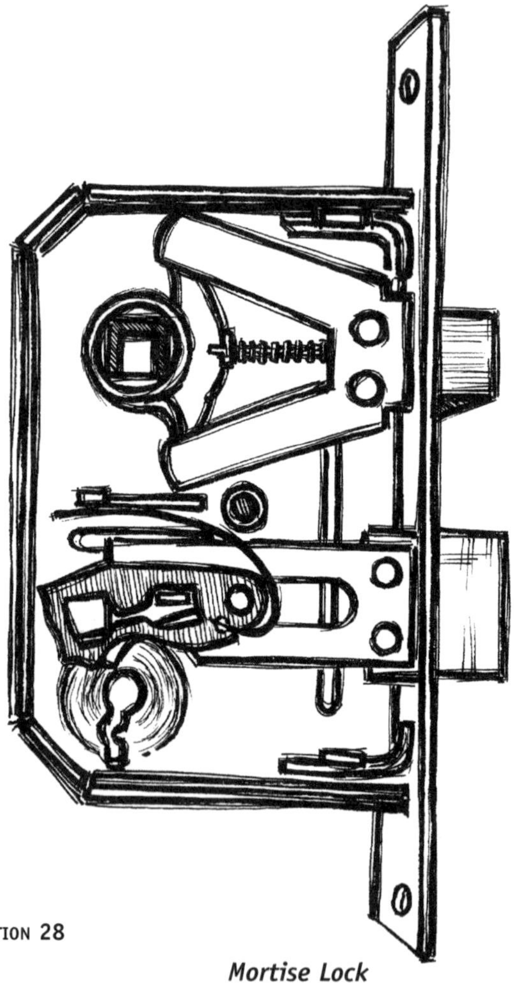

ILLUSTRATION 28

Mortise Lock

Looking at hidden locks, or mortise locks, encourages children to think about the many structures in their environment that are not in plain view.

Cupboard door fastenings are good items for students to examine since they include many hidden locks (see Illustration 29 on pg. 41).

Here are some questions about cupboard doors: What other shutting mechanisms can you find? How do they work? Why are they good for their job? What fastening could you invent?

Have students collect and make a display of shutting mechanisms. Have them make drawings of others that they see but cannot collect. Let them explain to one another how these shutting mechanisms work using words, models, and drawings. Encourage them to keep a list of all the places they see locks being used: at home, at school, when they travel, in the town, in the country, on things they use.

Turn buckle

Hook and eye

Simple lock

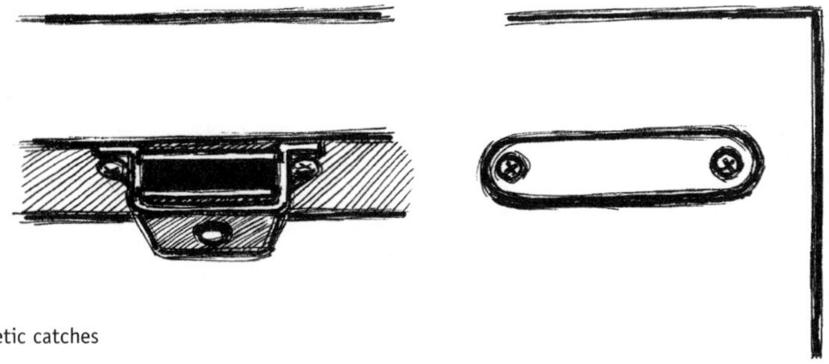

Magnetic catches

Ball catches

ILLUSTRATION 29

Cupboard Door Fasteners

Cupboard door fastenings are interesting items for students to examine because they include many different types of hidden locks.

Keeping It Together Mechanically ► *Activity 13*

DEVELOPMENTAL LEVEL
1–3

GROUP SIZE
Small

KEY EXPERIENCE
- *Designing, building, fabricating, and modifying structures or materials*

The materials we use are not always in the exact size we require; often they have to be joined. Large constructions call for special joins. Odd shapes need many joins, and sometimes joins need to be flexible to accommodate movement. Keeping things together is a real problem. Have students think about the simple problem of joining pieces of wood.

What solution do they think of first to join together pieces of wood? Perhaps they think of using nails. Nails are a good fastener to use with wood. They work by smoothly pushing their way in between the fibers of the wood (see Illustration 30). Nails can also be pulled out fairly easily to unfasten the wood.

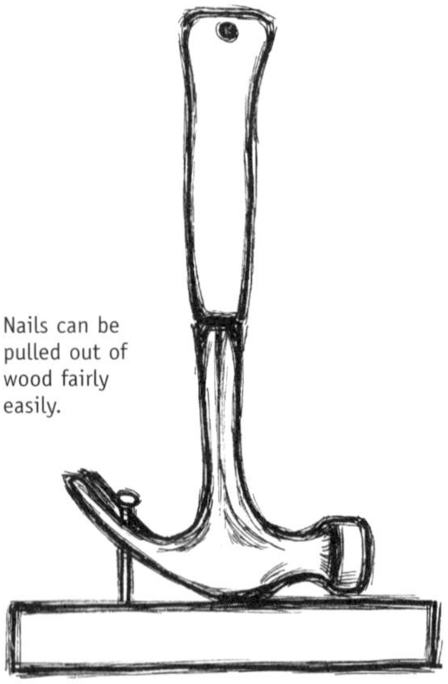

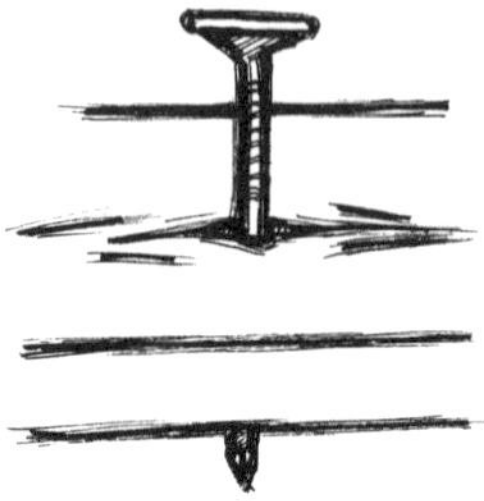

ILLUSTRATION **30**

Using Nails for Fastening Pieces of Wood

Nails are a good fastener for children to use with wood.

Perhaps the next thing students think of for fastening pieces of wood is screws. Screws draw themselves into the wood by their spiral thread (see Illustration 31 on pg. 43). As the screw enters the wood it chews a path through the fibers of the wood, holding itself firmly in. It is surprising how long the thread is on a screw. Have students see for themselves by winding cotton or thin string around the path of the thread on a screw. Then let them unwind it to see how long the string is. Let the students try this using 2", 3," and 4" screws. How long is the thread on each?

Screws will not pull out as easily as nails. Let students find out whether they can pull out a screw as easily as they can pull out a nail from a piece of wood (see Illustration 32 on pg. 43). Have the students do the following activities and think about the following questions:

- Drive a 2" nail a depth of 1" (5 cm) into a piece of wood.
- Screw a 2" screw a depth of 1" (5 cm) into a piece of wood.
- Try pulling each out with a claw hammer.
- Which is harder to pull out?
- Which would fasten wood together best?
- Which is quickest to use?

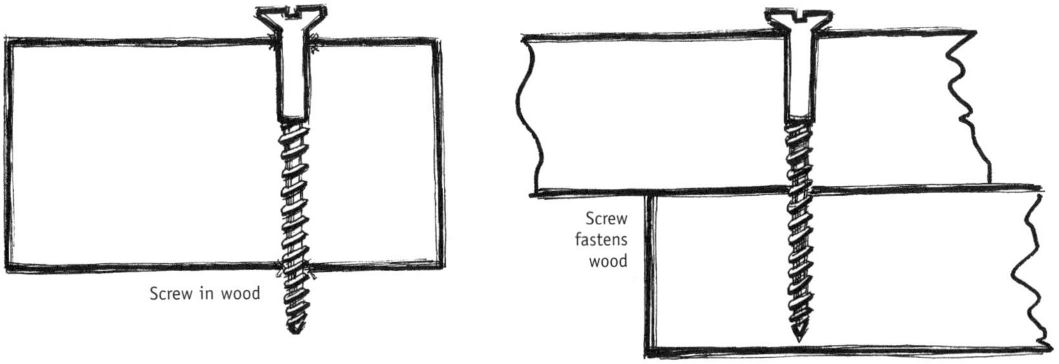

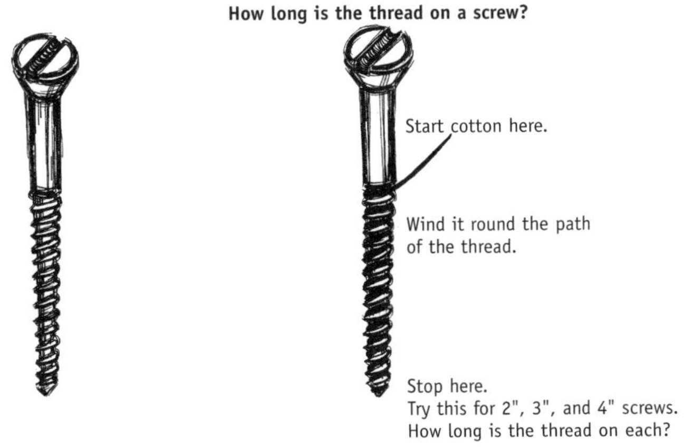

ILLUSTRATION 31

Fastening Pieces of Wood With Screws

Students can see for themselves how long the thread is on a screw by winding cotton or thin string around the path of the thread.

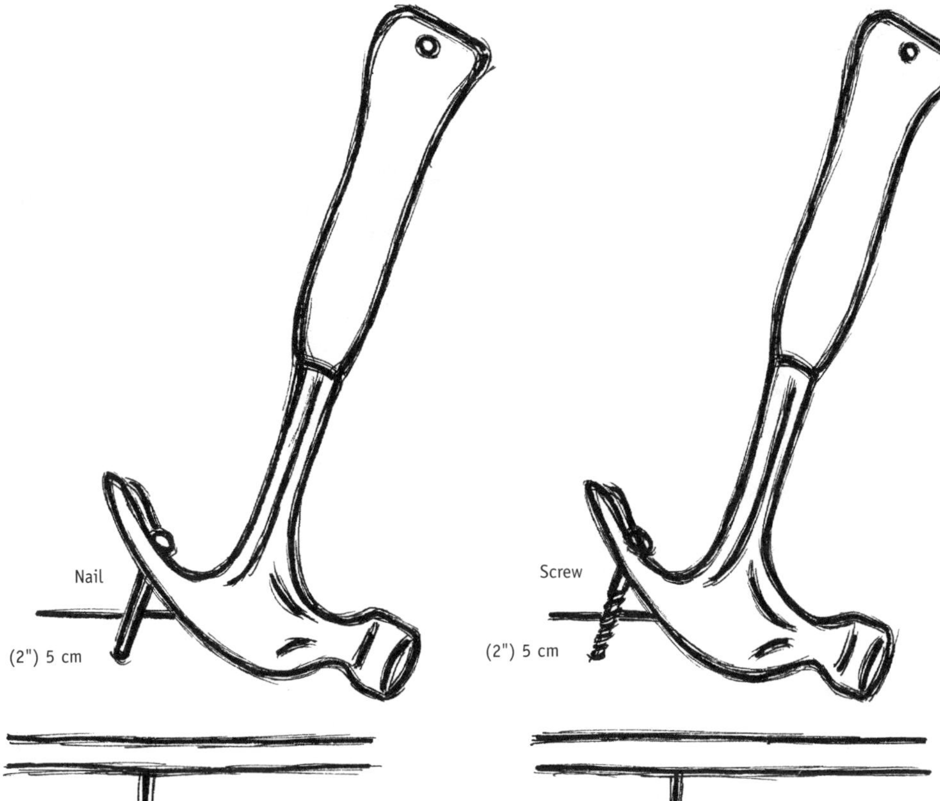

ILLUSTRATION 32

Removing Nails and Screws From Wood

Students can compare some of the structural properties of nails and screws by removing them from a piece of wood with a hammer.

• Which would you use just to fasten things down?

• Which would you use to hold things together the most strongly?

Now have students examine screws more closely:

• Why is there a cut across the head of the screw?

• How else could you take out the screw (i.e., turning in the opposite direction with the screwdriver)?

• Do some screws have different cuts on the head?

• Can you find a screw with a square head?

• What would you use to put this in with?

Finally, you or the students may come up with another way of fixing two pieces of wood together—using a nut and bolt (see Illustration 33). A bolt is a short metal rod with a thread cut all the way down in a spiral, like a wood screw only with the cuts closer together and the end flat instead of pointed. (You have to drill a hole in the

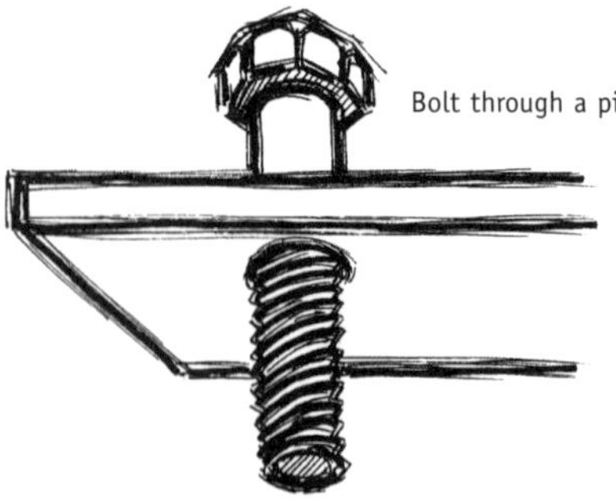

Bolt through a piece of wood

Piece of wood with a hole through for inserting the bolt and joining to the other piece

A thread on a bolt looked at under a magnifier

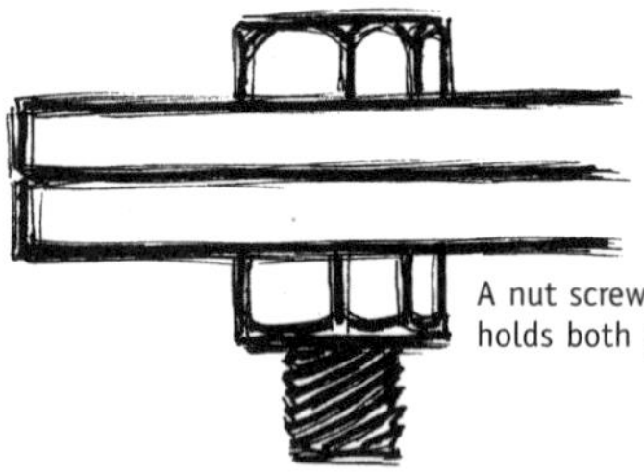

A nut screwed up to the bolt holds both pieces of wood together.

A nut screws up the spiral threads of the bolt.

ILLUSTRATION 33

Nuts and Bolts

Using nuts and bolts, how many ways can students come up with to fasten together two pieces of wood?

wood before you can put in the bolt.) A nut will screw up and down the thread of the bolt. Address the following questions and activities with the students:

- When would it be more useful to fasten things together with nuts and bolts?

- How do you tighten nuts and bolts? What do you use for this job?

- Find some large nuts and bolts and see exactly how they work. (There may be large plastic nuts and bolts in construction kits in the school.)

- Compare the length of thread on wood screws of many sizes with those of bolts of the same length. Use the method of winding strong cotton or nylon thread around the spirals. Display the findings by sticking the lengths of thread on charts beside the screws and bolts.

- Look around the school to see fastenings made with nails, with screws, and with nuts and bolts.

- Report these findings and try to explain why the different fastenings have been made for the different jobs.

Keeping It Together With Glue ► *Activity 14*

DEVELOPMENTAL LEVEL
2–4

GROUP SIZE
Small

KEY EXPERIENCE

- *Designing, building, fabricating, and modifying structures or materials*

Another problem in fastening is how to join wood without using nails, screws, or bolts. Nowadays we often use glues to fasten things together. Glues are certainly more convenient for joining things together than nailing or screwing or bolting. Sticking things together is not new; glues or adhesives for fastening wood have been known for a long time. But now there are even glues to fasten glass, metal, stone, and plastics.

Children will need to have a range of adhesives available—cold-water paste, white glue, rubber cement, liquid gum, wallpaper adhesives, balsa glue, woodworker's glue, and other general adhesives. (**Note:** Do not include any of the "super glues," as these are too dangerous.) The children may suggest other fasteners, such as chewing gum, double-sided adhesive tape, and putty or wax, so obtain these if possible. Avoid glues that need heating. Let students explore and become familiar with the texture and strength of these different types of adhesives.

To begin, provide students with plenty of pieces of wood about 12" (30 cm) long, 2" (5 cm) wide, and ½" (1 cm) thick. Plywood is excellent for this activity.

Younger children will test the adhesives in a random manner. They will put on different amounts of glue on different areas of the wood and will not always mark which glue is which. They will leave the pieces of wood overnight and then test them the next day by trying to pull them apart. They may put their subjects into two groups—good glues and bad glues—on the basis of this rough test-and-report procedure.

Keeping It Together With Glue ► *Activity 15*

DEVELOPMENTAL LEVEL
3–5

GROUP SIZE
Small

KEY EXPERIENCE

- *Measuring, testing, and analyzing: assessing the properties and composition of materials*
- *Reporting and interpreting data and results*

With older children, the natural testing process offers an excellent intervention point for the teacher. You can introduce a discussion about fair tests, that is, about controlling the variables so you can draw accurate conclusions. Teachers need to help children understand that they are investigating *adhesives.* The adhesives—the different kinds of glue—are the variables; all other things must be the same. Here are some questions to address:

• Why must tests be fair to be useful?

• What are some of the things that matter? For example: Will it matter if different wood is used for each test? Must the pieces of wood be the same size for each test? Will it matter how much glue is used? Must you use the same coating over the same area?

Through discussion, help children understand that for the scientific experiments with glue to be fair and accurate, the following "musts" need to be followed:

• The wood must be same kind, size, and thickness for all the tests.

• There must be the same amount and thickness of adhesive on each sample.

• The adhesive must be over the same area. (**Note:** Children often apply glue over so great an area that the joints are difficult to break. An area measuring between 1" and 2" square [2 to 5 sq. cm] is appropriate.)

• The same drying period must be given for all tests. Overnight drying is a good time period, with tests conducted during work time the next day.

Another discussion will certainly center around the testing method. For example, discuss with students the following types of questions:

• Was the pull-apart test good enough? Did it tell you how strong a glue was even though the joint gave way?

• How else could you measure the strength of the glues?

• Will the measuring units matter as long as they are the same for all the samples?

In addition to the testing ideas generated by the children, the teacher may suggest the following simple test rig (see Illustration 34 on pg. 48).

As students test the samples, have them set the tables at the agreed distance apart. Mark the center of the joint. Pass the test strip through the handle of the bucket. Clamp each end of the joined strip firmly to the table. The wood should extend about 2" (5 cm) beyond the end of the clamp. When the rig is set, students can place the bucket at the middle point of the joint marked *X.* (Some weak adhesives like cold-water paste or chewing gum may not even support the bucket!) They should put a large sheet of plastic under the bucket area to catch the sand when the bucket falls as the joint breaks. Add sand by the carton-full until the joint breaks. If children think an adhesive is weak, they should begin by using half carton measures. Keep a record of the loads in terms of carton units; this unit is quite sufficient for comparative purposes. If the weight of each carton of sand is known, students can also express the results in conventional terms by multiplying the number of units (cartons of sand) by the weight of each carton plus the weight of the bucket. Encourage students to record and order the results, as shown in the following table:

Adhesive	Carton Units to Break Joint *X*	Approximate Weight in Pounds	Approximate Weight in Grams
water paste	0 (bucket alone too heavy)	_____	_____
white glue	0 (bucket alone too heavy)	_____	_____
chewing gum	0 (bucket alone too heavy)	_____	_____
double-sided tape	½	_____	_____
gum liquid	½	_____	_____
wallpaper paste	2	_____	_____
balsa cement	22	_____	_____
woodworker's glue	38	_____	_____

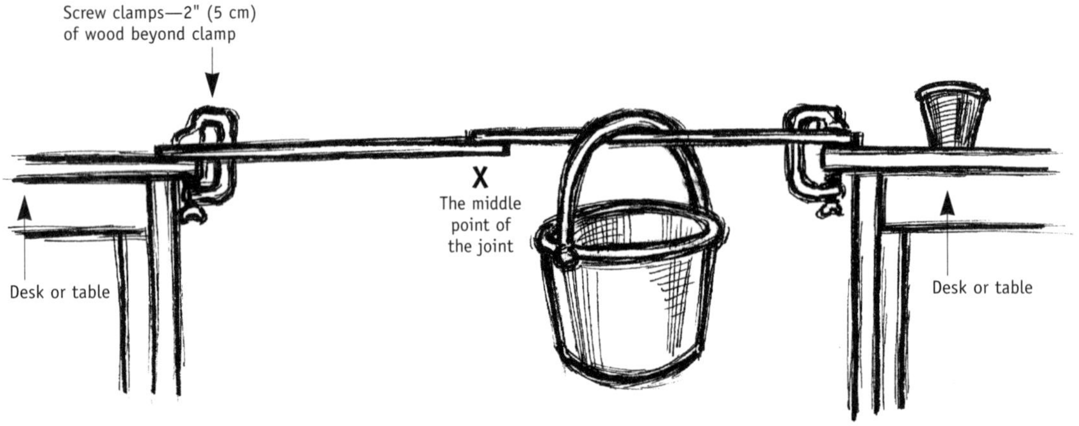

ILLUSTRATION 34

A Simple Test Rig

Students can make a simple testing rig such as this one. After setting two tables at an agreed distance apart, they mark the center of the joint, pass the test strip through the handle of the bucket, clamp each end of the strip to the table, and place the bucket at the middle point of the joint. They then test the strength by adding increasing amounts of sand in the bucket.

► *Part Four*

Natural Structures and Forms

The supply of interesting items for children to investigate is unlimited in the natural world; the variety of forms is enormous. From shells to plant stems to spider webs, the possibilities for active learning are endless.

Natural Structures and Forms

"Growth" and "form" are terms that are frequently used together when considering living things. In some cases, the forms of living things can be quite easily explained by growth and other physical considerations. In others, the somewhat vague word "growth" is used to describe a very complex matter. Sometimes growth is simply an increase in size without obvious alteration of form. At other times, growth brings about a gradual change of form and the slow development of a more or less complicated structure. The form of many living things is characterized by its symmetry. This symmetry is maintained by the organism; as growth and change produce one type of imbalance, another type of growth and change compensates for it and restores the balance.

The spiral is a common form of growth. It is often seen in plants, although it is not limited to them. Plants display many spiral forms. These range from the arrangement of leaves on the stem to the spiral growth of the stem itself. Looked at from above, for example, the head of the cauliflower shows spiral patterns of growth. Even more simple than spiral leaf arrangement and stem growth is the development of many one-piece shells. The tip is the oldest part and remains the smallest, while the rest of the shell gets bigger as growth continues.

Many things we take for granted reveal an interesting structure and form when they are looked at purposefully. For example, at first glance a fir cone seems a crowded mass of woody scales. But on closer inspection, patterns can be clearly seen, giving the cone a definite form with two spiral arrangements running up the cone from base to top. Almost everything has its own form; form may be seen in the shape of eggs, in the overall appearance of trees, in the cells of the beehive, in the spiral arrangement of the nautilus shell, in the horns of animals, and in the limbs of the human body. Equally amazing is the manner in which each form has features common to other living things within its own plant or animal group.

Shells: A Collecting Interest ► *Activity 16*

DEVELOPMENTAL LEVEL
K–2

GROUP SIZE
Large

KEY EXPERIENCES

- *Looking with a purpose: observing and collecting data*
- *Classifying and ordering materials according to their attributes and properties*

Shells provide many wonderful learning opportunities in the classroom. Shells of one sort or another can be found almost everywhere. Both saltwater and freshwater yield their own populations of shell dwellers, and young children love collecting shells! Wherever the collecting is done, be sure the students get empty shells. This is important for two reasons. First, we want to let living things survive. Second, shells with the bodies of their occupants still inside can smell unpleasant when brought into a warm classroom! Be sure to observe safety precautions. Never let children collect shells near the water on their own. Children near water should always be supervised.

As soon as students get a collection of shells, have them wash the shells thoroughly in a bucket of hot water. Swish the shells gently around in the water to get the mud and dirt from them. Do this several times to get them really clean. Look at the shells each time to see if you can gently scrape off any dirt. Wash them one last time. Pour away the water, shake out each shell, and put them on a cloth to dry.

When the shells are dry, they may look a bit dull and colorless. If so, have the students get a piece of soft cloth, moisten it with salad oil or some very thin machine oil, and gently rub both the inside and outside of each shell with the oil. The oil will bring out the natural color of the shells and help to preserve them. If after a time the shells lose their color and shine, wipe them again with the oil.

Collecting shells is not an end in itself. The value of the activity lies in deciding the purpose of the collection and its arrangement (see Illustration 35 on pg. 52). Should the shells be grouped according to some criterion, or should they be arranged serially along a continuum? Children can decide the arrangement(s) for themselves. For example, the students might come up with the following possibilities for arranging the shells:

- All the same species together
- Largest to smallest
- Lightest to darkest
- All the small shells together
- All the large shells together
- All the same colors together
- All the local shells together
- All those brought from other places together
- All the broken ones together

Having established criteria, the students can begin to sort the shells. Their next discussion will center on how to display the shells. Teachers can help by asking the following types of questions:

- What about using egg boxes or trays with compartments for each shell? Will you paint the compartments first? If so, what colors?
- Could you glue the shells to a cardboard box lid? Should this be colored first? If so, what colors?

• Would you like to put the shells in a clear plastic box or box lid so both the top and underside can be seen?

• How should we display broken shells? (**Note:** Don't discard broken shells; they can tell you a lot about the shell's structure. Look very closely at them.)

ILLUSTRATION 35

A Collection of Shells

Collecting shells is a fun activity for children. Let students decide how to sort and arrange the shells. Egg boxes or trays with compartments are good materials to have on hand for this activity.

Shells: A Collecting Interest ► *Activity 17*

DEVELOPMENTAL LEVEL
1–3

GROUP SIZE
Small

KEY EXPERIENCES

- *Looking with a purpose: observing and collecting data*
- *Classifying and ordering materials according to their attributes and properties*
- *Measuring, testing, and analyzing: assessing the properties and composition of materials*

Students can observe many things about shells. For example:

• If shells are in spirals, how many turns make the spiral?

• What colors are on the shell?

• What patterns are on the shell?

• What sizes do shells come in? How big is the largest shell in the collection? How small is the smallest shell? Measure to give precision to the answers to these size questions.

• Are the shells all in one piece? Do any shells have two pieces? Can you see patterns on the two halves? Do the patterns match? The columella is a kind of central pillar formed inside the shell (see Illustration 36).

• Make a display of the damaged shells to show the interiors of shells. Put them beside whole shells of the same kind.

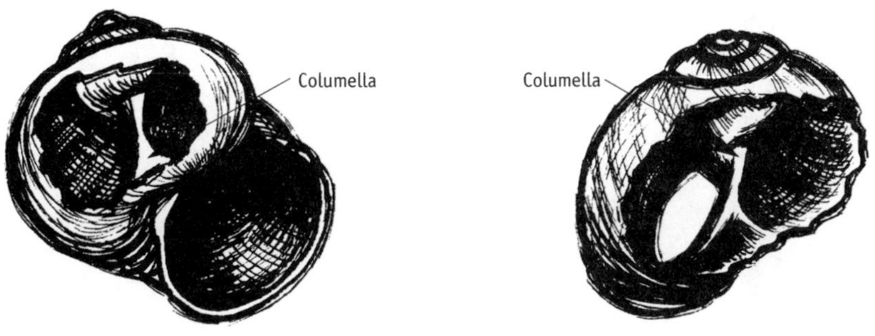

ILLUSTRATION 36

Looking at Broken Shells

Broken shells can also be displayed to show the interior structure and form of a shell.

Looking at Buds on Trees and Shrubs ► *Activity 18*

DEVELOPMENTAL LEVEL
K–2

GROUP SIZE
Large

KEY EXPERIENCE
- *Looking with a purpose: observing and collecting data*

Have children look at almost any tree or bush in winter, when the leaves have fallen, and they will see buds on the twigs—nearly always at the end of the twig and usually also along its sides (see Illustration 37).

Buds are interesting structures, so it is worth taking a close look at them. If trees or shrubs are being pruned, the students can easily get a supply of twigs to bring into school to examine. Otherwise, the class can visit a nearby place where a collection of twigs can be made. The teacher should take pruning shears to do the cutting. Students should be discouraged from tearing twigs from trees and bushes. If your school is in a town or city with little access to open places, students can observe living material on site without damaging it.

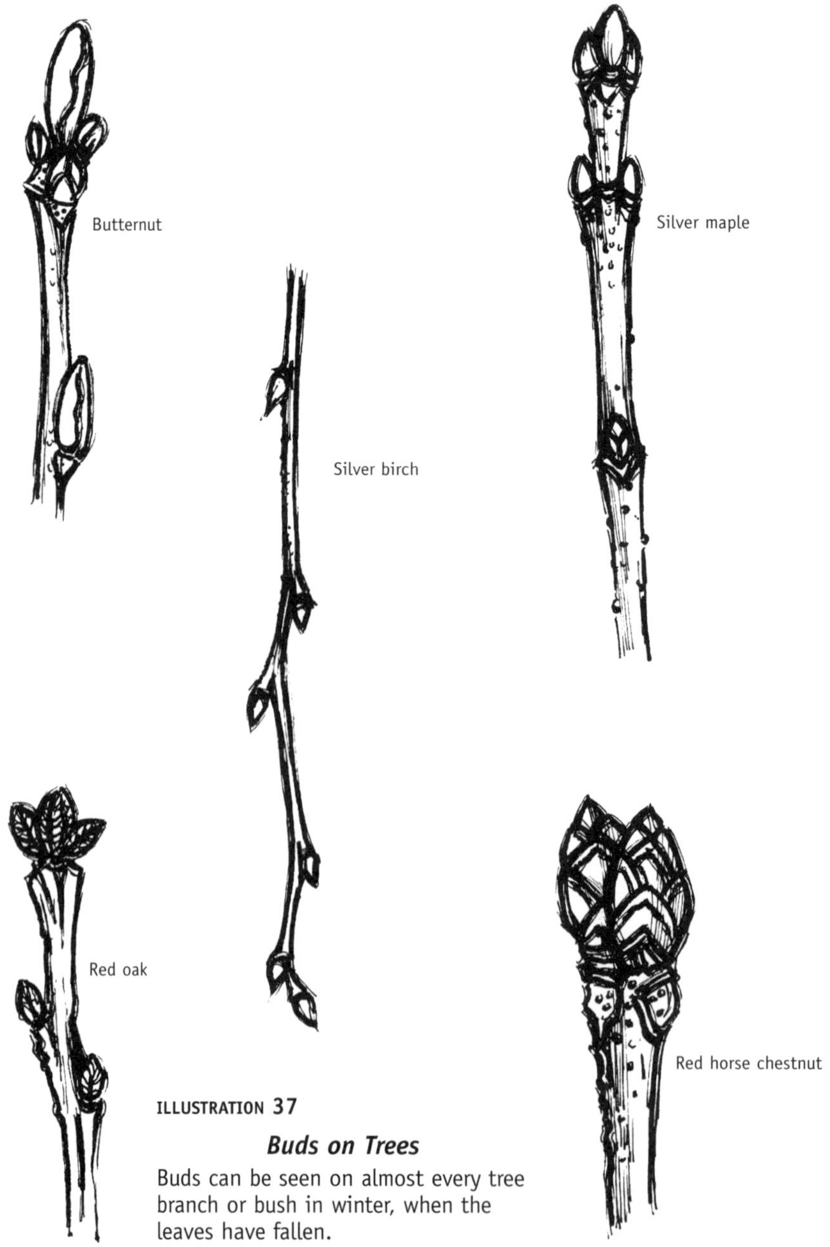

ILLUSTRATION 37

Buds on Trees

Buds can be seen on almost every tree branch or bush in winter, when the leaves have fallen.

Buds as Natural Structures

Most plants have buds. Buds are compressed embryonic shoots capable of developing into new shoots (which will themselves produce buds) or flowers. If the bud produces a flower, new stem growth must take place from another bud elsewhere on the stem. Most buds contain foliage leaves surrounded by tougher scale leaves. These scale leaves may give the bud protection—for example, by a covering of hair, as in the willow, or by a sticky substance as in the buckeye. When the bud begins to sprout, the scales are forced open and eventually drop off, leaving a scar. The foliage leaves inside expand, separate from one another, grow, and become green. While most buds grow, some do not, and these are called *dormant buds.*

It is convenient in a study of buds to use the twigs of trees and shrubs that lose their leaves in winter. Plants that lose their leaves in winter are called "deciduous," and they show the features of buds well. Winter buds of various trees differ a great deal. Some, like the beech, are long and slender with many bud scales. Others, such as the lime, hazel, and elm, are rather oval with few visible bud scales. The buds of ash are black, while those of the sycamore are green. Sometimes (as in the ash and buckeye) buds are placed in pairs opposite each other. In the lime, they are placed singly on alternate sides of the stem.

The way to get to know trees by their buds is by actively studying them, making drawings and photographs of good specimens, and describing them in detail. Children's work can be stimulated and assisted by a dialogue that raises real questions that children can answer through their own activities. By examining buds in the local area, children can address such questions as: Which type of bud opens first, which next, which last? Do buds all open in the same order? Do big buds open before little ones? Is there any connection between the position of the bud and how soon it opens? Which bud has the most leaves? Are the leaves all the same? Do all the buds on a tree or plant open at the same time? Is there a pattern to the opening of buds? Which buds open into flowers and which into leaves? Do flowers and leaves appear on trees at the same time? In additions to observations stimulated through dialogue, pose questions on how to record observations and how to continue observations over a period of time. Older children in the elementary school might study the development of a bud over a period by photographing the same twig and bud at intervals from its first swelling to its complete opening.

The Structure of a Cabbage: A Big Bud ► *Activity 19*

DEVELOPMENTAL LEVEL
K–2

GROUP SIZE
Large

KEY EXPERIENCE
- *Looking with a purpose: observing and collecting data*

Children will be interested to know what is inside a bud. They can get a good view of bud structure on a large scale if you bring in a few whole cabbages and cut them in half. These cabbage sections are ideal subjects for closely looking at a bud (see Illustration 38).

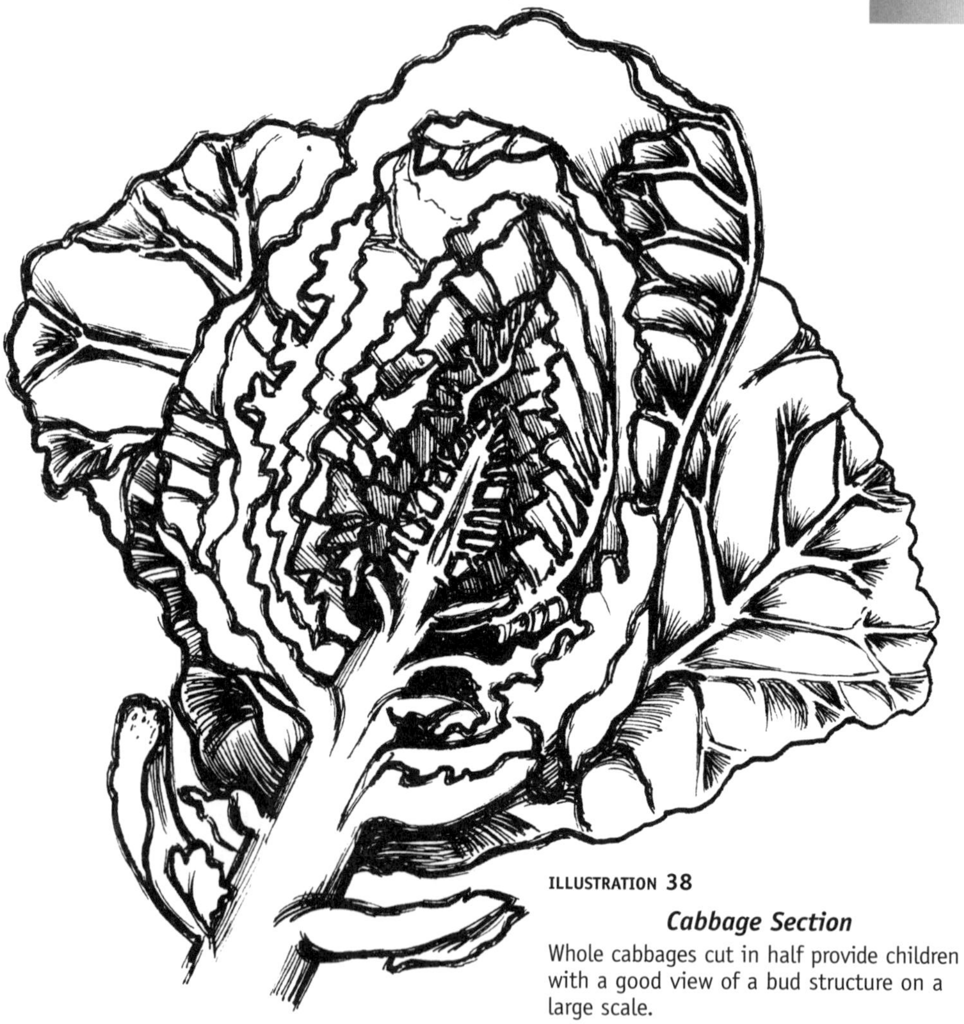

ILLUSTRATION **38**

Cabbage Section

Whole cabbages cut in half provide children with a good view of a bud structure on a large scale.

The teacher should guide this activity by posing questions such as the following:

- What is the structure of the bud? Can you see the thick, tight, outside leaves? Can you see the stem in the center?

- See how the side leaves are folded to fit into the bud. If this bud continued to grow, what would happen? When this bud opens, what would happen to the side leaves?

- What size of plant would this grow into? What evidence is there for this?

If there is a supply of twigs to examine in the classroom, or the group is outdoors looking at trees and bushes, ask the following types of questions:

- What shape are the buds? Are they pointed? Rounded?
- How are buds arranged on the twig? Are the buds separate from each other, or are they arranged in pairs? (See Illustration 39.)
- What color are the buds? Are all buds the same color?
- Look at the pattern on the outside of the bud—the bud scales. How many bud scales can you count? Are all bud scales alike (see Illustration 40)?

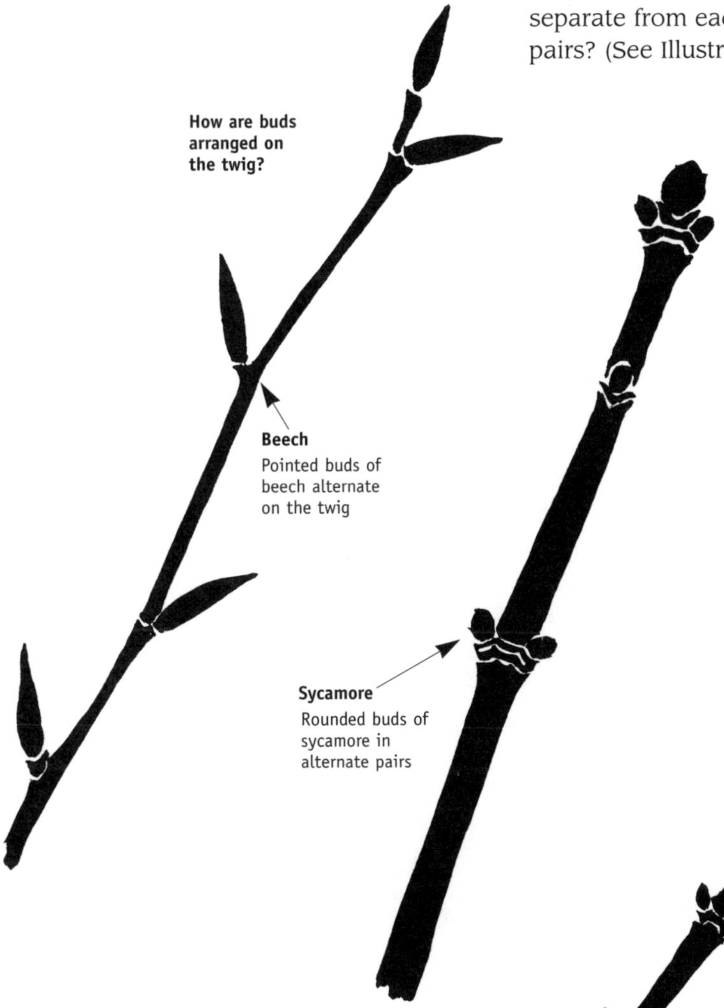

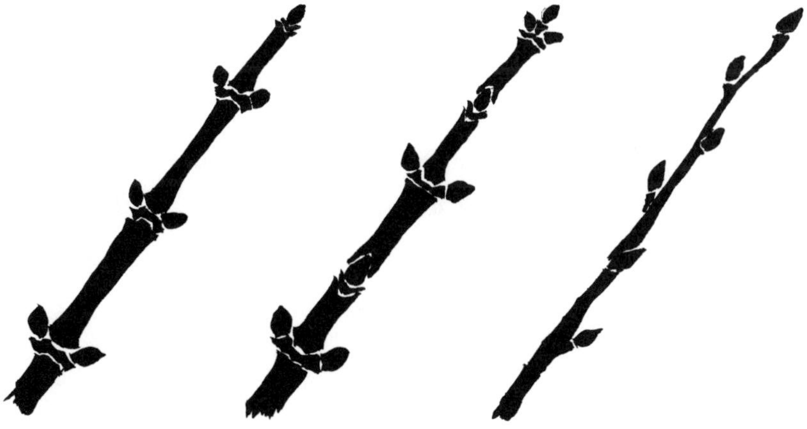

ILLUSTRATION 39

Bud Arrangement

Students can examine a supply of twigs in the classroom, or they can go outdoors to look at trees and bushes.

Single bud of horse chestnut showing the arrangement of bud scales

ILLUSTRATION 40

Single Buds of Horse Chestnut and Elm Trees

By looking at the buds of different plants, such as the elm and the horse chestnut, students can compare their color, pattern, and scale arrangement.

Single bud of elm showing the arrangement of the bud scales

Looking at Spider Webs ► *Activity 20*

DEVELOPMENTAL LEVEL
3–5

GROUP SIZE
Large

KEY EXPERIENCE
- *Looking with a purpose: observing and collecting data*

Spider webs are marvelous natural structures and are well-worth looking at closely. When children know something about webs and web-making they will look with more interest and insight at the next webs they see. This topic is a good example of something the teacher can introduce to the whole class after some personal preparation to have the facts right and to have illustrations on hand. Be on the lookout for webs—the beautiful ones are circular or orb webs. Sometimes children will see incomplete webs or broken webs awaiting repair; others are abandoned webs left by species that make fresh webs everyday. It is doubtful if children will have the patience to observe a spider spinning a whole web, for it takes about an hour. However, they may well see a spider at work making or repairing a web.

Spiders go through several steps when making an orb web (see Illustration 41 on pg. 59). When the web is spun, the spider strengthens it by tying it safely down with a few more boundary lines. Then the spider may go to a position in the middle of the web, or she may hide near, but outside, the web. If the spider hides outside the web, she always attaches herself to it by a lifeline, or telegraph thread, so that she can feel the slightest shake if the web snares an insect. When you see an empty orb web, always look for the lifeline or telegraph thread.

Together with the students, find an orb web. Look for the lifeline or telegraph thread and give it a very gentle tap with a very thin twig. What happens? Does the spider appear? What happens if she is in the center of the web?

Here are some questions to pose for children to think about:

- Can you make a model of a spider web?
- How will you anchor it?
- What will you use for thread?
- What will you use for glue? (**Note:** The spider uses her own glue.)
- How will you hang it up?

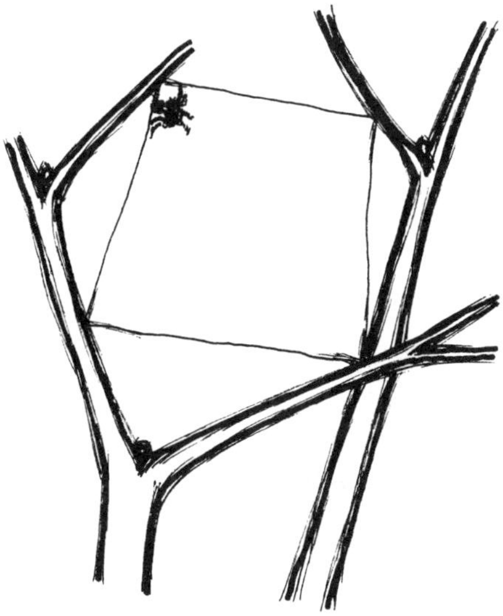

1. Making the boundary threads

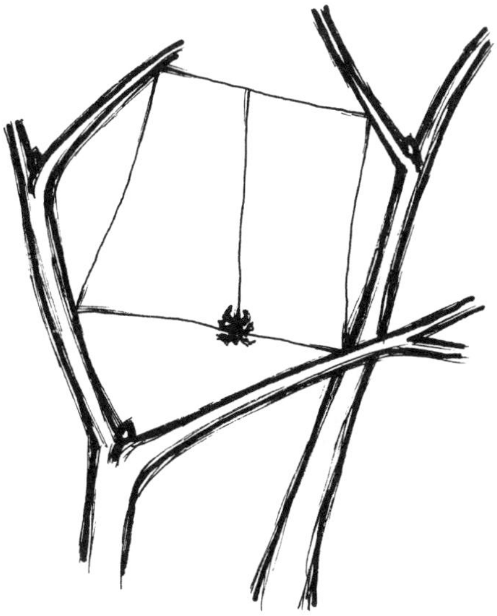

2. Dropping down to make the first spokes

3. Finishing the spokes

4. Making the central nonsticky platform—a scaffolding

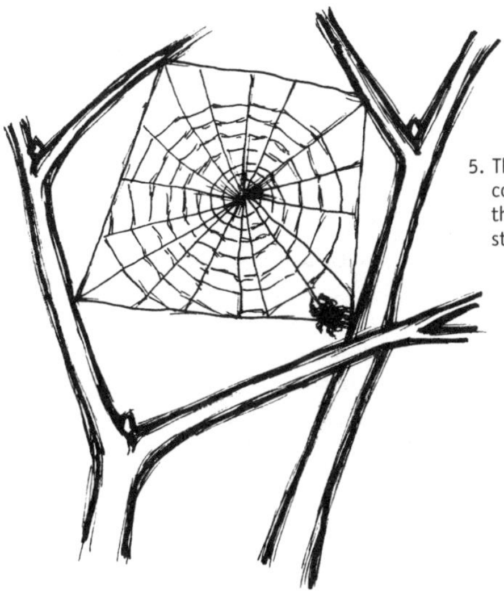

5. The real web is nearly completed starting from the outside with very sticky thread.

ILLUSTRATION 41

How a Spider Makes a Web

Spiders go through many different steps as they make an orb web.

The Structure of Plant Stems ► *Activity 21*

DEVELOPMENTAL LEVEL
4–6

GROUP SIZE
Small

KEY EXPERIENCES

- *Measuring, testing, and analyzing: assessing the properties and composition of materials*
- *Reporting and interpreting data and results*

A NOTE FOR TEACHERS

Plant Stems as Structures

One way of classifying flowering plants is according to their life cycles. Flowering plants can be put into the following three groups: (1) **Ephemeral** plants complete more than one life cycle in a year; (2) **Herbaceous** plants, such as the buttercup or nettle, are comparatively small plants with unthickened, soft green stems; and (3) **Woody** plants are comparatively large plants, such as the privet and oak, with hard brown stems covered in bark. Woody plants may be **deciduous**—shedding their leaves regularly at the end of the growing season; or they may be **evergreen**—shedding their leaves at irregular intervals. Woody plants are often described as trees or shrubs according to their size, but the differences are fairly imprecise. Shrubs are usually smaller and more bushy in appearance than trees. Some plants that are called herbaceous, such as wallflowers, have quite woody stems near the ground.

Stems are essentially cylindrical structures, though other ranges of shapes can be found, such as the four-angled stems of the mint family. Typically stems are upright, but some are horizontal and some even grow underground. Stems have the following main functions:

1. To hold the leaves to the light (for the plant to make food by photosynthesis)
2. To support flowers in a suitable position for pollination, that is, to be visible to insects or to catch the wind
3. To act as a pipeline between the root and leaves
4. To store plant food and to become an organ for vegetative reproduction
5. To make food by photosynthesis (in green stems)

Stems can be small, as in herbaceous plants, or very large, as in many trees. Their structure can be as simple as a hollow tube, or as complex as a tall tree. The simple stem will show the main features: the epidermis or outer skin; inside this the cortex or tissue storing plant food; and, possibly, some strengthening fibers. In thick stems, such as those of trees, the solid parts will be packed with tissues, each with different functions. The phloem contains tube-like cells for transporting food made as a result of photosynthesis, while the cambium makes a dense strong layer of cells. Altogether, the stem of any plant is a remarkable structure.

Students begin this activity by collecting the stems of plants. They then test the stems' stiffness by bending them gently with their hands, classifying the stems into two groups: (1) stiff and (2) pliable. Are there fairer and more accurate tests they could perform to study the stiffness of plant stems? What other rules (criteria) should there be to make good comparisons? Encourage students to consider the following questions:

- Should the stems all be the same length?
- Should they all be the same thickness?
- Should they be tested for bending or breaking?
- Why would bending be the best if students are holding the stems in their hands? (**Note:** Breaking stems held in students' hands may cause injury.)

Have students cut stems to the same length (12" or 30 cm) and test their bendability with a scale similar to that in Illustration 42.

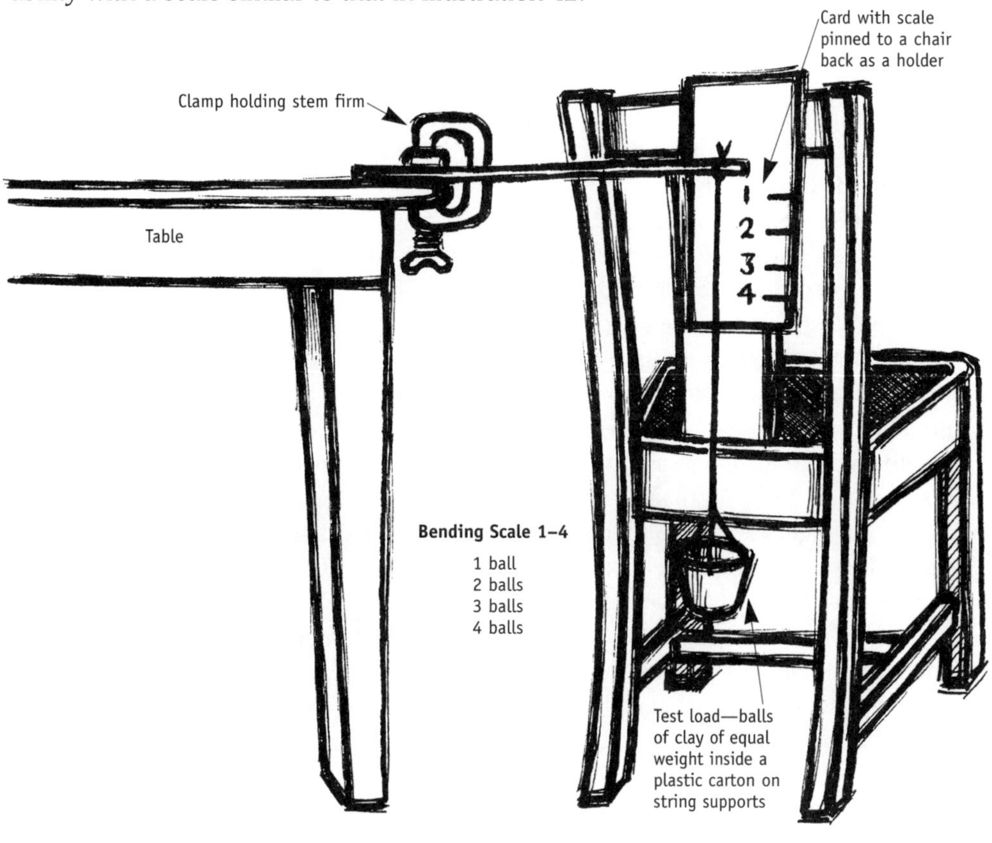

ILLUSTRATION 42

Testing the Bendability of Plant Stems

After collecting the stems of plants, students can test each stem's bendability with a scale such as this one.

Discuss an interpretation of the scale. For example, a score of 1 might indicate that a stem is very stiff; 2, stiff; 3, bendable; and 4, very bendable.

Compare the hand-tested results with the experimental testing. Let the students discuss which method of measurement is better. Place the stems in four bundles and mark each so that they will be known again according to their stiffness.

Together with the students, make another collection of stems. This time get many kinds, including woody stems from bushes or trees, stems of tall flowering plants, stems of wild plants in fields around the school, and stems from the produce department of the supermarket (such as celery or rhubarb). Have the students look at different stems using a magnifying glass to observe and answer the following questions:

- What shape(s) are the stems (for example, round, square, triangular)?
- How do the stems vary in thickness?
- What does the outer skin look like? Is it thick or thin?
- What colors are the stems?
- Can you see the ribs or stringy parts? Can you see soft stuff (pith) in the stems? Can you see the woody substance? What words can you use to describe all these different textures?
- Do the different stems feel alike as you hold them? What words can you use to describe their differences?
- Cut each stem with pruning shears. Look at the cross section. Are some stems nearly hollow? Look at the lengthwise cut. Can you see tubes running down the stem?

Encourage students to make drawings to illustrate their answers to these questions. Students should make the drawings as large as possible and show the actual stems beside the drawings.

Next, students can test for firmness by cutting a small section of various fresh stems that seem to be soft and watery and not very woody inside. Celery and rhubarb stems are good examples since they are kept firm by the water in them. Students should put a stiff stem of celery or rhubarb in the test apparatus used before, being careful not to squash the stem by clamping it too tightly. Put a plain sheet of paper on the marker position behind the stem. Mark the position of the free end every five minutes over a period of half an hour. Have the students record the results. Then have them put the stem in a jar of water to see what happens to the stem after an hour in water.

Encourage students to try these experiments with as many stems as possible, looking first at their cross sections and trying to forecast the result of the test based on the stem's structure. Have them record both their forecast and the actual results.

Water and plant stems are other interesting phenomena to study. Have the students get fresh leafy stems for this. They should put a collection of stems with the leaves still on into a jar of water colored with red ink. After half a day, have them cut across the stems at two-inch intervals to see where the water goes. In which stem does it travel most? In which the least? They can follow up these experiments by seeing what happens to a white flower on a leafy stem when the stem is put into colored water. Have them try a white daisy or a carnation or a rose.

At review time the teacher will need to help children organize some of these concepts in their minds to understand the fact that the woody parts of plants give them rigidity and that this rigidity is helped by the water in their stems. This water can pass right through the stems from root to flower.

A Seed Hunter's Guide—Wild and Garden Plants

► *Activity 22*

DEVELOPMENTAL LEVEL
2–4

GROUP SIZE
Small

KEY EXPERIENCE
- *Looking with a purpose: observing and collecting data*

A NOTE FOR TEACHERS

Fruits and Seeds

The Definition of "Fruit" and "Seed"

The *fruit* of a plant is the structure that contains the seed(s). It develops from the ovary of the flower after fertilization. The pericarp or fruit wall is formed from the ovary wall. Sometimes this becomes fleshy and forms part of the fruit, as in the apple. A *seed* is contained within the fruit. Fruits can be dry, such as those of the ash, acorn, sycamore, or poppy, or they can be succulent, such as the plum, sloe, tomato, orange, apple, or pear. It is popular to think of fleshy objects as fruits and dry ones as seeds, but this is a fallacy that is quite misleading.

Looking for and collecting seeds can be an exciting and interesting activity for children throughout the year. Flowering plants can produce seeds in nearly all seasons if they are allowed to go on growing. Some seeds will need a lot of hunting down while others are easy to see. Children will need clues to help guide their searches for plants producing fruits.

The Formation of the Fruit and Seed

It is important for teachers to know how fruits and seeds are formed; then they can better guide children, via suitable questioning clues, to the main features of the fruits they discover. After fertilization has occurred most of the flower parts wither away, as their purpose has been served. Interesting traces of them may persist after the fruit has formed. In apples, the remains of petals and sepals may be seen at the point opposite the stalk. In oranges, they may be seen at the point of attachment. In certain plants, some of the flower parts persist, but with different functions. The style may form a hooked spine in some animal-dispersed fruits; for example, the pappus forms a parachute for the dandelion seed. The receptacle sometimes swells and becomes succulent as in the apple. In all plants, the main changes after fertilization involve the ovary and its contents, as summarized below:

The *ovary* wall is now called the "pericarp." It increases in size, becoming leathery as in the buttercup; woody as in the oak or hazel; dry and brittle as in legumes; or fleshy as in succulent fruits.

The *ovule* becomes the seed itself.

Children in the elementary grades will not need to know this much detail, but their keen eyes may be able to pick out evidence of the remains of the former floral parts. Certainly, teachers will be asked about the diverse structures that plants have developed to produce, contain, and disperse their seeds.

Fruits and Seeds as Plant Structures

Following is a list of some common wild plants and garden plants that teachers and students can easily obtain to examine plant structures:

- **Buttercup.** These have very small seeds that will be found on the top of the stem that carried the flower. At first they are green fruits; later they turn brown and woody. When very ripe, they fall off the stem. The best time to collect them is just before they fall but this will not be easy for beginners.

• **Sweet Pea.** The pods containing the seeds are easy to see even at an early stage. When ripe, they are quite long and contain a number of seeds that can clearly be seen. Collect these before the pods become completely dry and split open, spilling the seeds.

• **Sunflower.** No one can miss these seed heads. But if you want really ripe seeds, the collector must wait until the petals have all fallen and then get to the seed heads before the birds discover them.

• **Dandelion.** These fruits are easy to see as the ripe seed heads show as "dandelion" clocks. To collect them, put a plastic bag carefully over them and cut the stem at the base. Close the bag carefully and don't crush the contents.

• **Thistle.** Heads soon fill with the fluffy hairs of the fruit. These hairs act like parachutes carrying the tiny seed at the end. Again, use the plastic bag method for collecting.

• **Snapdragon.** Look on the stems where the flowers had been and find the dry box-like fruits with an opening at the top. If you shake this box, seeds will fall out. Use the plastic bag method for collecting or you may lose the seeds.

• **Poppy.** The seed capsule of the poppy is easy to see soon after the flowers fall. Look at the row of holes near the top, just under the cap. It is from these that the seeds can escape. Shake a ripe capsule and look! Use the plastic bag method to collect these fruits.

• **Trees.** Most trees have their fruits ready to fall in late autumn, and if you know the trees, you will easily find their fruits. Some common trees and their fruits, found in both woodlands and parks, are as follows: oak (acorns), ash (ash keys), sycamore (wings), horse chestnut (buckeyes), and hazel (nuts).

A Seed Hunter's Guide—Fleshy Fruits

►*Activity 23*

DEVELOPMENTAL LEVEL
2–4

GROUP SIZE
Small

KEY EXPERIENCES

- *Looking with a purpose: observing and collecting data*
- *Reporting and interpreting data and results*

Fleshy fruits are worth looking at as sections cut two ways—*vertical* (lengthwise), and *transverse* (cross sections). The tomato is an easy item for students to cut and observe (see Illustration 43). Teachers should ask students questions such as the following:

- Can you find the seeds in the tomato?
- Can you see the remains of the flower parts of the tomato?
- How many tomato seeds can you count?

ILLUSTRATION 43
Tomatoes
Fleshy fruits, such as the tomato, can be cut both lengthwise and crosswise to provide interesting views of the seeds that are inside.

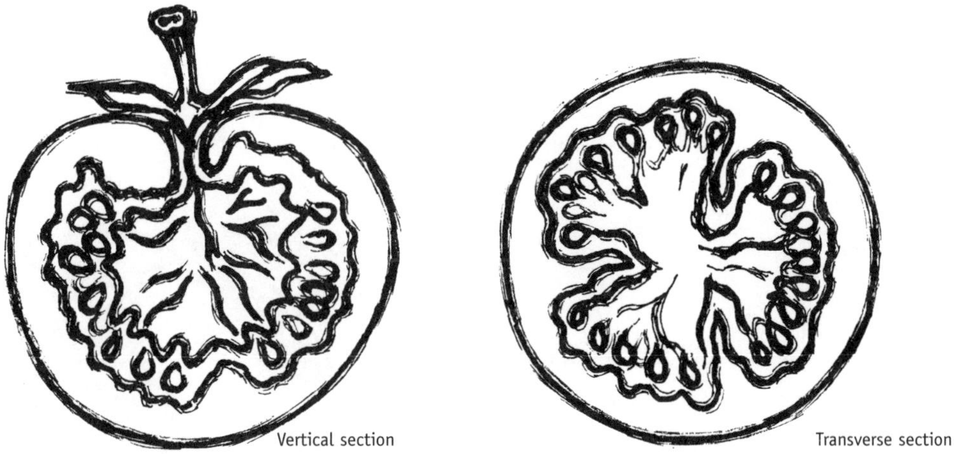

The apple can also be cut two ways (see Illustration 44). Ask questions such as the following:

- Where are the apple seeds?
- How many seeds are there in the apple?
- What part is the apple core?

ILLUSTRATION 44
Apples
As students look at the inside of an apple, encourage them to look at the arrangement of the seeds. When the apple is cut into a transverse section, what pattern or shape do the seeds make?

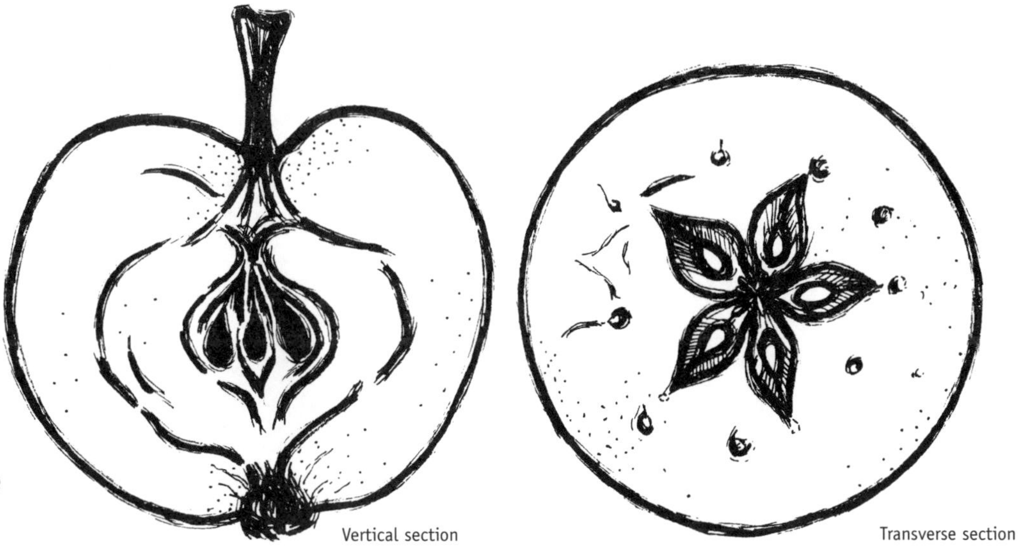

The plum is another fruit; varieties include the damson, cherry, and sloe plums. Students will learn to cut only one way—vertically—as they discover that they cannot cut through the stone (see Illustration 45). Ask students the following types of questions:

- Where is the seed of the plum?
- How many seeds are there in the plum?
- What surrounds the seed of the plum?

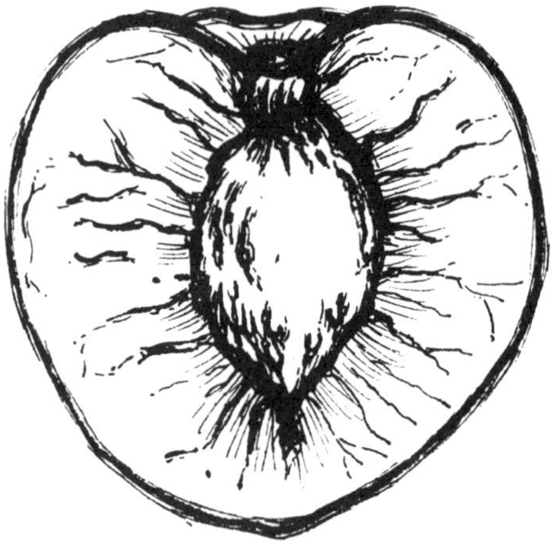

ILLUSTRATION 45

Plum

Children will discover that plums can only be cut one way—vertically—because of the hard interior core.

If you want a surprise fruit to examine, get a complete coconut—not just the "nut," the whole fruit. You will need a hacksaw or fine-toothed tenon saw to cut a half section. The teacher may need to do this as it may too difficult for the children (see Illustration 46).

ILLUSTRATION 46

Section of a Coconut

Coconuts are another type of fruit that students can examine, although the teacher will need to cut the fruit in half.

1. Can you find the part we eat?
2. How many seeds does a coconut have?
3. What protects the seed?
4. What else might protect the seed?
   (Hint: Coconuts grow by water and the fruits could fall in.)

Have students record their observations about the fruits and their seeds. They can make separate displays of the fruits and seeds, or they can attach the seeds on paper or cardboard and put them beside the complete fruits. Have students make some sections of fruits and label the seeds.

► *Part Five*

Structure, Size, Symmetry, and Shape

It is important to help children develop the ability to perceive differences in the size, symmetry, and shape of an object. Examining these elements is a major component of the scientific study of structure and form.

The Importance of Measurement

Understanding measurement is an important component of the development of scientific thinking in young children. Measurement is the process of making objective assessments. It allows scientists to communicate results using commonly understood terms and standard units. Children naturally make comparisons, and measurement becomes a way of making such comparisons systematically and accurately. Although children may not realize it, measurement is an everyday part of their lives; shopping for clothes, preparing food, being weighed at the doctor's office, lining up in place by size—all of these activities involve measurement.

Modern society depends on the ability of its members to measure a wide range of quantities accurately, and above all, to understand what measurement implies. Measuring can be thought of as an extension of the use of number—from counting to stating the quantity contained in a continuous whole. Separate objects can be counted one by one. However, some things are continuous, with no discernible subdivisions. Time runs continuously, although we can divide its passage in terms of minutes and hours, day and night, or the seasons. The distinction between "numbers" and "measures" is important. *Number* is a concept quite free from the nature or the arrangement of the objects in a particular set. The concept of the number 9, for example, is independent of time and place; it does not change if the sets contained within it vary. *Measurement,* however, always refers to real situations, such as the length of a room, the weight of a person, the temperature of the air, and so on. Numbers ascribed to measures of these situations provide the means for making useful comparisons of the properties being considered.

The primitive way of assessing quantity was based upon a visual or manipulative estimation. Since earliest history people have used measuring rods, which were generally based on the size of the human body. Such estimates could be remarkably accurate after many repetitions. For example, the ancient Egyptians used the *cubit,* the earliest known unit of linear measure. The cubit was the distance from the elbow to the tip of the middle finger. The cubit was divided into twenty-eight digits. A digit was the width of the middle finger. The Greeks introduced the concept of the *foot,* which they divided into 16 fingers; the Romans modified the Greek system and divided the foot into twelve equal divisions called *inches.*

The attempts to measure length by building up a succession of equal lengths, which will make a graduated strip leading to the idea of counting the parts, paved the way for measurement as we now know it. Once counting could be carried out, it became possible to state a measure as a number of units. As children become aware of their own use of measurement, they may become curious about how certain standard measures developed. The history of measurement makes a fascinating study in its own right.

What Size Is It? ► *Activity 24*

DEVELOPMENTAL LEVEL
K–2

GROUP SIZE
Large

KEY EXPERIENCES

- *Measuring, testing, and analyzing: assessing the properties and composition of materials*
- *Reporting and interpreting data and results*

Working in pairs and using string, have children measure one another's "cubits" (the distance from the elbow to the tip of the middle finger) and "digits" (width of the middle finger) (see Illustration 47). As they complete each measure, students should cut the string to size. Have them place all these cut strings together and stitch or staple them to cards for comparisons, writing each student's name below his or her length of string. Put all the cubits on one card and all the digits on another card.

Use these displays to discuss questions such as the following:

- Whose cubit is the longest?
- Whose cubit is the shortest?
- Whose digit is the widest?
- Whose digit is the narrowest?
- Why is it unsatisfactory to use personal measures like these?

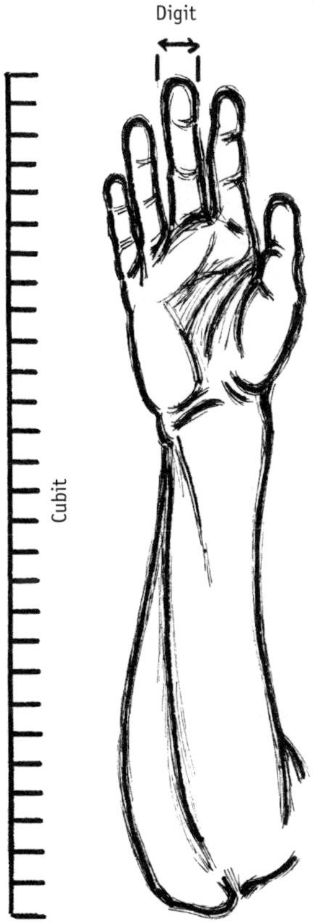

ILLUSTRATION 47

Cubits and Digits

A cubit is the distance from the elbow to the tip of the middle finger; a digit is the width of the middle finger.

The "yard" and the "foot" were also originally based on the human body. The yard was the distance from the tip of the nose to the end of the thumb when the arm was fully outstretched. The foot was the length of the foot. An inch was based on three barleycorns. (See Illustration 48 on page 70.) For the students' next practical work, barleycorns as well as string will be needed. Barleycorns are available at pet stores or in the section of the supermarket where packaged or bulk grains are sold.

Working in pairs as before, have each child measure the other's "yard" and "foot." Stick all the yards together or staple them side by side on a card. Put all the names below the strings appropriately. Place all the foot lengths on another display card with the student's names below them.

Using these displays, discuss the following types of questions:

- Whose yard is longest? Shortest?
- Whose foot is shortest? Longest?

Now give every child three barleycorns. They should carefully put them end-to-end and then measure the resulting length with string. Tell them to be careful to cut the string to the exact length. As above, mount and label the strings on a display card. Again, have the children discuss the different lengths of the "inch."

Review all these results (yard, foot, and inch) with the students and then turn to a discussion of standard measurements. Talk about variable versus standardized measures. Have children discuss how issues of accuracy and fairness would be disrupted if measures varied from one time to another. Have a range of rulers and yardsticks so that children can compare to see that they all measure the same lengths when standardized measures are used. You can tell them that the official length measures used to be set by *rods,* which were kept by the federal government in the Department of Standard Weights and Measures. Today, scientists have advanced procedures for defining standard units, such as measuring the length of the path traveled by light in a vacuum during a fixed interval of time.

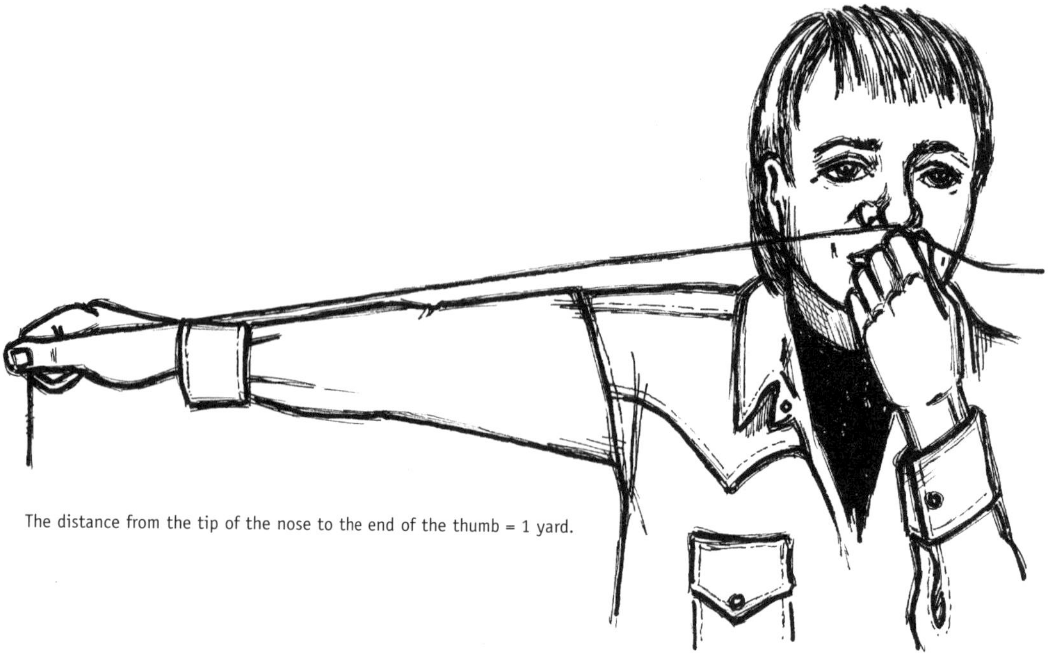

The distance from the tip of the nose to the end of the thumb = 1 yard.

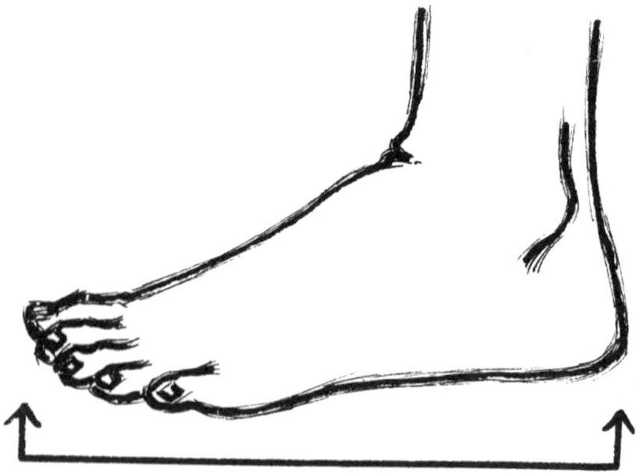

The length of a human foot = 1 foot.

Three barleycorns = 1 inch.

ILLUSTRATION 48

Early Forms of Measurement

By exploring these early forms of measurement, children discover for themselves how inconsistent these measures of length can be.

Using Metric Measures of Length ► *Activity 25*

DEVELOPMENTAL LEVEL
2–4

GROUP SIZE
Small

KEY EXPERIENCES

- *Measuring, testing, and analyzing: assessing the properties and composition of materials*
- *Reporting and interpreting data and results*

A NOTE FOR TEACHERS

Getting the Size Right

In the past, before the development of the metric system, every nation had its own measurement units. The English used "three barleycorns round and dry" as their standard for one inch. Grains of corn varied in size, so the inch varied also! As a result, no one could be really sure measurements of the same thing would be equal. People began to see the need for a single accurate measurement that everyone could use. During the 1600s and 1700s, especially in France, scientists and mathematicians thought about the problem and sought solutions based on linear measurement, not on human or mathematical sources. In 1790 the National Assembly in France asked the Academy of Sciences to create a standard system of measures. Out of this came a system that was simple and scientific: the metric system. This original system was based on a unit of length that equaled a fraction of the earth's circumference. This fraction was 1/10,000,000 of the distance from the North Pole to the equator. The French scientists named this unit of length the *meter,* from the Greek word "metron," meaning a measure. As time has gone on the measures of the world's circumference have become more accurate, but basically the metric system remains unchanged.

No other system of measurement equals the metric system in its simplicity, for its relationships are all based on tens. In a decimal system, a unit is 10 times larger than the next smaller unit. So a meter equals 10 decimeters, just as a dollar equals 10 dimes. Most metric units have a Latin prefix indicating its relationship to the basic unit: "deci" is 1/10, "centi" is 1/100, and "milli" is 1/1,000. Thus, millimeters, centimeters, and decimeters are the three parts measuring the meter. This uniformity makes metric measurement simple for all to use. Long distances are measured in "kilometers"—which are equal to 1,000 meters, or about 5/8 of a mile. There are metric units for all other measures, in addition to linear measurement. Scientists everywhere measure in metric units. Additionally, many countries of the world now use the metric system measures for their everyday measurements.

To begin this activity, divide the class into groups. Each group will measure a different set of items and report back to the whole class. Provide the students in each group with metric measuring devices, such as metric sticks, metric rulers, and metric tapes. Have them record their results in meters, centimeters, and/or millimeters, as appropriate. The following types of groups can be formed (see Illustration 49 on pgs. 72 & 73):

- ***Personal Measurement Group.*** This group can measure heights, size of feet, hand spans, length and width of fingers, tip of nose to thumb when the arm is extended (the old yard), and the tip of the elbow to the end of the middle finger (the old cubit).

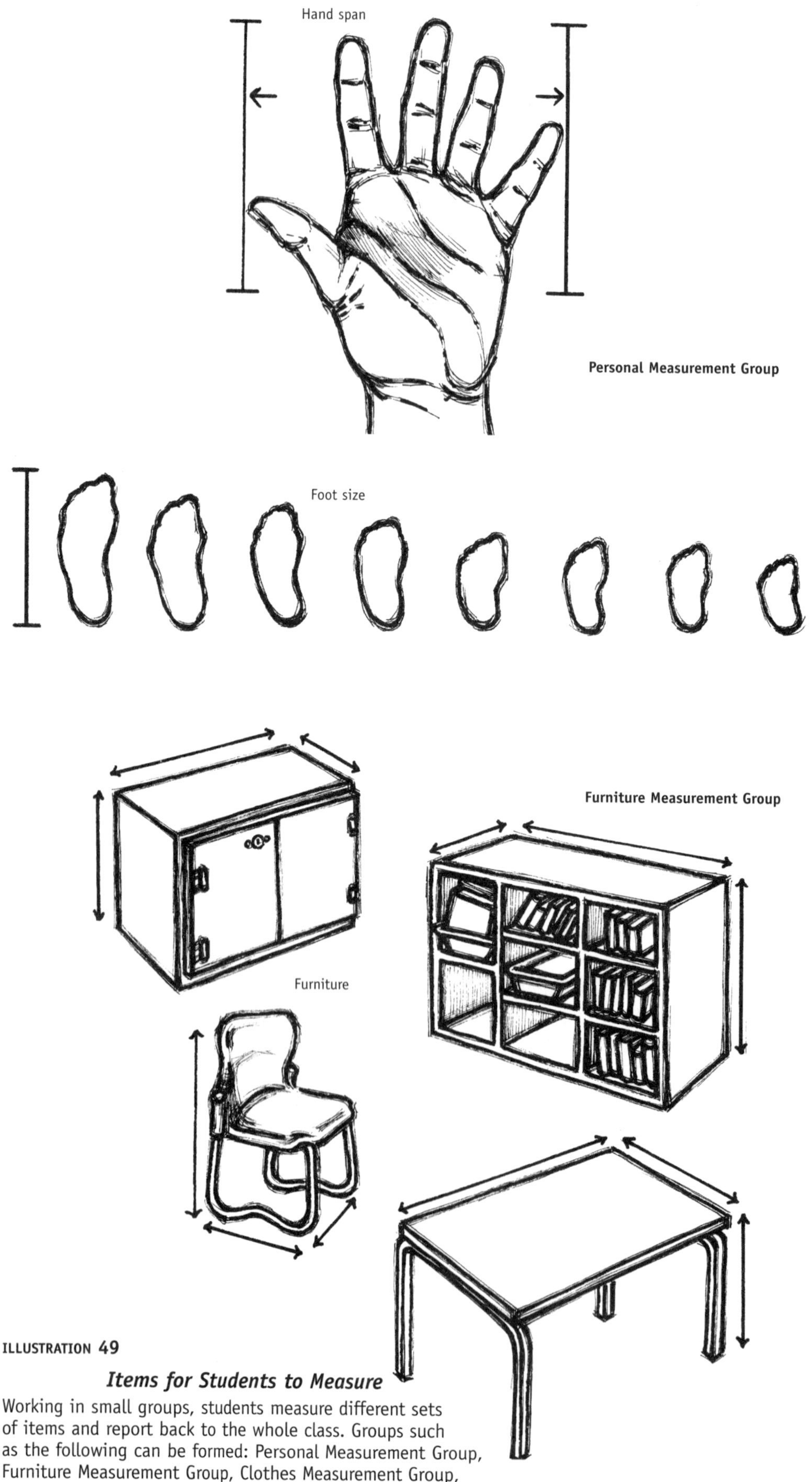

ILLUSTRATION 49

Items for Students to Measure

Working in small groups, students measure different sets of items and report back to the whole class. Groups such as the following can be formed: Personal Measurement Group, Furniture Measurement Group, Clothes Measurement Group, and Room Measurement Group

Clothes Measurement Group

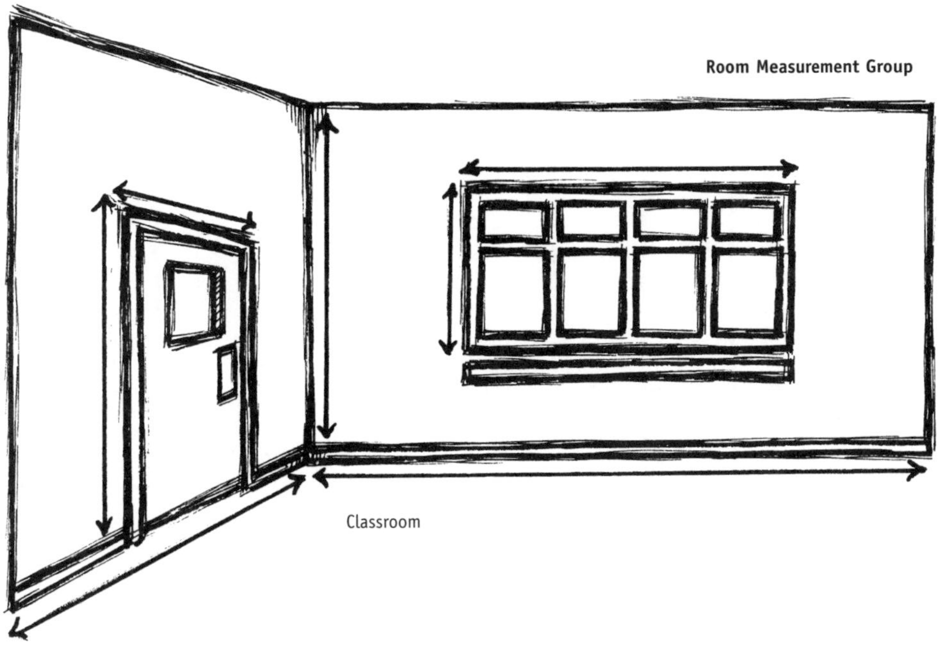

Room Measurement Group

• ***Furniture Measurement Group.*** This group can measure the height, width, and length of tables and desks, chairs, cupboards, and shelves.

• ***Clothes Measurement Group.*** This group can measure garments, such as jacket lengths, sleeve lengths, chest measurements, jeans waist sizes, leg lengths, raincoat lengths, and hat openings.

• ***Room Measurement Group.*** This group can measure the principal dimensions of the room, such as the height and width of doorway(s), window openings, windowsill sizes, and the length and width of the floor.

After the groups have finished their investigations there will need to be a discussion on how to record, report, and review the results. Discuss questions such as the following: How should results be presented? Can they be mounted on a display? Who from the group will speak about the measurement process, about how students worked in pairs or teams to complete the measuring? What questions should students ask about the data; for example, what item was the biggest, longest, tallest, widest? Can these results be put in an order, largest to smallest? Are there other ways to represent the results; for example, what about the use of cutout paper patterns to represent the size of clothes? (See Illustration 50.)

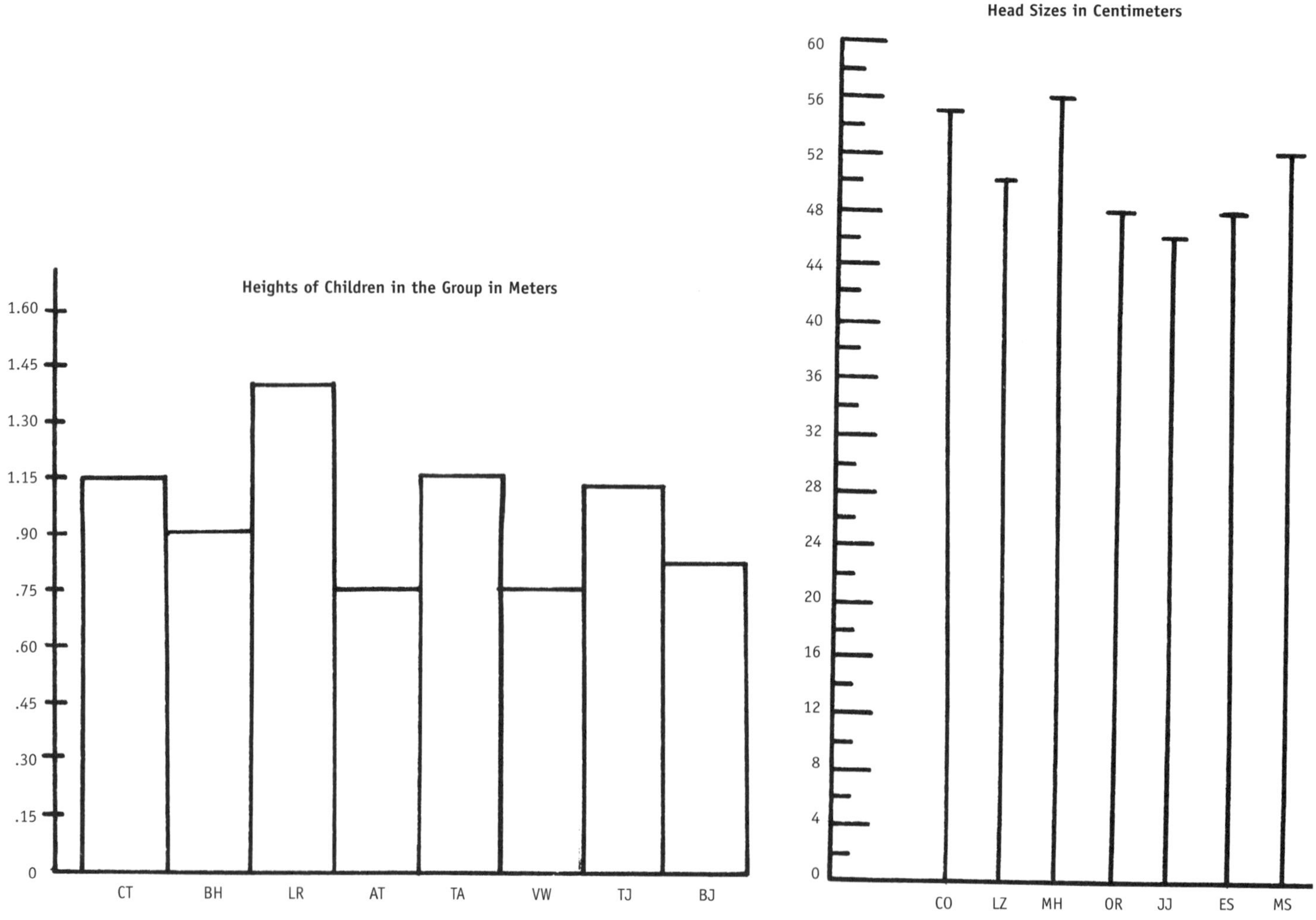

ILLUSTRATION 50

Displaying the Measurement Results

Children can display the results of their measurement activities by creating graphs, charts, and other visual displays.

Symmetry and Shape

Through active learning that includes repeated activities with the same object or sequence of events, children develop a sense of both stability and change. They become aware of similarities and contrasts and appreciate the effects of time and movement upon structure.

By carefully examining objects, for example, children become aware that some shapes are invariant, or unchanging, regardless of how they are manipulated. An initial approach to studying the stability of shape is by observing the *symmetry* of objects. Balance in a shape—for example, balance between the right and left sides of an object—is a property that gives us aesthetic pleasure. A symmetrical shape retains this balance between the two halves no matter how it is rotated.

The dynamic study of shapes opens up new possibilities. Movement may cause an object to change its position but it can still retain its shape. For example, an object moving in a straight line will retain its original appearance. The movement may be forward, backward, or up and down; such movements are called "translations." But when an object turns or moves around, either wholly or partially, this is called "rotation." Appreciating the significance of rotation is the basis for understanding the turning movement of many measuring dials, such as clocks, electric meters, and compasses, as well as many types of weighing devices.

It is also possible for the shape of an object to remain the same while its size changes. Examples of an increase in size are when a balloon is blown up or a picture is enlarged on the screen. Here the overall shape—the ratio of the various parts—remains the same; only the dimensions change. Similarly, if all the dimensions of a shape are made smaller by the same ratio, reduction takes place. Altering size while keeping shape invariant is the basis of scale drawings and map-making. Students develop an understanding of the relationship between size and shape through repeated observations of an object. Experience lets them establish an object's absolute or relative size from various aspects of observation, for example, seen from up close or far away. Similarly, repetition allows children to recognize an object's shape from different directions, for example, viewed from above or from the side.

Children also begin to understand that changes in size or shape may occur with time as well as movement. The structural properties of living and nonliving things alter with the passage of time—things grow or shrink with age; they swell or dry up under changing natural conditions. Observing and understanding these transformations is part of the growing base of knowledge by which children construct reality. Teachers can provide students with ample opportunity for observing the shape and size of objects. Natural processes and human activities allow children to see how objects can either remain the same or change as forces act upon them. Examining the static and dynamic properties of objects is an important component of the scientific study of structure.

Types of Symmetry ► *Activity 26*

DEVELOPMENTAL LEVEL
3–5

GROUP SIZE
Small

KEY EXPERIENCES
- *Looking with a purpose: observing and collecting data*
- *Observing, predicting, and controlling change: understanding causality*

Children develop their powers of observation as they explore an object's position. Since children generally stand and move in an upright position, they see things from that perspective—from a level base with a vertical axis. Thus, shapes come to be identified most easily from this position. At a young age, before children develop the idea of "conservation of shape," they often think that if an object's position changes, then the object itself is a different shape.

The notion of upright—verticality—is reinforced when children build towers. The idea of vertical or graduated levels grows much more slowly, often out of children's experiences of objects rolling or running down slopes and then stopping on level stretches, such as when they roll marbles, balls, or toy cars down a hill or a ramp. Somewhere between grades 2 and 3, children begin to understand the meaning of vertical and horizontal. Engaging children in relevant experiences helps them to grasp these concepts. One such activity involves using a simple beam balance (see Illustration 51).

This type of balancing device helps children find shapes in which the two halves look alike. Children like making shapes that balance. Ample experience with balancing and balanced shapes leads children to an appreciation of the important concept of "symmetry."

Some well-known experiments with blobs of paint and folded paper, such as the experiments described next, form excellent introductions to the idea of bilateral symmetry (see Illustration 52 on pg. 77).

ILLUSTRATION **51**

Beam Balance

Experimenting with a beam balance helps children appreciate and understand the important scientific concept of symmetry.

Experiment 1

1. Fold a piece of paper in half. Open it up again.
2. Put a blob of colored ink or paint (not too much, a little goes a long way) on the fold.
3. Refold the paper, pressing the two halves firmly together.
4. Open the sheet carefully and see the symmetrical pattern that results.
5. Make a variety of patterns in different colors and display the results.

Experiment 2

1. Fold a piece of paper in half.
2. Cut a pattern or shape along the edges.
3. Open the paper and see the symmetrical shape that results.
4. Make a variety of shapes this way and display the results.

Experiment 1

1. Fold a piece of paper then open it out.
2. Put a blob of color (not too much, a little goes a long way) on the fold.
3. Refold the paper, pressing the sheets firmly together.
4. Open out the sheet carefully and see the symmetrical pattern that results.
5. Make a variety of patterns in different colors and display the results.

Experiment 2

1. Fold a piece of paper in half.
2. Cut a pattern or shape along the edges.
3. Open the paper and see the symmetrical shape that results.
4. Make a variety of shapes this way and display the results.

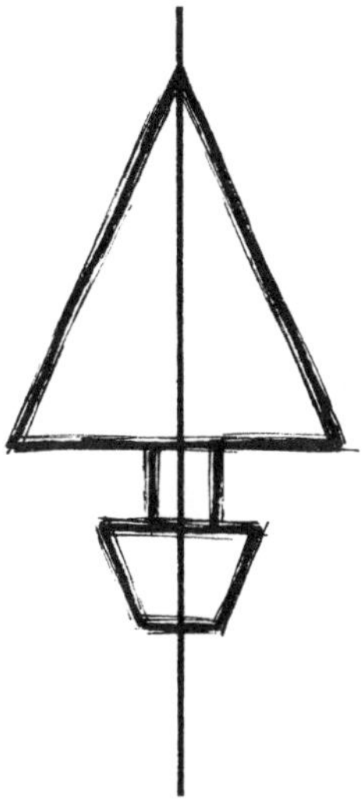

ILLUSTRATION 52

Experimenting With Symmetry

These experiments with blobs of paint and folded paper introduce students to the idea of bilateral symmetry.

Up to the age of seven, and sometimes beyond, children often do not distinguish between "left" and "right" with any certainty. This is true mainly because the interpretation depends on the point of view of the observer. Children cannot "decenter" from their own perspective to know which point is seen as left and which is seen as right by another person. Making symmetrical shapes helps children know left from right. Shoes, gloves, and double doors, for example have left–right symmetrical relationships; therefore, one of the pair must be identified as left. If you turn a pair of shoes upside down, it is difficult for the young child to identify which one is left and which one is right.

Folding a paper into quarters (two folds—one vertical and one horizontal) is a way of introducing symmetry about two axes. Using this fact, children can make interesting patterns, cutting and tearing around the edges and cutting holes from the center.

ILLUSTRATION 53

Flower Illustrating Rotational Symmetry

No matter which way students turn this flower, it appears the same.

Eventually, children can begin to recognize three kinds of symmetry—rotational, translational, and bilateral. The following activities can help bring these concepts into focus for children.

• **Rotational Symmetry.** Rotational symmetry occurs when an object appears the same even when it is rotated. For example, however much you rotate the flower shown in Illustration 53, it appears the same. How many flowers can the students draw (or photograph or point out) that display rotational symmetry?

• **Translational Symmetry.** Things with translational symmetry show repeating patterns. The caterpillar in Illustration 54 exhibits translational symmetry. Have you seen animals like these?

ILLUSTRATION 54

The Translational Symmetry of a Caterpillar

Things with translational symmetry, such as this caterpillar, show repeating patterns.

• **Bilateral Symmetry.** Bilateral symmetry is present in an object when opposite halves are identical. Illustration 55 (below and on pg. 79) provides examples of this kind of symmetry. For example, can students find leaves that exhibit bilateral symmetry? Can they find those that are not symmetrical? Can students identify insects with bilateral symmetry? Does the human form have bilateral symmetry? Can the students find other things in the classroom with bilateral symmetry (such as the wallpaper pattern, certain letters of the alphabet, items of furniture)?

Wallpaper design
Can you see the symmetry in this wallpaper design?

ILLUSTRATION 55

Examples of Bilateral Symmetry

These items all exhibit bilateral symmetry because the opposite halves are identical.

Leaves
Can you find other leaves that have bilateral symmetry?

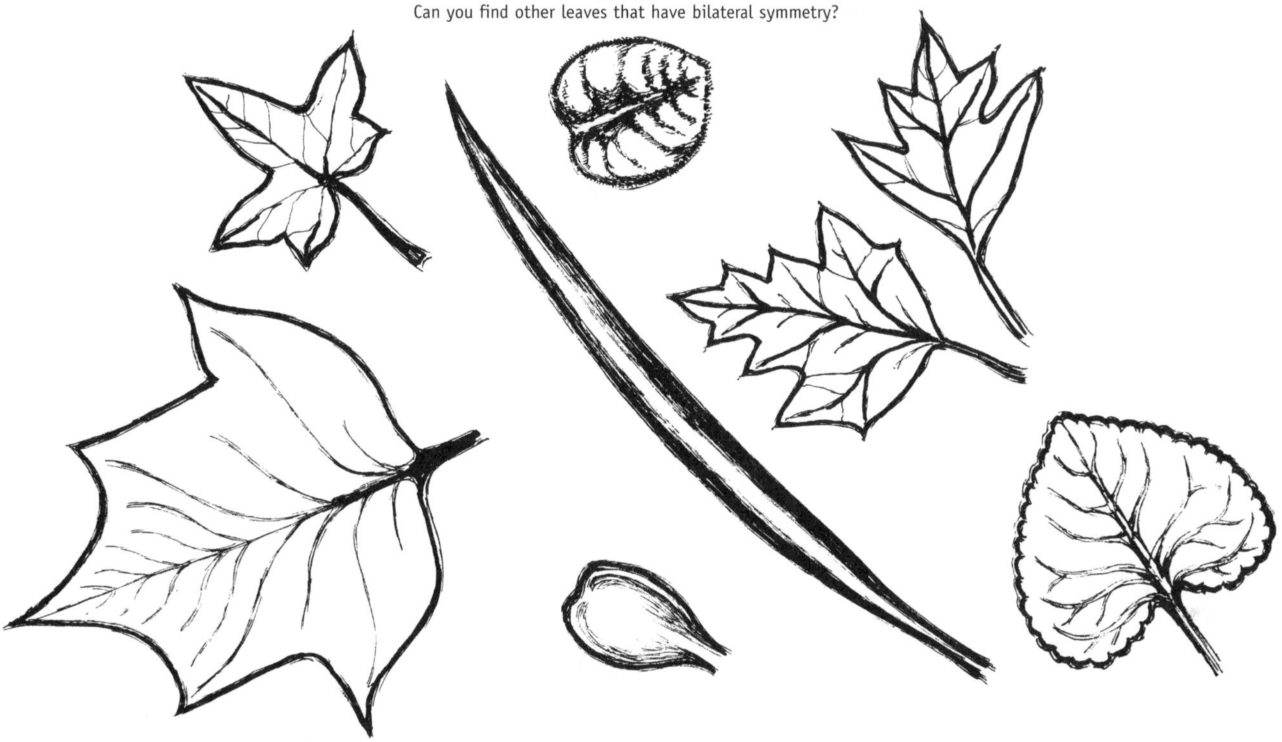

Insects
Can you identify insects that have bilateral symmetry?

Other Activities in Symmetry and Shape

►*Activity 27*

DEVELOPMENTAL LEVEL
4–6

GROUP SIZE
Large

KEY EXPERIENCES

- *Looking with a purpose: observing and collecting data*
- *Designing, building, fabricating, and modifying structures or materials*

As an additional activity, encourage students to look for symmetrical objects in nature (animals, flowers) and decide what kind of symmetry is shown. (Remember that most natural objects are not exactly symmetrical; however they are close enough to be classified as such for this activity.) Let the students make sketches of the shapes and then use the shapes to make patterns and designs. Have them make different designs based on each of the three kinds of symmetry. Illustration 56 shows how students can turn a nonsymmetrical pattern into patterns exhibiting both bilateral and translational symmetry.

There are many other ways to extend the study of symmetry. For example, see if children can find symmetrical rhythms in music and clapping. Have them look at the written music to find symmetry in the sets of notes on the page. They may find translational symmetry in the repetition of sounds.

Nonsymmetrical pattern

Pattern with bilateral symmetry

Pattern with translational symmetry

ILLUSTRATION 56

Creating a Symmetrical Pattern

Using some simple shapes, students can change a nonsymmetrical pattern into one exhibiting both bilateral and translational symmetry.

► *Part Six*

Structure and Patterns

Children do not always need complex equipment and supplies to explore scientific concepts. In fact, some of the most rewarding activities in science involve the simple observation of everyday items. This is particularly true with respect to the activities in this section, which revolve around the study of the various patterns in our environment.

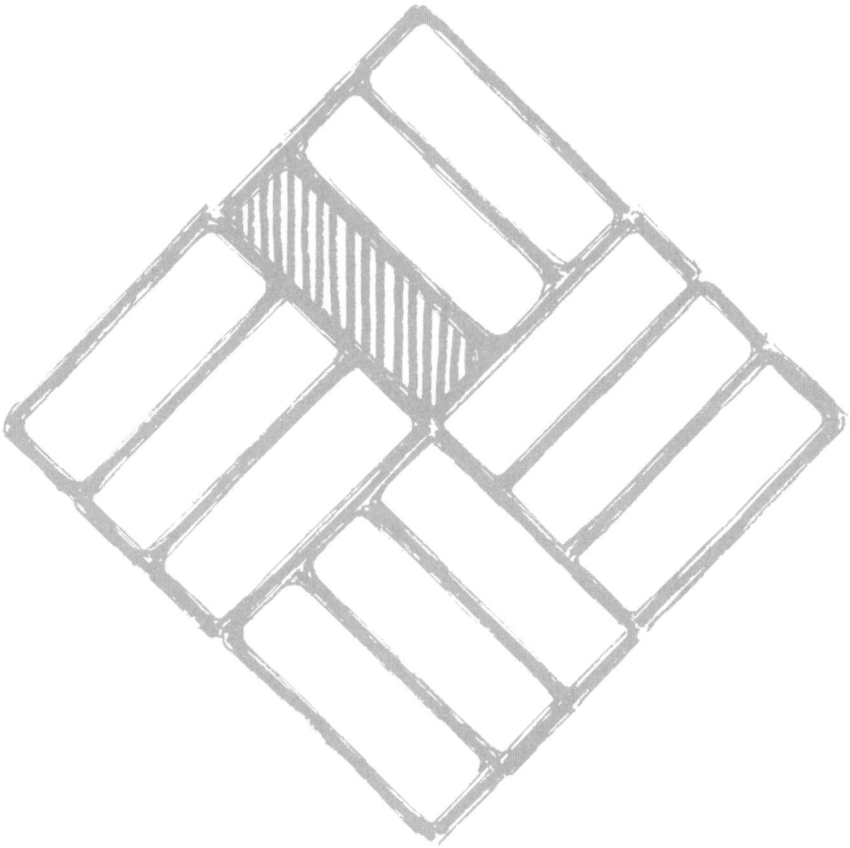

Tessellations

Brick walls, tiled areas, and floor surfaces are often made from materials of regular shapes that fit together. When a surface is covered completely so that no gaps are left between the tiles, the pattern is called a *tessellation.* The tiles are the "faces," and the points where two or more corners meet are the "vertices." A study of tessellation—and the various shapes and angles of the fitted tiles—can provide the springboard for basic experiences in geometry.

For example, simple squares can be arranged in the three basic patterns shown in Illustration 57 (see pg. 83). Rectangular shapes can be arranged in more ways than simple squares because they can be turned vertically, horizontally, and in combinations of these two orientations. By looking at the tessellations of squares and rectangles, children can see that the area around any vertex is completely filled by either four right angles or by two right angles and a straight angle. (This observation also reinforces the concept that two right angles make a straight angle and that four right angles together completely fill a space round a point.)

Patterns of tessellation become more interesting, especially for older children, when shapes other than rectangles are introduced. As children experiment with making shapes for tessellations, they may find great success with the isosceles right-angle triangle (a right triangle in which two of the sides are of equal length). These triangles can be combined to make polygons. A hexagon (six-sided figure) can be made from six such triangles. Children can also discover that a regular hexagon (six sides of equal length) can be made out of six equilateral triangles. Regular hexagons can in turn be tessellated to make a honeycomb pattern. Other shapes, such as dodecagons (twelve-sided figures), cannot be tesselated into such regular patterns. As students will discover, there will be success only if the angles at the vertex completely fit and fill the space.

By the time children are able to handle practical work such as this, they should be able to understand and use a protractor. They can find that the sum of the angles of any triangle equals a straight angle, or two right angles, or 180°. Children can make regular polygons, that is, shapes having all their sides equal in length and all their angles equal in the number of degrees. Children are most likely to discover the following types of polygons: the *equilateral triangle* (three sides and three angles each at 60°); the *square* (four sides and four angles each at 90°); and the *regular hexagon* (six sides and six angles each at 120°). It will become clear that only these regular polygons are possible for tessellations because only they fulfill the following conditions:

- The sum of the angles that surround any vertex of the tessellation is 360° because the space must be entirely filled.

- At least 3 polygons meet at each vertex and the only possibilities are:

  six equilateral triangles meeting at each vertex ($6 \times 60^\circ = 360^\circ$)

  four squares meeting at each vertex ($4 \times 90^\circ = 360^\circ$)

  three regular hexagons meeting at each vertex ($3 \times 120^\circ = 360^\circ$).

By studying simple brick and tile patterns on the classroom floor or walls, considerable insights in geometry can be opened up for older children. For the younger child, the simple shapes of brick and block patterns make excellent starting points for their introduction to geometry in a real setting. Such work is not only good science, but good math too.

Studying Patterns of Square Floor Tiles ► *Activity 28*

DEVELOPMENTAL LEVEL
K–2

GROUP SIZE
Large

KEY EXPERIENCE

- *Looking with a purpose: observing and collecting data*

Patterns on the Floor

Elaborate equipment and supplies are not necessary for children to engage in science activities. All that is needed for the following activity is a patterned floor, some graph paper, pencils, rulers, and keen young eyes.

To begin, students look at a pattern of square tiles and then use graph paper to copy the pattern for at least four rows of tiles in either direction. Ask them to identify which of the three patterns in Illustration 57 is shown.

Pattern 1

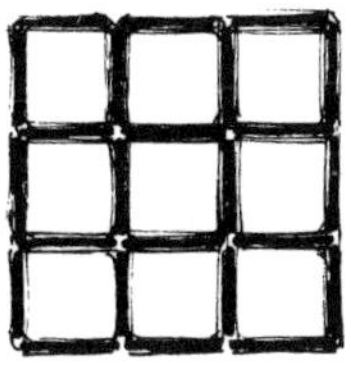

Pattern 2

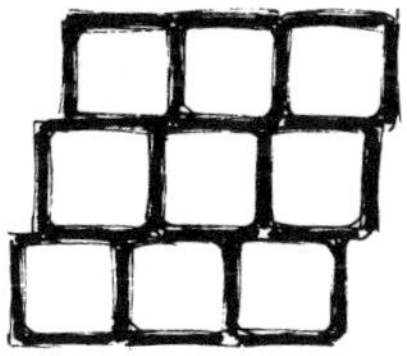

Pattern 3

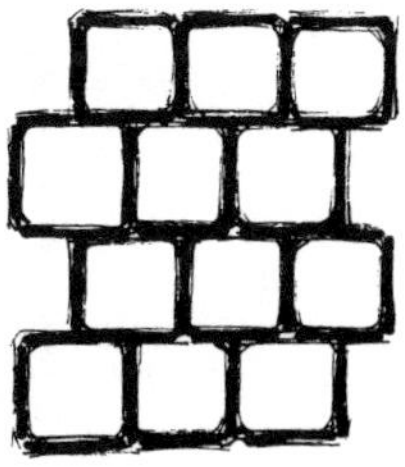

ILLUSTRATION 57

Three Patterns Created With Square Tiles

These are the three basic patterns that can be made with square tiles. However, they can be made more interesting by adding color. Invent some patterns using color and identify which type each one is.

These are the three basic patterns that can be made with square tiles: the tiles in each row directly above the ones beneath; the tiles in each row slightly to the right or left of the ones beneath; and the tiles in each row at the midpoint above the ones beneath. However, these patterns can be made more interesting by adding color. Have the students invent some patterns using color and ask the rest of the class to identify which type it is.

Studying Patterns of Rectangular Floor Tiles ►

Activity 29

DEVELOPMENTAL LEVEL
K–2

GROUP SIZE
Large

KEY EXPERIENCE
- *Looking with a purpose: observing and collecting data*

Students begin this activity by looking at patterns of rectangular tiles. They should use graph paper in units of two squares to make rectangles and then copy each pattern they find for at least four rows of tiles in either direction.

Now the students have a choice of five patterns (see Illustration 58). Which of these are on the floor or wall of the school?

When rectangular tiles are used instead of square ones, more patterns are possible. In Illustration 58, the pattern moves from tile to tile. Each tile pattern is derived from the shaded one by translation or rotation.

Pattern 1

Pattern 2

Pattern 3

Pattern 4

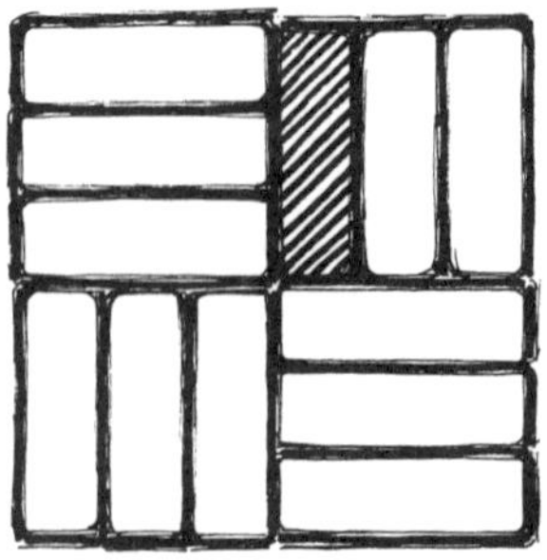

Pattern 5

ILLUSTRATION 58

Creating Patterns With Rectangles

When rectangular tiles are used instead of square ones, more patterns are possible. In this illustration, each tile pattern is derived from the shaded one by translation or rotation.

Studying Patterns All Around Us ► *Activity 30*

DEVELOPMENTAL LEVEL
K–2

GROUP SIZE
Large

KEY EXPERIENCE
- *Looking with a purpose: observing and collecting data*

Patterns on a Variety of Surfaces

To help children see the patterns in a wide variety of surfaces, have them collect different repeated patterns from wallpapers, floor coverings, fabric designs, computer printouts, and so on. Encourage them to observe the patterns that bricks and tiles make on walls, pathways, countertops, and other areas they see every day. They can make a display of patterns discovered in this way. The students can also invent their own patterns for special places and purposes (for example, to cover bookshelves or line their cubbies) and make a display of them. The tiles for the display can be made of cardboard, colored paper, or flat wooden blocks.

► *Part Seven*

The Structural Properties of Materials

By examining and classifying the structural properties of various materials, students can engage in many active learning activities. They learn how objects are assessed and analyzed, and they discover how to display their findings on graphs and charts.

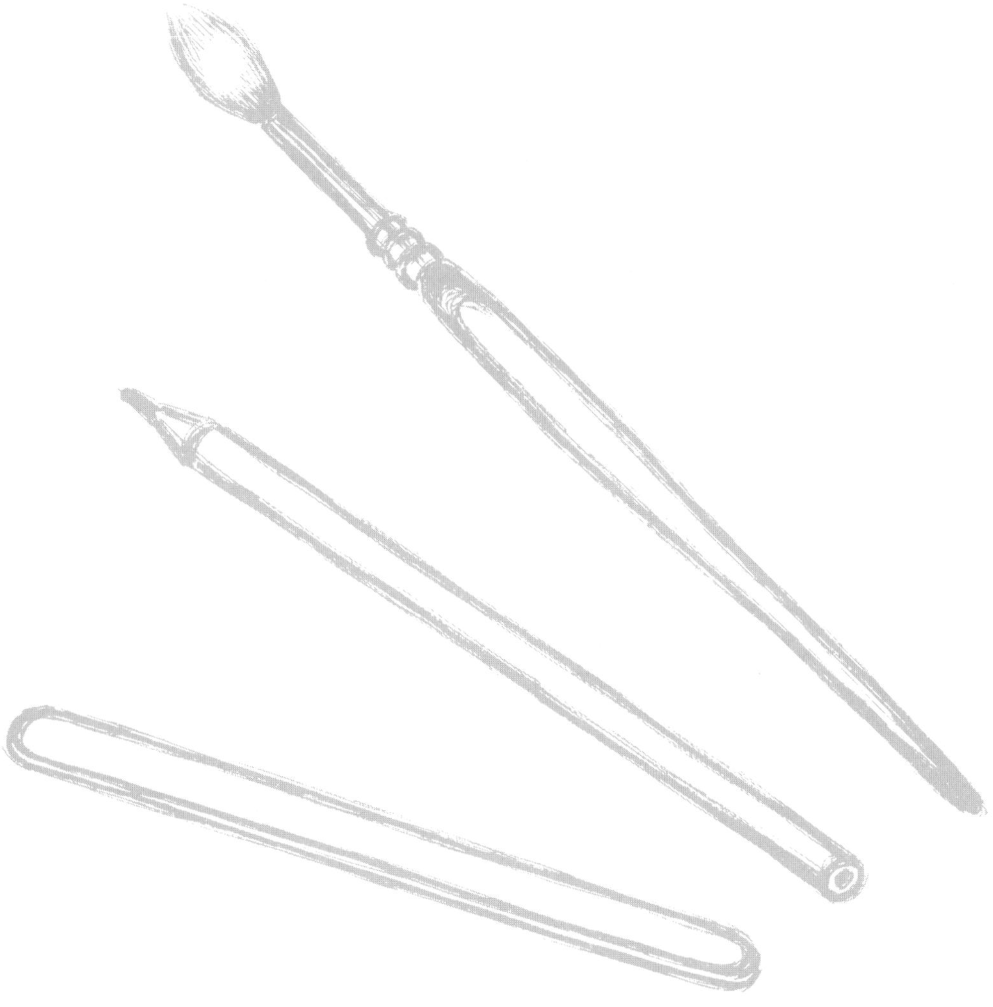

Plastics

In recent decades, plastics have become so commonplace in all facets of our lives that we sometimes refer to our times as the "Age of Plastic." It should be made clear to children that we use the term *plastic* rather loosely to describe a range of products that are based on "hydrocarbons," which are composed of hydrogen, oxygen, and carbon. Sometimes chlorine and nitrogen are added to make other plastic products. Plastics all consist of chains of giant molecules that give them their strength and flexibility. All plastics can be molded or shaped by heat. Some can be reheated and reshaped, while others are set forever after they are manufactured.

We generally use the term plastic as a noun to refer to synthetic materials made of these hydrocarbon molecules. Yet the term plastic is also an adjective referring to something that can be molded or receive form. Thus natural as well as synthetic materials may be described as plastic. For example, glass can be plastic because it can be shaped and molded. Many other natural materials are also plastic, including amber, casein, rubber, shellac, and gutta-percha.

While the range of synthetic (hydrocarbon-based) plastics is enormous, and new ones are created all the time, there are five common types that children will encounter in their everyday lives: polyethylene, polyvinyl chloride (PVC), polystyrene, perspex, and nylon.

Plastics, like all materials used in science, should be handled with care, even though they may be said to be unbreakable. Teachers should know what children propose to do with materials beforehand and should provide adequate supervision. When bending plastics by hanging weights on them, take care when weights fall off because the test strip may fly back. Remember broken plastics can have sharp edges and need careful handling. Children should not burn plastics or do tests involving flames because some plastics are inflammable and give off toxic fumes.

The Properties of Materials ► *Activity 31*

DEVELOPMENTAL LEVEL
2–4

GROUP SIZE
Small

KEY EXPERIENCES

- *Classifying and ordering materials according to their attributes and properties*
- *Measuring, testing, and analyzing: assessing the properties and composition of materials*
- *Reporting and interpreting data and results*

Divide the class into four groups and ask each group to find things in the classroom made from one of the following materials: (1) metal, (2) wood, (3) ceramics, and (4) plastics. The four groups will quickly be supplied with what they think are objects made of these materials (see Illustration 59). But ask students how they determined which items to put in which categories. For example, if an item floats, is it wood? When an item is smooth or light, is it plastic? Is a heavy item always metal? What other criteria did they use to determine the materials?

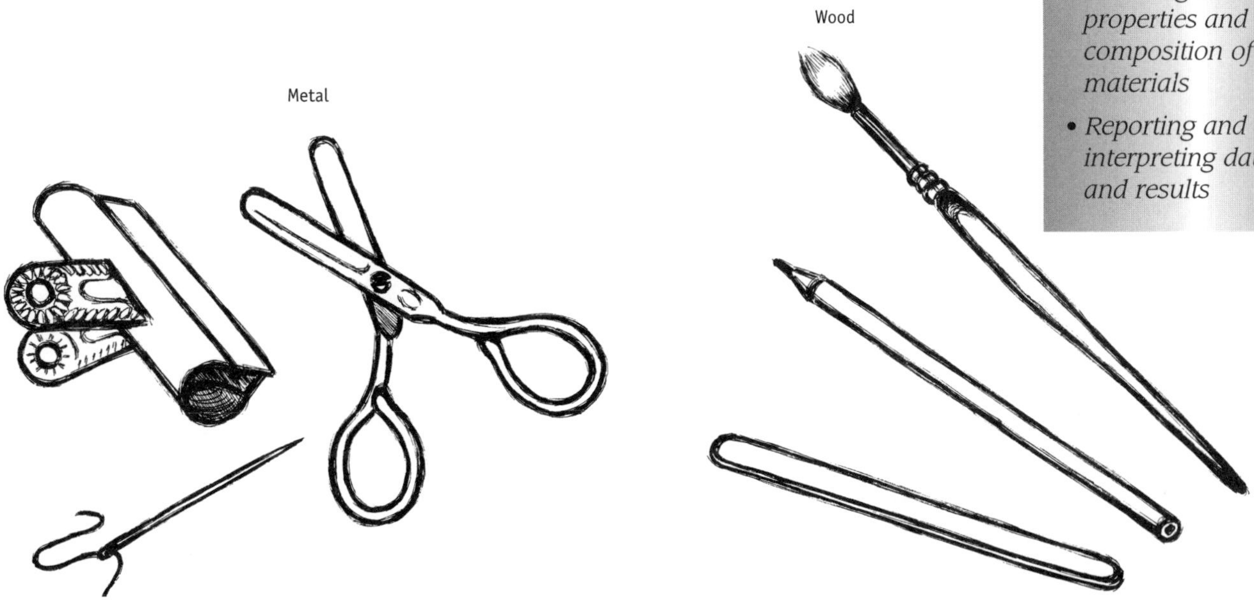

ILLUSTRATION 59

Classroom Items Made of Various Materials

After students collect classroom items made of various materials, discuss with them the criteria they used to sort and group the objects.

Next, have students discuss the criteria they used to sort and put the objects in their groups:

• **Feel.** What does the object feel like? Is it smooth or rough? Warm or cold? Hard or soft?

• **Weight.** What is the heft? Is it light or heavy?

• **Sound.** What noise does the item make when tapped? Is it dull? Ringing? Hollow?

• **Appearance.** What does the surface look like? Is it shiny? Grainy? Rough? Uneven?

• **Flotation.** What happens when you put the object in water? Does it float or sink?

The groups should exchange items so that every group has some materials claimed to be of a certain sort. Let the children test their materials according to the agreed criteria. After a time for experiments and tests, let the groups report their findings. They can summarize the results in a chart that lists some of the properties of each type of material. For example:

- **Ceramics**
  - Hard
  - Smooth
  - Cold
  - Sometimes ring when tapped
  - Sink
  - Sometimes heavy
- **Wood**
  - Hard
  - Rough and smooth
  - Dull noise when tapped
  - Floats
  - Not cold
  - Medium weight
- **Plastic**
  - Hard, but sometimes soft
  - Smooth, but sometimes rough
  - Dull or no sound when tapped
  - Generally sinks, but some may float
  - Warm, sometimes very warm
  - Light to very light weight
- **Metal**
  - Hard
  - Smooth
  - Rings when tapped
  - Sinks
  - Feels cold
  - Heavy in weight

Have the students make a display of typical objects that illustrate the attributes summarized on the chart. All of the objects should be labeled by name, material, and function.

Another comparative study of materials can be made with paper bags versus plastic bags. Two lines of inquiry can emerge from this activity: (1) How much does each type of bag hold when you go shopping? and (2) Which type of bag is the strongest? A third question can be asked: (3) Which type of bag is best for what job?

To answer the first question, you will need to discuss with the class the meaning of "how much." Does it refer to how much bulk (capacity carrying) or how much weight? Two groups may be formed, one to test the bags in terms of capacity and the other to test them in terms of weight. The group testing for carrying capacity must decide what "how much" means in shopping terms, for example, what size load one could manage if one were going to the supermarket. The group testing for weight must decide what weighty object to use; for practical purposes this could be the weight of two house bricks or about 10–12 pounds (5 kilos). The question will arise: Does this test the strength of the bag or the handles? Illustration 60 presents a simple and safe method for finding out the answer to this question. Another comparative test can be made in the same manner with a thick paper bag of the same size.

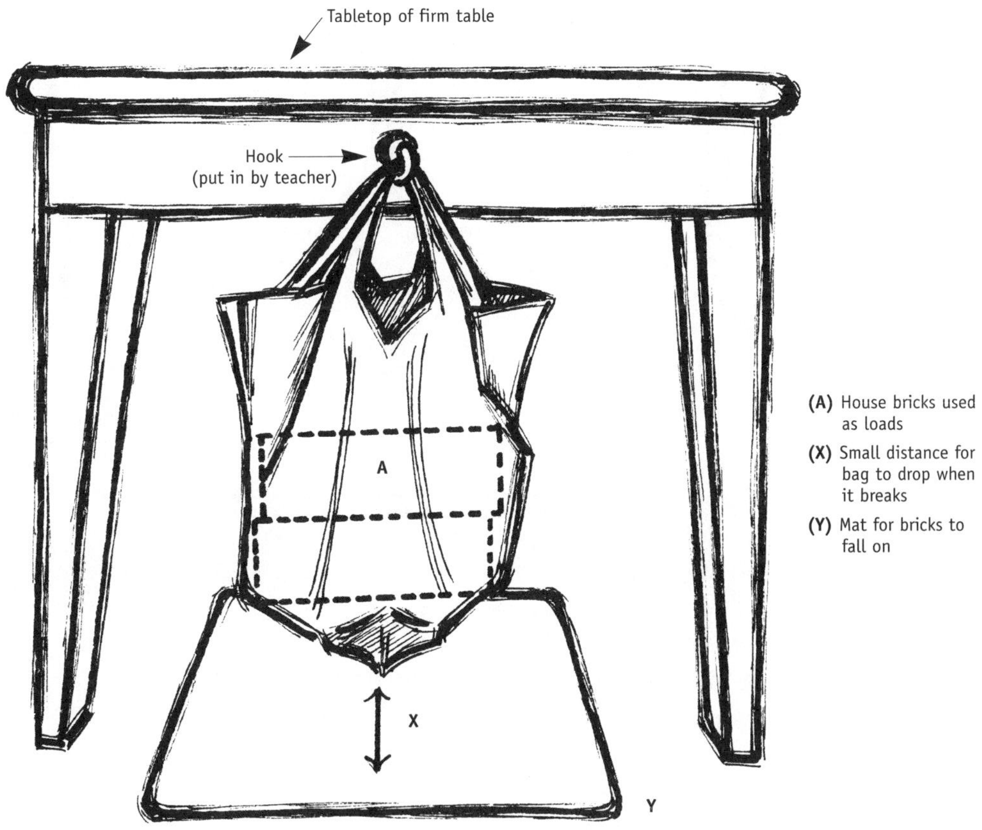

ILLUSTRATION 60

Testing the Strength of a Bag's Handle

This simple test helps children assess the strength of a bag's handles.

Other questions will also arise. For example, some items, such as fresh produce or frozen foods, may be damp or wet; these items in turn make the bag carrying them wet. Which bag will be best for carrying these items when it becomes wet? Children could test the strength of plastic and paper bags when they are dry versus wet.

This testing in turn raises questions about the strength of the actual plastic and paper. Have the students cut test strips—about 8" x 12"—from each type of bag and test as shown in Illustration 61 on page 92, using the hook in the side of the table to suspend the test apparatus. Fill the suspended plastic container with gradually increasing weights (such as nails). Test wet and dry strips of both materials. Record the results in a chart.

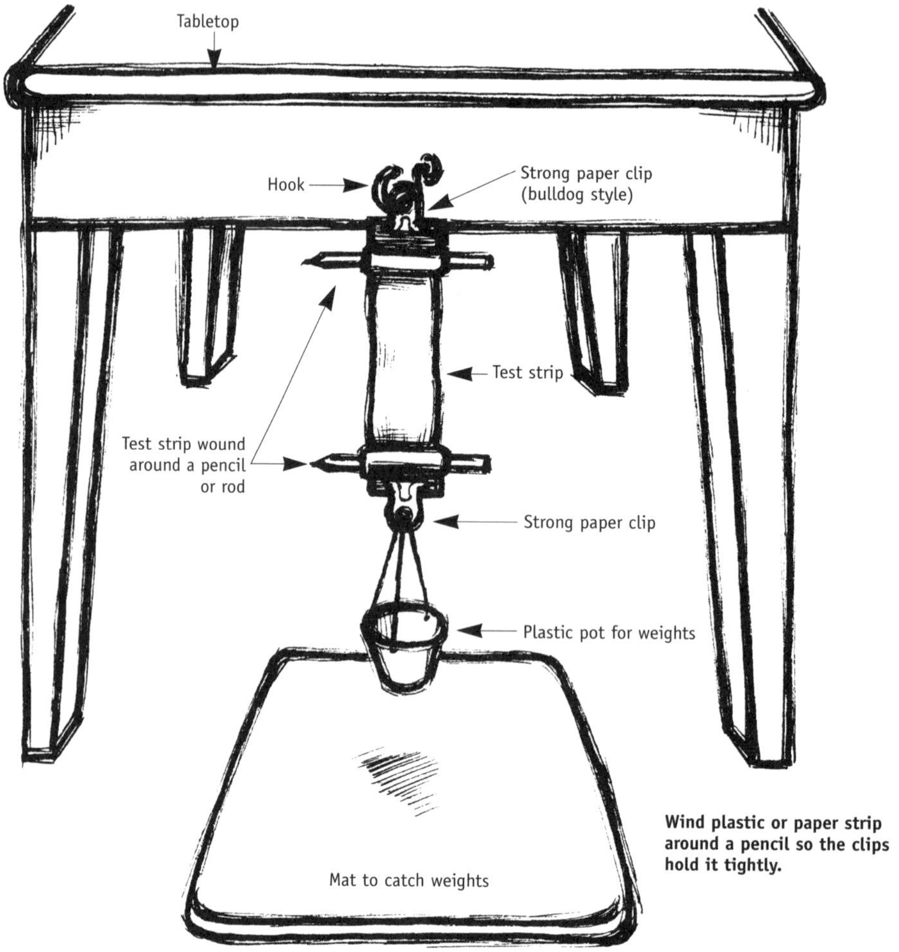

ILLUSTRATION 61

Testing the Strength of Wet Bags

For this activity, have students cut test strips from each type of bag and compare the strength of these strips when they are wet and when they are dry.

► *Part Eight*

Skin: A Living Structure

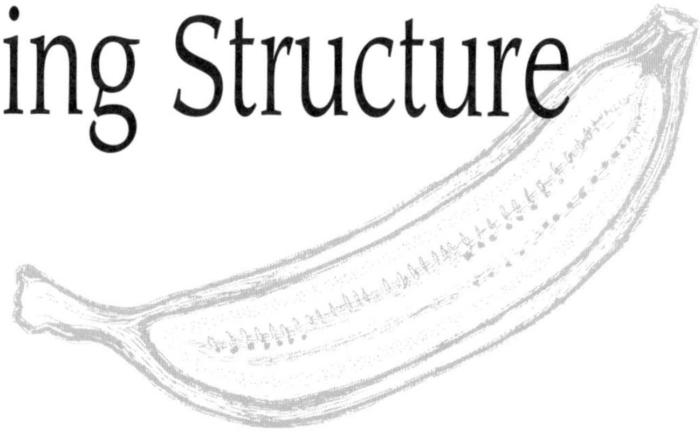

Skin is a substance that provides a protective covering. It is found in many different forms on various living structures. In addition to its more obvious forms, such as human skin and animal skin, encourage children to think of other places that skin can be found, such as on fruits and vegetables.

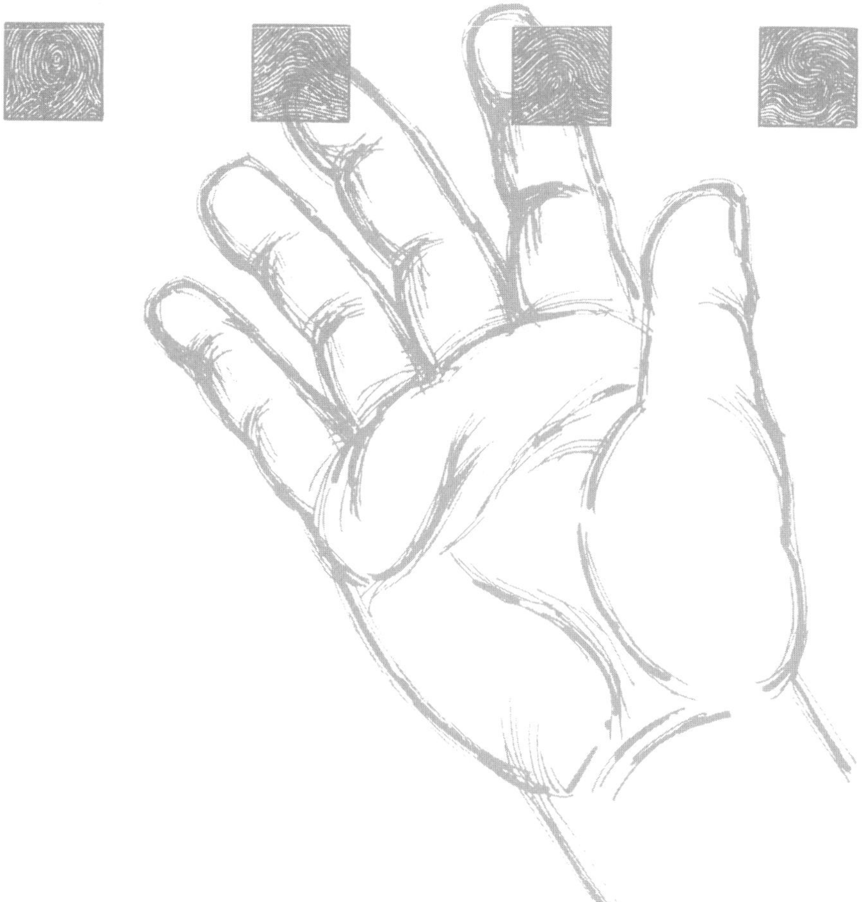

Looking at Human Skin ► *Activity 32*

DEVELOPMENTAL LEVEL
2–4

GROUP SIZE
Large

KEY EXPERIENCE
- *Looking with a purpose: observing and collecting data*

Children can begin by looking at their own skin, for it is a good representative example. Provide magnifying glasses for the children to use in observing their skin closely and clearly. Have them look at both the front and back of their hands and at their arms. Here are some questions and topics for discussion:

- Is skin really smooth?
- What differences do you see?
- Look at the front of your hand—can you see how the skin folds? To be useful, skin must be flexible.
- Look at the patterns on your fingers. These are called fingerprints. Fingerprints are really very small folds in your skin.
- Look at the back of your arm. Can you see small holes in its skin? These are called pores (see Illustration 62).
- Can you see fine hairs growing on your arm?
- Skin has many functions. What do you think they are? For example, skin protects the softer parts of the body underneath it. Where there is a lot of friction that might damage the body, the skin is thickest. Where could this be? Have children look at their hands again, then think of the parts of their body they walk on (see Illustration 63).
- Is skin waterproof? How could you test it?
- How does human skin differ from plastic? Think what happens to plastic if it is cut. What happens to skin?

Fingerprints

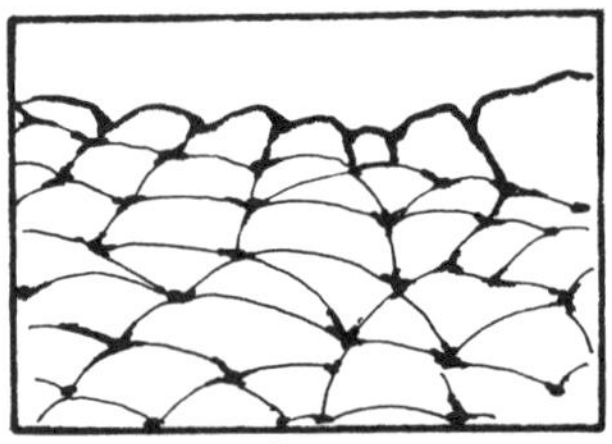

Pores

ILLUSTRATION 62

Skin Patterns

Children can use a magnifying glass to examine the fingerprints and pores on their skin.

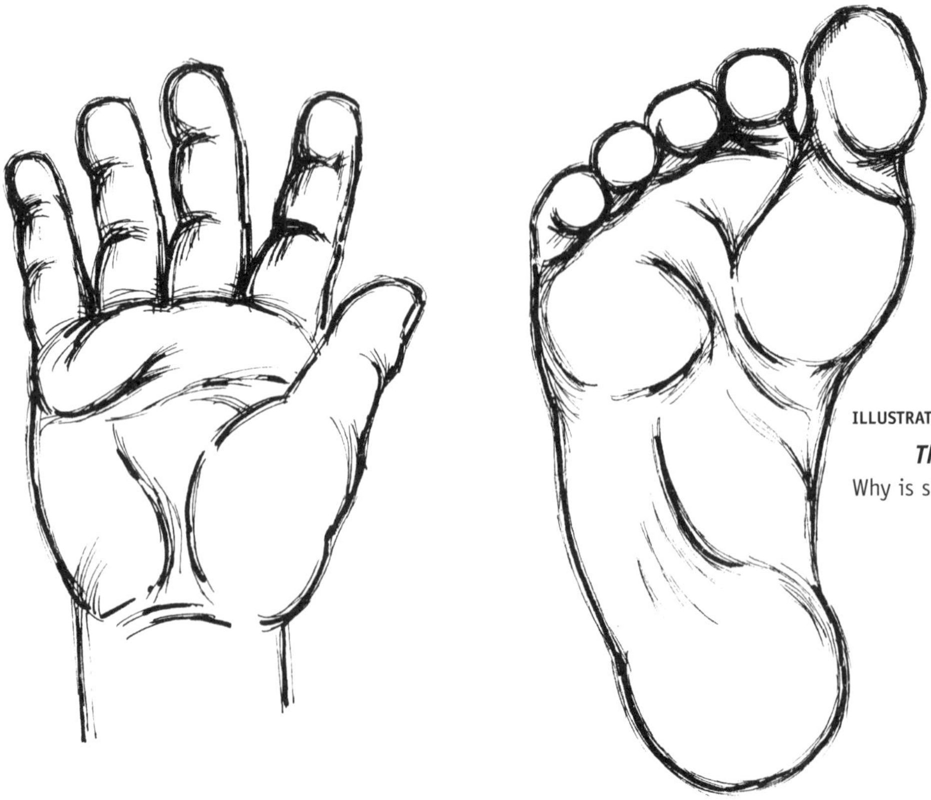

ILLUSTRATION 63

The Protective Function of Skin

Why is skin thickest on the hands and feet?

Here is a practical question children will be curious about: How much skin covers your body? Let children debate this and then try the following activity to determine an approximate answer to this question.

Working in pairs, students should follow these steps:

- One child lies on his or her back on top of paper spread on the ground with arms and legs outstretched (see Illustration 64).

- The other child draws around this silhouette. Pose the question: Would this be all or only part of a complete skin? Help the children realize that humans have front and back sides. Also, we are not flat but rounded in shape. Therefore, a complete skin also has right and left sides.

- Have the children cut out the silhouette of the back section.

- Now have the child lie down, on top of more paper, on his or her stomach. Let the other child trace the silhouette and cut around the outline. This is the front section.

- Have the child lie down on paper on his or her side and let the partner draw around the outline and cut it out (see Illustration 65). Let them make another from this shape as a pattern (discuss the idea of two equal sides).

ILLUSTRATION 64

Lying on a Mat With Arms and Legs Outstretched

Students begin this activity by lying on a large piece of paper on the ground, with arms and legs outstretched. Another child traces the silhouette. The first student then lays on another piece of paper on his or her stomach and the silhouette is again traced.

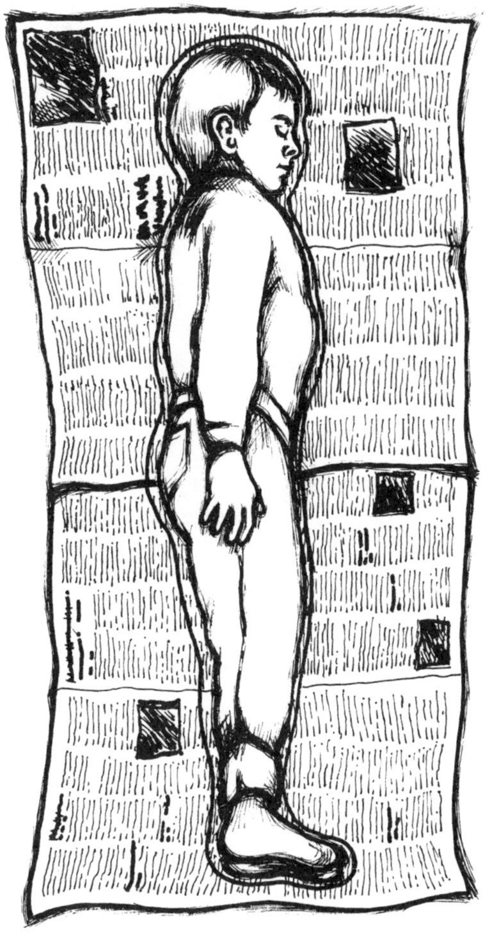

ILLUSTRATION 65

Lying Sideways on a Mat

Next, the child lays down on his or her side (both left and right sides), and the partner again traces the outline.

- Now the students have a whole skin—front, back, and two sides.
- Have them put this on a large display board (see Illustration 66).

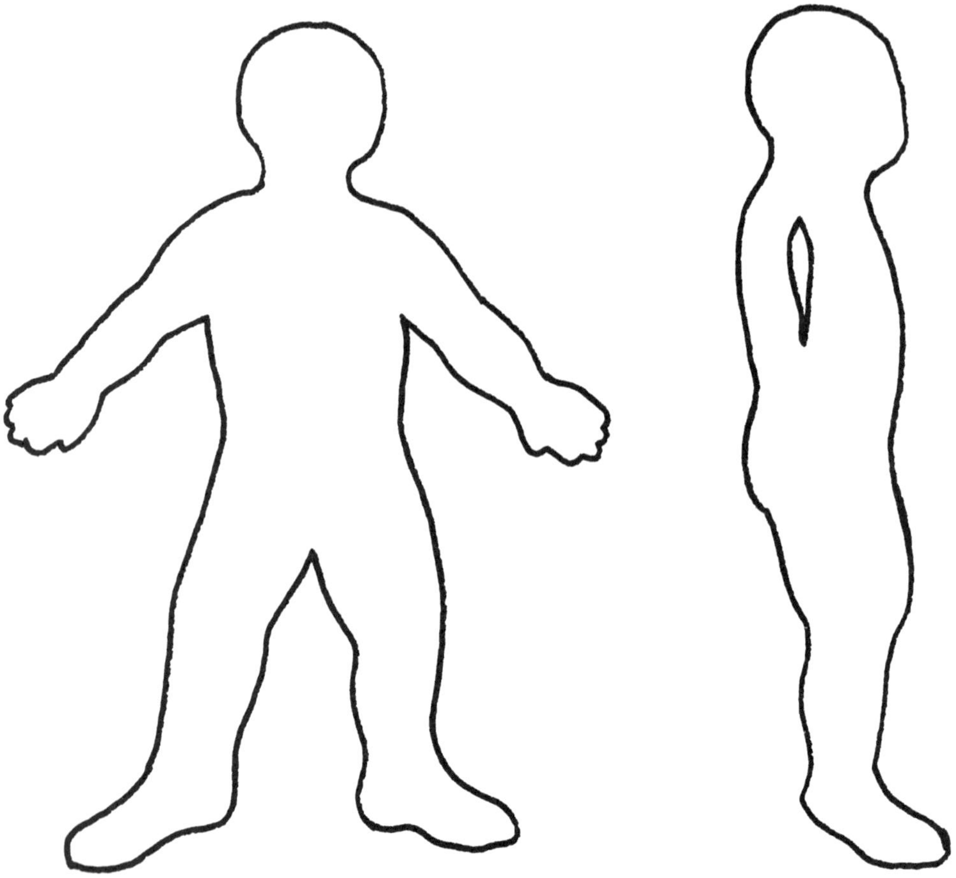

ILLUSTRATION **66**

Displaying Cutout Patterns

Students now have their "whole skin"—front, back, and sides.

Looking at Fruit and Vegetable Skins ► *Activity 33*

DEVELOPMENTAL LEVEL
2–4

GROUP SIZE
Large

KEY EXPERIENCES

- *Looking with a purpose: observing and collecting data*
- *Measuring, testing, and analyzing: assessing the properties and composition of materials*

Together with the students, collect some fruit and vegetable skins. Good ones to collect include orange, apple, banana, tomato, potato, and (in season) peach and plum skins (see Illustration 67).

Have the students look at the skins closely and discuss the following:

- Is there more than one layer of tissue? What is the outer layer like? The inner layer?
- What is the job of the skin? How does it carry out its job?
- How does the skin of fruits and vegetables compare to human skin? For example, do you see holes (pores) as in human skin?
- Are these skins waterproof? How can you test this?
- Can you see places where the skin has been damaged? What has happened to it?

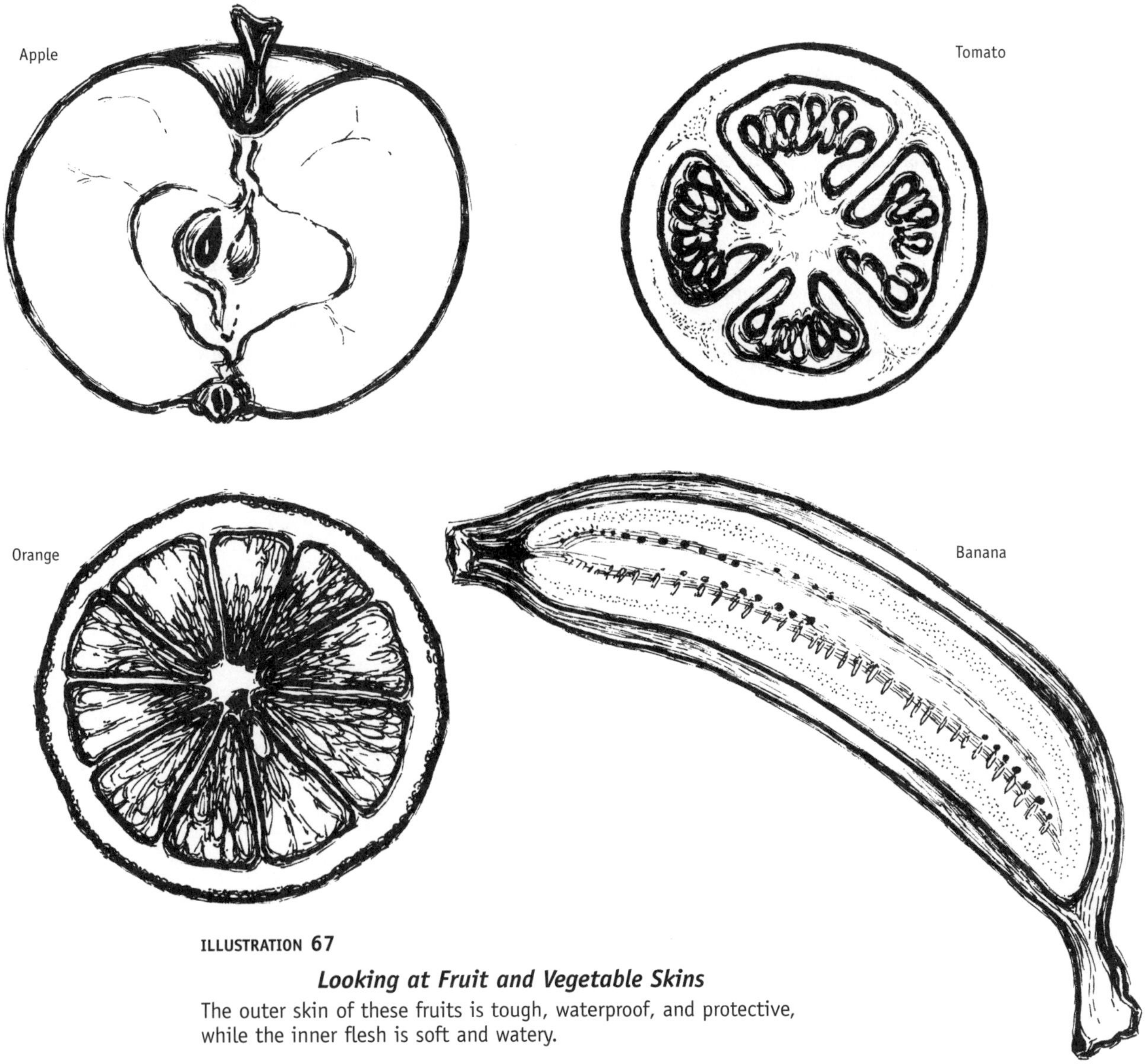

ILLUSTRATION 67

Looking at Fruit and Vegetable Skins

The outer skin of these fruits is tough, waterproof, and protective, while the inner flesh is soft and watery.

Looking at Animal Skin ► *Activity 34*

DEVELOPMENTAL LEVEL
2–4

GROUP SIZE
Large

KEY EXPERIENCE
- *Looking with a purpose: observing and collecting data*

Examining animal skin is a good way to make students aware of the great diversity of skin in living creatures. They may be surprised to discover, for example, that whiskers (hairs) are structurally part of the skin. In addition, nails, claws, and hooves are thick plates of dead horny material produced by the outer layer of the skin (the epidermis).

• **Whiskers** are very long stout hairs or bristles that grow near the mouth of many mammals. Whiskers act as extended touch receptors in animals. Discuss with students which animals have whiskers and how they might use them.

• **Nails** occur at the edges of the digits and act as protective shields. The dead cells of the nail are pushed out toward the tip as the nail grows. Fingernails grow faster than toenails, and nails of individual fingers of the same hand grow at different rates. The growth rate is thought to be greater in people from about age 10 to 30, with a slight decline thereafter. Growth increases during the summer months, and growth rates are slower in cold climates. Nails may also grow more slowly during illness. Encourage students to discuss the following types of questions: How much do their nails grow in a week? How much do their pets' nails grow?

• **Claws,** found in birds, reptiles, and some mammals, are strongly curved and narrow nails that occur at the end of a finger or a toe. They are used for scratching, clawing, and clutching. The claw is made up of two types of materials: one (called the "unguis") produces a harder claw on the top surface; the other (called the "sub unguis") produces a softer surface at the front of the claw. Discuss the following: What animals have claws? How do they use them?

• **Hooves** are nails whose unguis layer completely surrounds the end of the digit. They occur only in certain mammals, called "ungulates," and protect the ends of the toes. Hooves have the same placement and composition as do nails and claws. Because hooves grow throughout life, their length is normally controlled by wear.

Looking at Fingerprints ► *Activity 35*

DEVELOPMENTAL LEVEL
4–6

GROUP SIZE
Large

KEY EXPERIENCE

- *Looking with a purpose: observing and collecting data*

No two people have the same fingerprints. Fingerprints are of four types—whorls, arches, loops, and composites. Most prints are loops; few are arches; the rest are whorls and composites (double loops). (See Illustration 68.)

ILLUSTRATION 68

Fingerprints

Using magnifying glasses, let students see how many of these patterns they can find on their fingers.

Students may find all or only one of these types on the fingers of both hands. Provide them with magnifying glasses and let them look at their fingers for the four patterns: whorls, arch, loops, and the composites (double loops).

It is not always easy to get a clear fingerprint; here are some tips for students to follow:

- Work very carefully and use a fairly dry ink pad (from a home printing set or stamp pad).

- Roll one finger only on the surface of the pad.

- Press the inked finger very firmly on clean white paper, rolling it once from side to side. Press firmly but not hard. (It is important to press it only once or the print will smudge.)

- Experiment to get good prints. What technique works best?

Using the magnifying glass to look carefully, students can discuss the following questions: Is the fingerprint of your index finger the same for both hands? Is this so for your other matching fingers (pinky, ring finger, etc.) on both hands? Are the fingerprints of different fingers on your hand the same or different? For example, compare the fingerprint of your index finger with that of your ring finger. How are they the same? How are they different?

► *Part Nine*

The Structure of Everyday Items In the Science Context

Everyday items, such as rocks, string, and fibers, can provide students with many interesting ways to explore form and structure. These items can be assembled into collections. In addition, various types of natural and man-made fibers can be tested, studied, and compared.

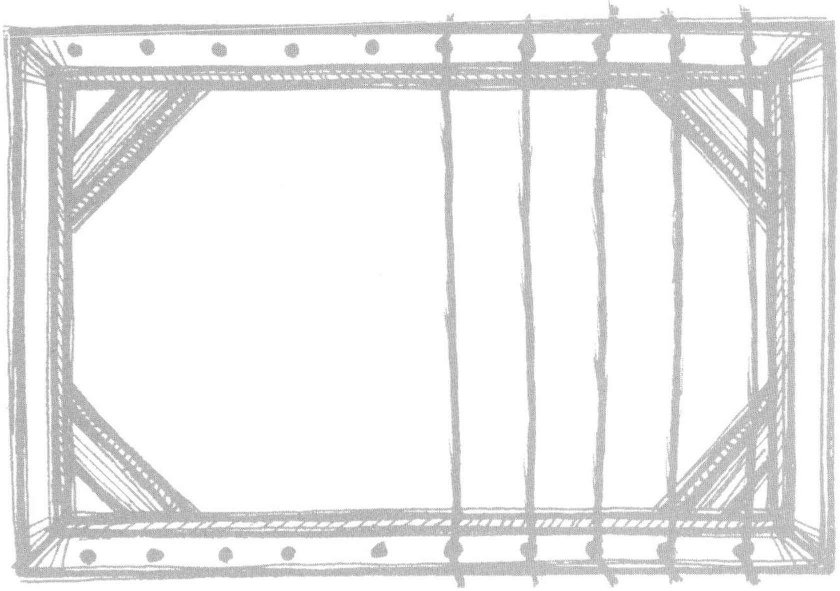

Making Collections of Everyday Items ► *Activity 36*

DEVELOPMENTAL LEVEL
K–2

GROUP SIZE
Large

KEY EXPERIENCE
- *Looking with a purpose: observing and collecting data*

Many common, everyday items can be easily assembled into collections. The following lists contain examples of the types of items that can be found around us.

• **Rocks.** Rock collections are easily assembled from the neighborhoods surrounding children's homes and schools. In addition to local rocks, it is useful to have examples of two major groups of rocks to add to children's collections:

Igneous (formed by fire)	*Sedimentary* (put down in layers)
granite	sandstone
quartz	clay
pumice	limestone
basalt	conglomerate
	coal

Pieces about the size of the palm of a child's hand are ideal for examination. To help children get the feel of the rocks, let them scratch the rocks, first with a fingernail, and then with a metal nail. Let them look at the rocks with magnifying glasses.

• **Artificial stones.** Children can make a collection of various artificial stones:

House bricks of various kinds, colors, sizes, shapes
Concrete in various forms
Tiles (roofing tiles, floor tiles, and wall tiles)
Plaster of Paris objects

• **Animal and vegetable fibers.** Fibers of all types are wonderful for children to examine with magnifying glasses. Include the following:

Paper, cardboard (all kinds)
String, rope (all kinds)
Sackcloth, wood shavings
Cloths of all kinds, wool, cotton, man-made fibers, silk

Samples of cloth can be useful as examples of pattern formation and pattern design. Get samples that can be replicated on squared paper to inspire child-invented patterns and designs. Samples of materials of all kinds can be used for weaving, design making, and art work.

Working With Fibers ► *Activity 37*

DEVELOPMENTAL LEVEL
1–3

GROUP SIZE
Small

KEY EXPERIENCE
- *Measuring, testing, and analyzing: assessing the properties and composition of materials*

Students can test the strength of fibers by unraveling them, noting how they are twisted and woven. Illustration 69 shows a simple way to test the strength of a single thread or fiber.

Tie one end of the fiber to the hook of a spring scale. Pull the other end of the fiber with a pair of pliers. Record the strength of the fiber, that is, the maximum weight reading on the scale before the fiber breaks.

Several tests should be made on each fiber, and the results averaged to get an accurate reading. Test fibers for water absorbent properties, and for water resistant properties, for dyeing and color fastness when treated.

ILLUSTRATION 69

Testing the Strength of a Fiber

To begin this test, tie one end of a fiber to the hook of a spring scale. Pull the other end of the fiber with a pair of pliers. Record the fiber's strength, which is the maximum weight reading on the scale before the fiber breaks.

DEVELOPMENTAL LEVEL
4–6

GROUP SIZE
Small

KEY EXPERIENCE
- *Designing, building, fabricating, and modifying structures or materials*

Plaiting and Weaving With Natural Fibers

How can natural material be used to make things today? Not long ago, many things—such as baskets and clothing—were made of plaited and woven natural materials. Natural fibers are still useful for people to work with today.

Here are some questions for students to think about: Have you ever made a daisy chain? Can you plait long grasses using three strands? Is it possible to plait with five strands of grass? What about making a rough basket from thin twigs? Think of a bird's nest. Can you get a basket to look at as a model and see if you can copy it?

Pose this challenge to the students: Can you make a natural fiber rope by twisting long plant stems together? Try using the long trailing stems of ivy or the creepers of honey suckle. Try plaiting these fibers into various lengths. The best time to get the long fibrous stems is in the autumn and spring when there is the least sap in the stems. For the purposes of experimenting, however, these fibers can be tried at any time of the year. It is best to look for long scrambling stems.

Plants can also provide the basic materials for weaving wall decorations from natural fibers of all kinds. Long grasses can be used either singly or in bunches of several strands for weaving. Plaited grasses and twisted grasses can be inserted into loose weaves to give them a patterned surface. Colored twigs that are long and flexible also weave well into patterns. Some form of weaving frame is needed for these experiments with natural materials (see Illustration 70). Old picture frames strengthened at the corners with a diagonal slat are excellent for small scale work. Nails along the top and bottom can be used to tie down the warp (vertical or fixed) threads.

To begin this activity, set up the loom. Make sure that the warp threads are a sturdy material such as cotton or linen threads that will support the weft (horizontal) threads of natural fibers. Begin the weaving at the bottom end. First, insert three or four rows of "heading" using a thick material such as heavy twine or even several

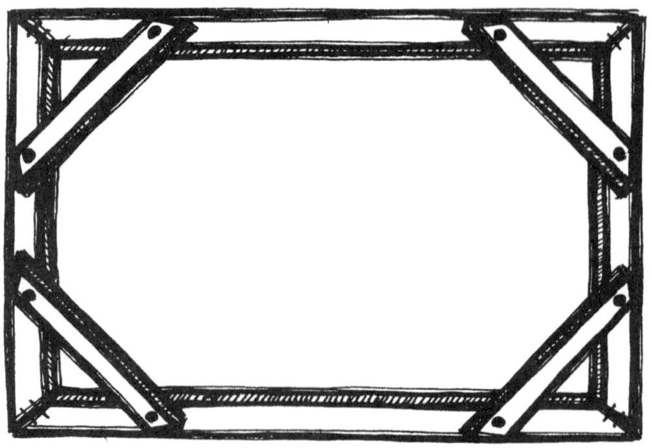

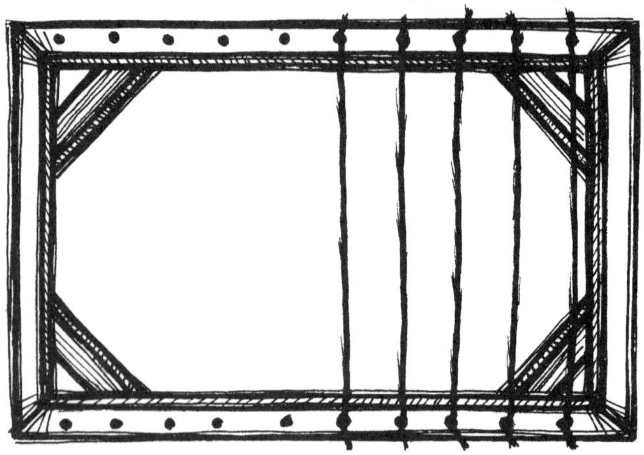

ILLUSTRATION 70

Creating a Frame for Weaving
Using common, everyday materials, students can create a simple frame for weaving.

sheets of twisted paper towels. The heading will keep the warp threads from unraveling when the finished weaving is cut off the loom and will also provide an even base. Once the heading is in place, students can begin to use natural materials in a simple weave (the weft thread goes over one warp thread, under the next thread, and so on), in a basket weave (two over, two under), or in combinations of the two. Threads can be left hanging in the middle of a row for a shaggy effect, perhaps shredded at the end or with a small bead attached. Students can create beautiful patterns by the use of a variety of materials in the weft. For example, they can try long shavings, twisted paper inserts, and colored twigs as well as long trailing stems of obviously useful material. When the weaving is a few inches from the top, the students should insert another three or four weft rows of heading to anchor the weaving in place and keep it from unraveling when it is cut off the loom. Then the students can cut the top and bottom ends of the warp threads near the nails where they are attached. They should gently remove the heading rows and tie the ends of the warp threads. The weaving is now ready for display!

The principles used in the simple frame loom can be adapted for many variations on this device. Basically, the loom needs a fixed axis on which to secure the warp threads. In some Latin American and Asian countries, weavers tie one end of the loom around a tree and the other end around their waist. As they sit away from the tree and lean back, the pull of their bodies creates the tension to make the warp threads fixed and ready to receive the weft threads. Warp threads can also be made fixed and taut by weighing them down with rocks, bricks, or other heavy objects, as in Illustration 71, and students may be able to set up looms such as these. When the warp threads are not fixed at the bottom, students should being weaving with their weft threads at the top. Let them experiment with different types of headings or other alternatives to prevent the finished weaving from unraveling.

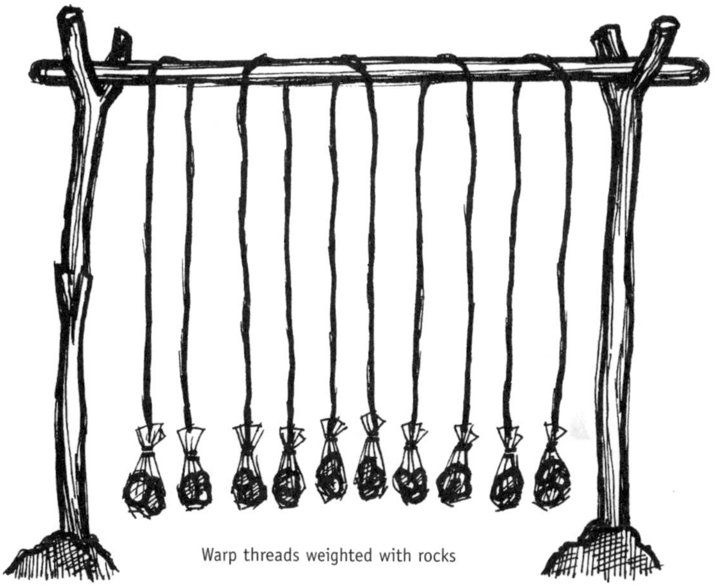

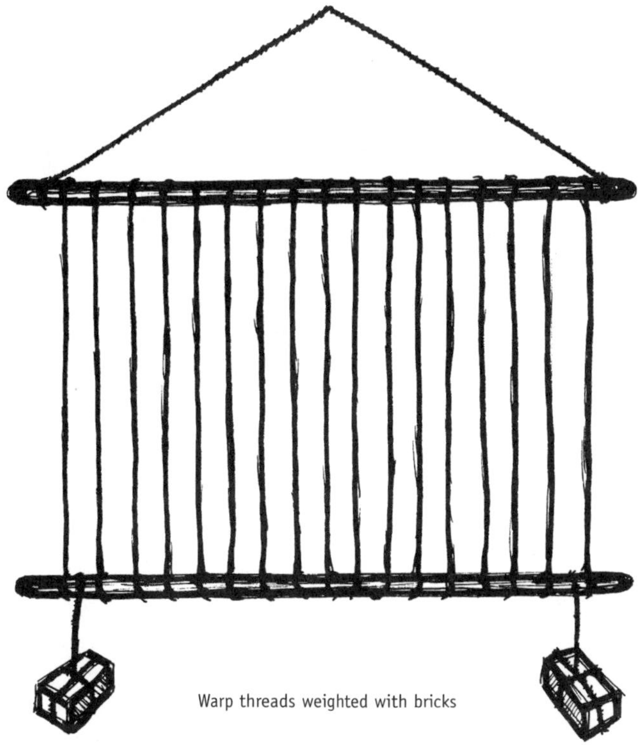

ILLUSTRATION 71

Setting Up Warp Threads for Weaving on a Loom

Warp threads can be made taut by weighing them down with rocks, bricks, or other heavy objects.

► *Part Ten*

Common Textbook Topics On Structure From a New Perspective

Air and water are common and essential substances in our daily lives. Consequently, they form natural topics for the study of science. Children's spontaneous curiosity about these materials becomes a wonderful starting point for hands-on learning activities. Some simple air and water experiments are described in this section, experiments that can be carried out with easily obtainable materials.

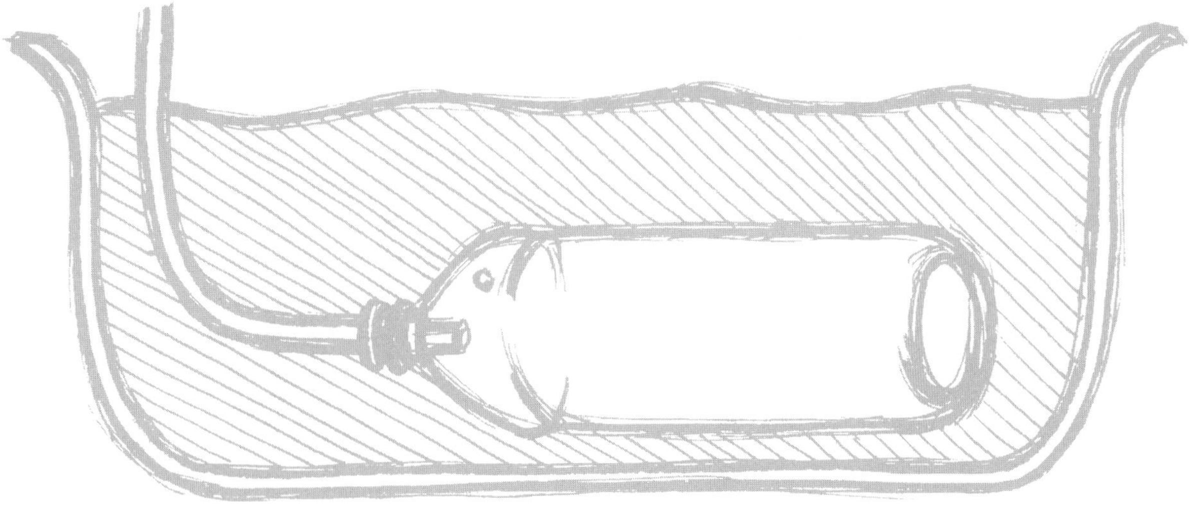

Air Is Real and Takes Up Space ► *Activity 39*

DEVELOPMENTAL LEVEL
K–2

GROUP SIZE
Small

KEY EXPERIENCE
- *Measuring, testing, and analyzing: assessing the properties and composition of materials*

Many simple and everyday materials can be used to investigate the properties of air. It is easy for teachers to keep a ready supply of them on hand for the following activities as well as for improvised experiments by the students.

- Small plastic bags without holes enable children to get a bag full of air. They can investigate its properties and compare a bag of air with a bag of water, or with a bag with a solid wooden block in it.
- Large plastic bags provide the raw materials for parachutes and kites.
- Paper can be used to make gliders.
- Plastic bottles and funnels can be used to investigate how air is real enough to prevent water from running into a bottle.

To begin this activity, have students first try pouring water through a funnel and into a bottle stoppered with a cork without an airway (see Illustration 72). What happens when water is poured into the funnel? Next, have students repeat the activity using

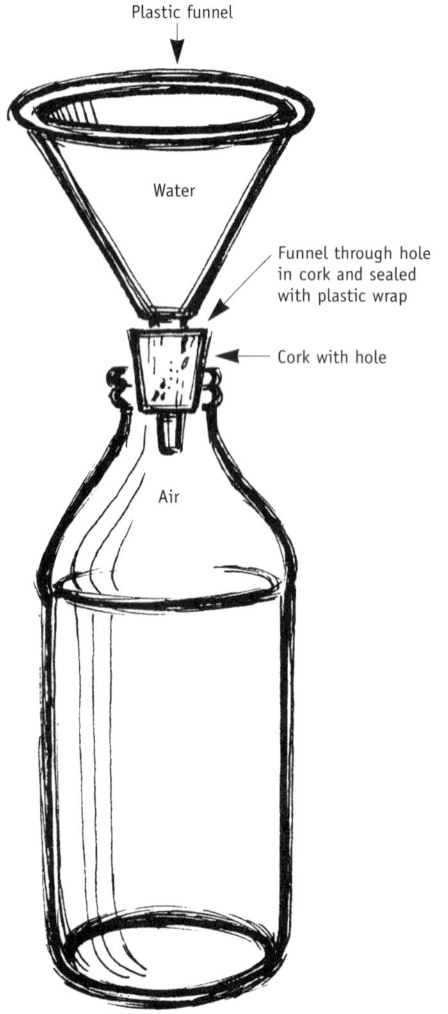

ILLUSTRATION 72

Pouring Water Through a Funnel

To begin this activity, first try the cork without the airway. What happens when water is poured into the funnel? Change the corks over; what happens now? Why?

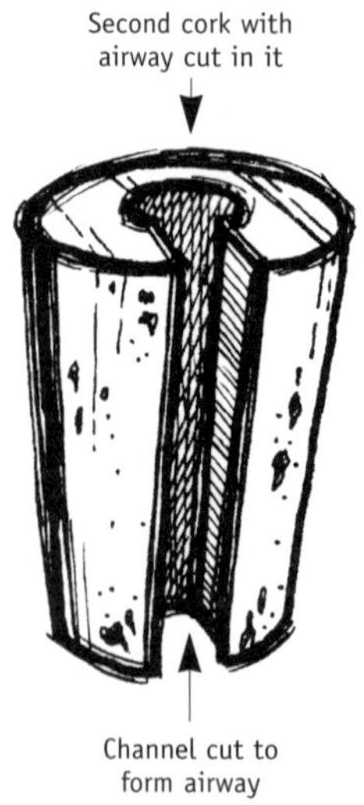

a cork that has an airway cut through it. What happens now? Why does the water go into the bottle differently under these two conditions?

Plastic bottles and a bucket will be needed for children to pour air from one container to the other, one filled with air, the other water. Tins with tight lids make good materials for magic water suppliers. Have students make a tin with one hole in the lid and three holes in the bottom (see Illustration 73). Immerse the tin in a bucket of water until it is full. Quickly press the lid on tightly. Take the tin out of the bucket and keep a finger over the top hole until someone in the group says "go." Take the finger off the hole, hold the tin over the bucket, and then watch what happens. Why? Students can control the flow on command by releasing or pressing a finger on the top hole.

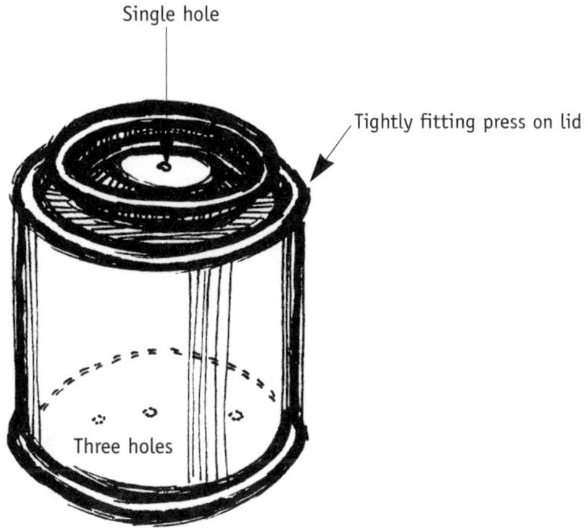

ILLUSTRATION 73

Experimenting With Air and Water

Tins with tight lids make good materials for magic water suppliers.

Air Is Real and Takes Up Space ► *Activity 40*

DEVELOPMENTAL LEVEL
2–4

GROUP SIZE
Small

KEY EXPERIENCE

- *Observing, predicting, and controlling change: understanding causality*

Materials for the study of hot air and moving air are usually easy to find. Students can use tissue paper for streamers, for example, to detect moving air indoors over radiators and outdoors in the wind. In addition, children might try cutting a metal snake from thick aluminum cooking foil to use as a hot air detector (see Illustration 74). Have them mark out a spiral on a flat sheet of foil and cut it out carefully. Place one end on the needle and allow the coil to fall freely. See what happens when the coil is placed near moving air currents—both warm and cool.

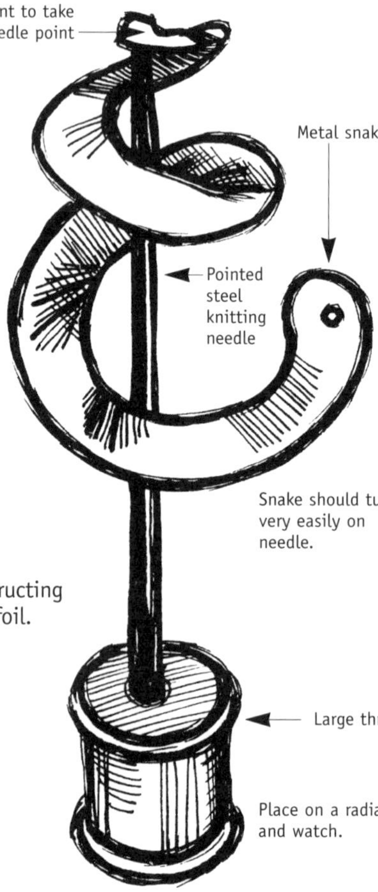

ILLUSTRATION 74

The Study of Moving Air

Students can investigate the study of moving air by constructing a simple metal snake made from thick aluminum cooking foil.

Students can investigate the study of moving air using windmills, propellers, toy aircraft, balloons, and other ordinary materials.

Air Is Real and Takes Up Space ► *Activity 41*

DEVELOPMENTAL LEVEL
K–2

GROUP SIZE
Small

KEY EXPERIENCE

- *Measuring, testing, and analyzing: assessing the properties and composition of materials*

Children are always interested in how much air is in their lungs. Again, simple everyday items suffice to test this.

To begin this activity, have the children blow into a tube (as shown in Illustration 75) and then measure the amount of water they displace. The amount of water they displace into the beaker is equal to the amount of air in their lungs. Have them try this first without taking a deep breath and then again after they take a deep breath. Do their lungs hold different amounts of air in each case? (**Note:** This is always a popular experiment, so it pays to have several "sterilized" tubes available. If several children are to use the same plastic tube, clean it by putting it in mild disinfectant each time after use. Clean the whole tube well with disinfectant before putting it away.)

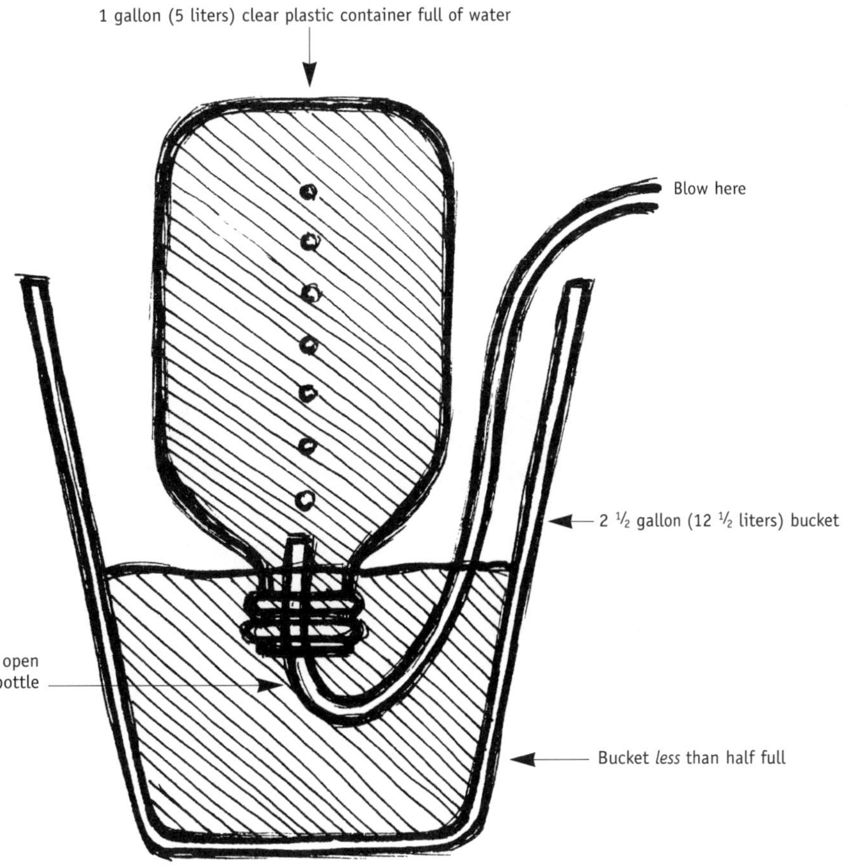

ILLUSTRATION 75

Measuring the Amount of Air in Our Lungs

Simple, everyday items can be used by children to discover how much air is in their lungs.

Ships and Submarines ▶ *Activity 42*

DEVELOPMENTAL LEVEL
3–5

GROUP SIZE
Small

KEY EXPERIENCES

- *Measuring, testing, and analyzing: assessing the properties and composition of materials*
- *Observing, predicting, and controlling change: understanding causality*

Water, like air, is a universal element of interest to children. Ordinary materials can be used to study water. Practical activities can start with tests of floating and sinking. Have on hand a supply of wood, metal, and stone objects of various weights. Here are some suggestions:

• Collect equal size blocks of various woods and have the students closely observe their levels in the water when floating. Include balsa, which floats very well, and oak, which just barely floats. If you can get some ebony, you will see this sink! Pose the following questions: Do all kinds of wood float? Do all woods float equally well?

• Have a collection of stones including pumice stone and coke. Ask the students: Do all stones sink?

• Have various types of plastic on hand, both heavy and light. Ask the students: Does all plastic float? How well does a plastic sponge float when it is dry? When it is wet?

Ships and submarines are also fascinating to children and can be the source of many investigations. Provide students with aluminum foil and have them mold it into a simple boat shape. Does it float? Now have the students scrunch up the foil into a ball. Does it float? (It probably will.) Have them scrunch it up tighter. Does it float now? (It may.) Finally, have them hammer the foil into the flat metal that sheets are made from. Does it float now? Try the same experiment with plastic wrap. What are the results? How does this help to explain why metal ships float?

Raising a sunken submarine is also possible with simple materials (see Illustration 76). Fill a plastic bottle with water and insert a stopper with a hose. Submerge the bottle in a basin of water. Gradually let the water out of the bottle through the hose, replacing the water with air. When does the submarine rise—before or only after all the water is out? How could water be pumped out of a real submarine?

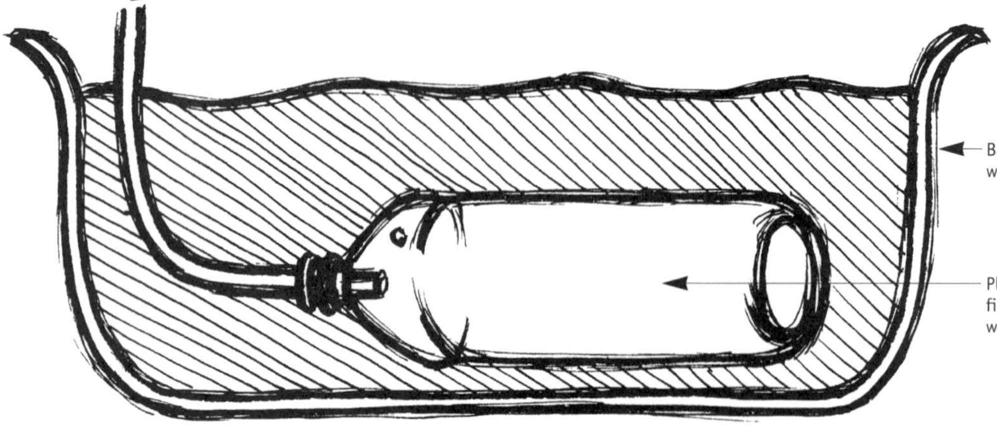

ILLUSTRATION 76

Raising a Sunken Submarine

Ships and submarines can be the source of many interesting science activities for elementary-aged children.

Water as a Solvent ► *Activity 43*

DEVELOPMENTAL LEVEL
1–3

GROUP SIZE
Small

KEY EXPERIENCE
- *Measuring, testing, and analyzing: assessing the properties and composition of materials*

Students can test household materials and list those that are soluble (dissolve) and insoluble (do not dissolve). Have them try salt, sugar, washing soda, chalk, talcum powder, baking powder, soap powder, coffee, tea, scouring powder, and sand. They should take equal amounts of each to test for solubility. To begin, have them dissolve some sugar or salt in water in a clean cup. It disappears. Ask them: Has it gone forever? How could you tell it is still there? (For example, by tasting it.) Could you get it back? Leave some of the solution in a clean saucer sitting on a warm radiator until it dries up. What do you find? Look closely! Touch the dry saucer with a clean finger. Can you taste anything?

Water Penetrates Many Substances ► *Activity 44*

DEVELOPMENTAL LEVEL
3–5

GROUP SIZE
Small

KEY EXPERIENCE
- *Looking with a purpose: observing and collecting data*

Water penetrates many substances but some soak up water better than others. Children can investigate the properties of paper towels, cotton towels, diapers, and so on for this property. Have them cut test strips all of the same size and let them hang about 1″ into water colored with a few drops of ink or food dye. Have them test strips of several different kinds of material. How will they determine how much colored water each strip absorbed (for example, looking at the color with their eyes, squeezing it into a measuring cup)? What test methods are most accurate? Which materials which would make the best toweling?

Many Things Absorb Water ► *Activity 45*

DEVELOPMENTAL LEVEL
3–5

GROUP SIZE
Small

KEY EXPERIENCE

- *Measuring, testing, and analyzing: assessing the properties and composition of materials*

Many things absorb water. Have students set up tests for comparing different building materials: wood, concrete, bricks, wallboard, and so on. Also include rocks and metal.

Begin with a brick (see Illustration 77). Have the students weigh the dry brick. Then set a brick in a bowl of water. Watch what happens. Does the brick begin to turn a darker color from the bottom up? Have the students time how long the water takes to rise 1 inch up the brick, then 2 inches, and so on. Will it reach the top?

Set this up and observe what happens overnight. Have the students try the experiment with other things used in building. Weigh each one dry and then weigh it wet to see how much water is absorbed. Have them time how long it takes each material to dry out. Which materials are best for building? Why?

Set brick in a bowl of water.

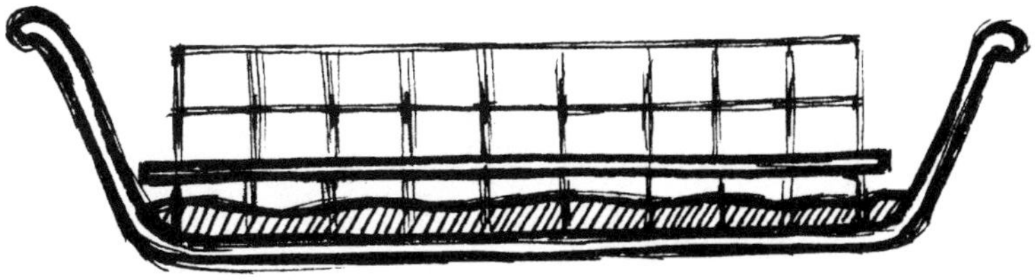

Observe the brick as it begins to absorb water and darken.

ILLUSTRATION 77

Testing How Things Absorb Water

After setting up a brick on two pieces of wood in a bowl of water, students can time how long the water takes to rise 1 inch up the brick, then 2 inches.

► *Part Eleven*

Structure and Form Case Studies: Some Classroom Experiences

The following case studies describe what happens when ideas on paper or in the teacher's mind are actually used with children. Teachers begin a science project with specific learning experiences in mind. While students may indeed generate these experiences, their own interests will also lead to the development of other activities and insights. The classroom experiences presented in this section provide real-life examples of how planned activities may evolve into unanticipated explorations in science. In all cases, the children are actively engaged and the teacher is flexible enough to respond to the students' leads. The resulting learning is rich, varied, and exciting.

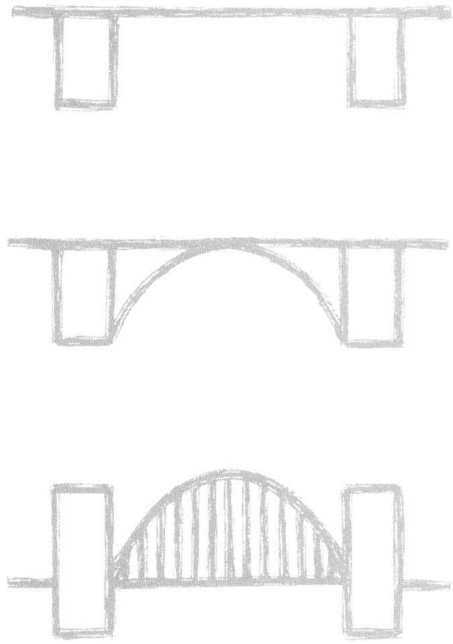

Patterns in Nonliving Objects—Color Matters

► *Activity 46*

DEVELOPMENTAL LEVEL
2–4

GROUP SIZE
Large

KEY EXPERIENCES

- *Looking with a purpose: observing and collecting data*
- *Measuring, testing, and analyzing: assessing the properties and composition of materials*
- *Reporting and interpreting data and results*

General Experiences the Teacher Had in Mind

• To enable children to gain a greater awareness of color as a factor in their surroundings and in their everyday lives

Other Experiences the Teacher Hoped to Encourage

• To investigate color preferences in the immediate surroundings of the classroom and handle the resulting data

• To consider the uses and effects of color

Follow-Up Activities the Teacher Hoped to Stimulate

• To survey favorite colors using colored candies as one means of information and a questionnaire as another means of measurement

• To define colors and establish criteria for sorting colors

• To examine color and background camouflage outdoors

• To examine color changes and colored lights

• To examine the effects of colors on other background colors

Activities That Actually Resulted

• Favorite colors were investigated by four children using the whole class as the survey base. They offered each individual in turn a choice of colored candies (jelly-beans). The colors available were red, orange, pink, purple, black, brown, and yellow. The color preference was judged by the candy selected and eaten. (The teacher raised doubts about this criterion, arguing that children could also be selecting for taste!) The results were shown by putting pieces of the candy on a chart (see Illustration 78 on pg. 119).

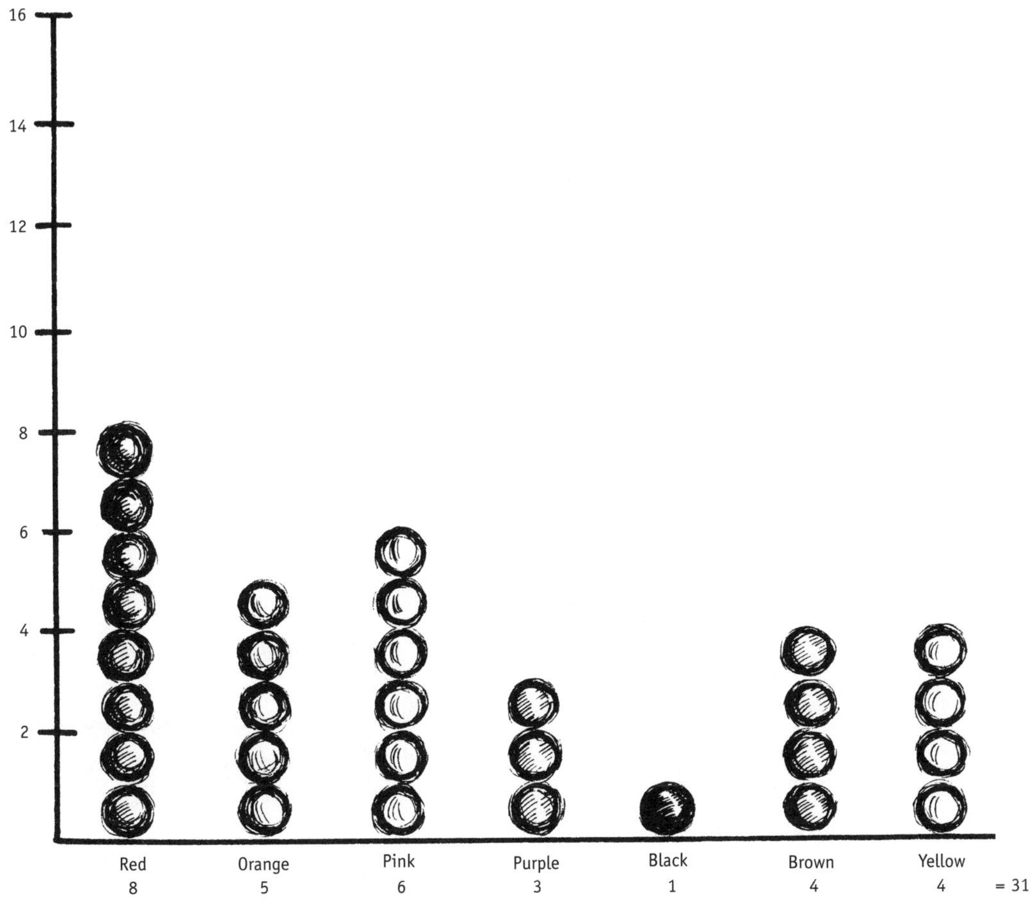

ILLUSTRATION 78

Charting Color Preferences

Students were offered jellybeans in a variety of colors and their preferences were recorded on a chart.

• Another group of students conducted a questionnaire asking others to choose their favorite color from the same choices as above: red, orange, pink, purple, black, brown, and yellow. The results were shown with check marks (see chart below).

Colors Reported As Favorite Colors

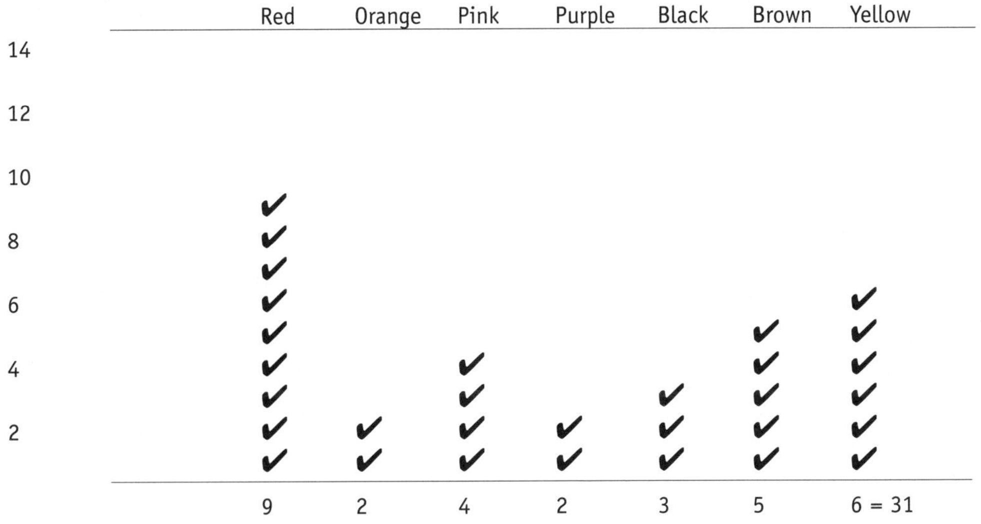

There was plenty of class discussion of these results and demands for further surveys, especially when the teacher asked, "Do different colors have different tastes?"

• Two groups of students each set out to list all the colors of objects they could find within the classroom. A first snag was to decide what is blue, what is green, and so on. A color card was adopted with the seven colors of the candies as standards. When the statistics were collected, the two groups of children sorted their results. They looked for answers to the following questions: What is the most common color? What is the least common? They compared their results and scrutinized them for differences. How could they explain these differences? They decided that it was because some interpretations of blues and greens, and oranges and reds were not the same.

• The same two groups then set out to apply the same technique to a survey of colors of children's clothing. They put a cross beside colors they thought fell on the boundary between two colors and were therefore doubtful.

• Two other groups of five students each investigated how easy it was to see colors when different colors were used as the background. They adopted a standard pattern of a 6" test square on an 18" x 12" background. They used the seven colors of the candies plus white for their work. While four members from each group made the test cards, one student from each group went into the hall and measured out test distances in paces for the trials. They chose 10, 20, 30, 40, and 50 pace intervals to test how easily they could recognize colors against different backgrounds. The students asked the teacher for help in deciding how to record their judgments. The teacher suggested a simple scale ranging from clear/good to unclear/poor. The students then recorded their results for each color-background combination. The teacher noted that this investigation could lead to a discussion about the visibility of such things as road signs, posters, and advertisements.

• Yet another group in the class had taken up the theme of setting criteria for labeling colors: What is blue? What is green? The members of this group worked individually on the problem and then pooled their results. One child produced the greatest range of greens by mixing varying amounts of blue and yellow paint. Another collected all the blue things in the classroom. A third investigated the effects of placing colored papers first under a blue cellophane sheet and then under a green sheet. A fourth child made a color viewing box to look at different colored objects through the light of the differently colored windows made of colored cellophane (see Illustration 79). The students concluded that colors vary greatly depending upon how they are made and how they are viewed.

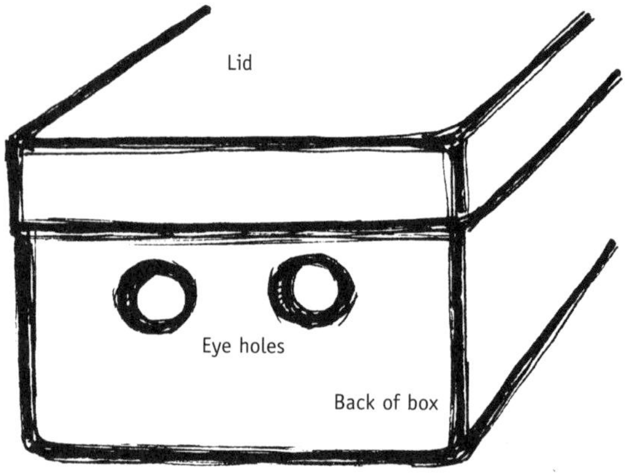

Eye holes placed as far apart as the designer's eyes

ILLUSTRATION 79

Making a Color Viewing Box

One child made a color viewing box to see how different colored objects look through the light of various pieces of colored cellophane.

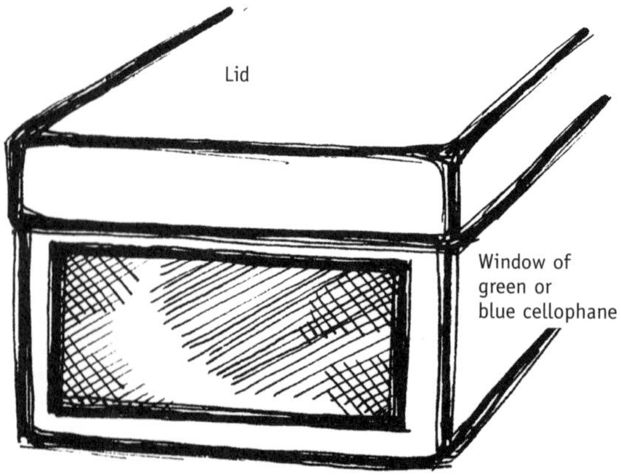

Cellophane fixed tightly around the edges of the window

Relationships/Compositions/Properties—More About Solids ► *Activity 47*

DEVELOPMENTAL LEVEL
3–5

GROUP SIZE
Large

KEY EXPERIENCES
- *Classifying and ordering materials according to their attributes and properties*
- *Measuring, testing, and analyzing: assessing the properties and composition of materials*

General Experiences the Teacher Had in Mind

• To give children an increased awareness of the significance of the concept of solids as one of three states of matter

• To make children familiar with the standard units of weight for measuring and comparing

Other Experiences the Teacher Hoped to Encourage

• To get children to appreciate through first-hand experience that solids have a shape of their own and occupy a definite space

• To make children aware that solids of the same size can have different weights

• To introduce the units of weight we encounter in daily life, including the metric system

• To help children understand that weighing is a method of measurement

• To help children understand that weighing is a method of comparison

• To make children aware that it is convenient and important to have standard measures of weights, such as the pound (and the kilogram)

Follow-Up Activities the Teacher Hoped to Stimulate

• To examine a variety of solid objects and establish the attributes that are necessary to classify an item as a solid

• To discuss the idea of weight and its convenience in measuring

• To compare arbitrary measurements and standard measurements

• To explore the metric system

• To experiment with everyday weighing devices such as balances, spring scales, scales with weights, electronic weighing machines, and weighing bridges

Activities That Actually Resulted

• The children put small objects into opaque plastic bags and tried to determine their fixed shapes by feel alone. They recorded the number of correct guesses.

• Working with collections of small objects such as books, a box of crayons, a box of chalk, a pack of cards, and a pencil box, the children determined that they were all solids by answering the question: Do they take up space? They listed the objects from the smallest to largest and from the shortest to longest to emphasize the idea of taking up space.

• Using the same collections of small objects, the children weighed each by "feel." They arranged the objects in an order from lightest to heaviest. Each child made his or her own list and then compared results. The children discussed similarities and differences in their lists and how these came about.

• The children discussed the idea of weight and its convenience for measuring and comparing. They discussed why we need standard weights.

• The children made sets of weights using sand in bags or boxes and a kitchen scale for checking.

• The children tried to get a sense of different weights—¼, ½, ¾, and 1 pound. They used unlabeled opaque plastic or cloth bags, filled with different weights of objects (such as candies) and tried to guess the weight of each. They compared their guesses to the actual weight (see Illustration 80 on pg. 123).

• The children filled two identical sized boxes, one with sand and the other with cotton wool. They compared their weights to investigate whether same-sized objects are always the same weight.

• From the materials box, the children collected as many items as possible of the same size. (The teacher had prepared such a box with identical size pieces of styrofoam, wood, rubber, iron, chipboard, and carpet.) They again discussed whether objects of the same size were the same weight. They arranged the objects according to their weights.

• The children found objects that weighed the same but took up different amounts of space, such as two paperback books that were equal in weight to one hardback book.

• The children used a range of weighing machines including balances with homemade weights, kitchen scales, spring scales (balances).

• Students explored the metric system. They made sets of metric weights in labeled bags or boxes filled with sand—50 grams, 100 grams, 250 grams, 500 grams, and 1 kilogram.

• The children devised weight charts for the whole class, representing the results in pounds (see Illustration 81 on pg. 123).

• Students made a survey of the weights and sizes of goods on the supermarket shelves.

• The students wondered how to weigh an elephant. They planned a visit to a local weighing station such as that found on highways to weigh trucks.

Presentation 1

Guessed weight	Less than 5 oz	5–9 oz	10–14 oz	15–19 oz	20–24 oz
Number of children	7	14	12	5	1

Presentation 2

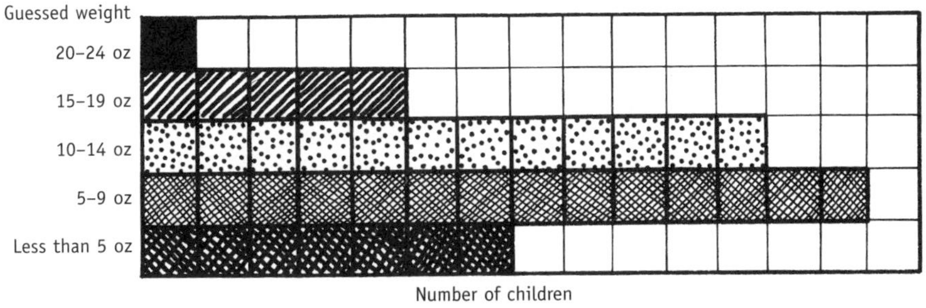

Presentation 3

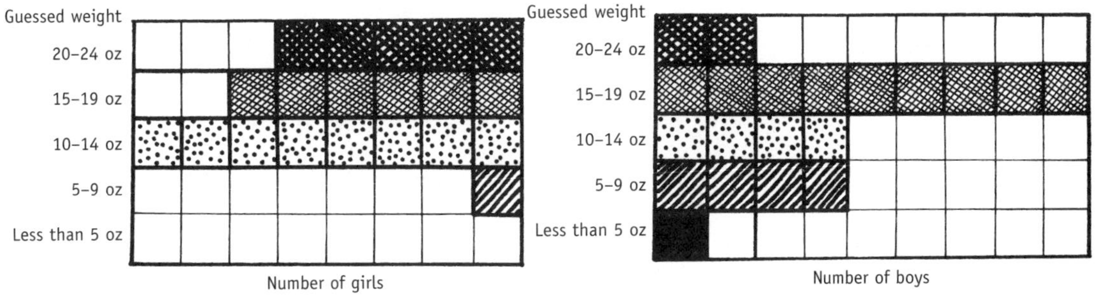

ILLUSTRATION **80**

Three Ways of Presenting Weight Estimates

Students tried to guess the weights of different objects and then compared their guesses to the actual weight. They presented their results in three different ways.

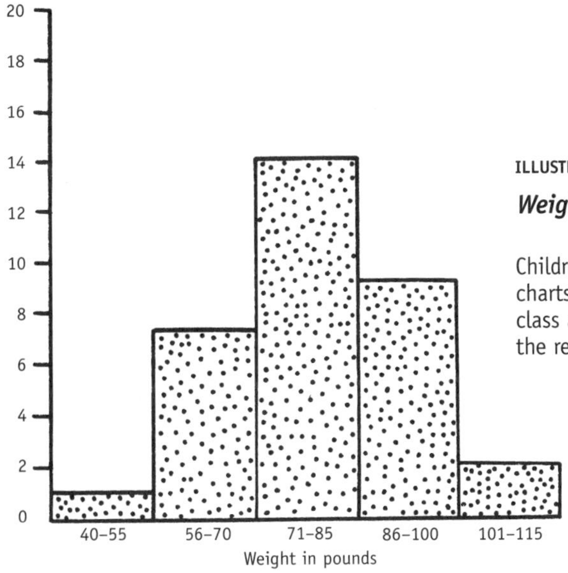

ILLUSTRATION **81**

Weighing Children in the Class

Children devised weight charts for the entire class and represented the results in pounds.

Relationships/Compositions/Properties—Some Properties of Air ► *Activity 48*

DEVELOPMENTAL LEVEL
1–3

GROUP SIZE
Small

KEY EXPERIENCES

- *Looking with a purpose: observing and collecting data*
- *Measuring, testing, and analyzing: assessing the properties and composition of materials*

General Experiences the Teacher Had in Mind

- To help children appreciate the presence of air all around us
- To help children understand that air is a form of matter called a "gas," and that it possesses certain properties they can investigate

Other Experiences the Teacher Hoped to Encourage

- To help children perceive that there are three states of matter—solids, liquids, and gases—and that air is an example of the last
- To allow children to establish for themselves some of the properties of gases and to compare these properties with those of solids and liquids
- To let children find out that air is invisible but that its effects can be felt and sometimes seen
- To help children appreciate that air is always moving and that the wind is moving air

Follow-Up Activities the Teacher Hoped to Stimulate

- To examine samples of air collected in plastic bags
- To discuss how something can be real yet invisible (defining what invisible means)
- To discover where there is moving air—inside the room and outside the classroom
- To experiment with moving air; to invent ways of making air move
- To discuss wind as moving air and how its power can be used

Activities That Actually Resulted

- Children collected air in plastic bags and twisted the tops to imprison the sample of air. They examined the air by feeling it through the bag.
- The children described the properties of air. Although they did not use scientific terms, they identified fluidity, compressibility, and shapelessness. The teacher helped them attach labels to their descriptions.
- Children put solid objects (wooden blocks, shoes) and liquids (water, lemonade) in the plastic bags and subjected them to the same examination. They compared the properties of air, solids, and liquids. The teacher helped them to enlarge their vocabulary as they described the properties of each type of matter.
- The children looked for air currents in the room. They attached feathers on thread fixed to a short stick and moved about the room to detect air currents. They recorded where they found them and how strong each one was (how much it blew the feather).

• Children examined the effects of moving air using various means. They fanned a feather with a card fan; they blew air through a straw to move a Ping-Pong ball across a table; they used the air stream from a bicycle pump to blow up a balloon.

• The students observed moving air outdoors and made up wind speed estimates from such observations. They made wind socks to detect the direction and strength of the wind.

• The children investigated wind power. They made simple windmills and kites (see Illustration 82). The students organized a schoolwide kite flying competition. Parents became involved in designing and making kites.

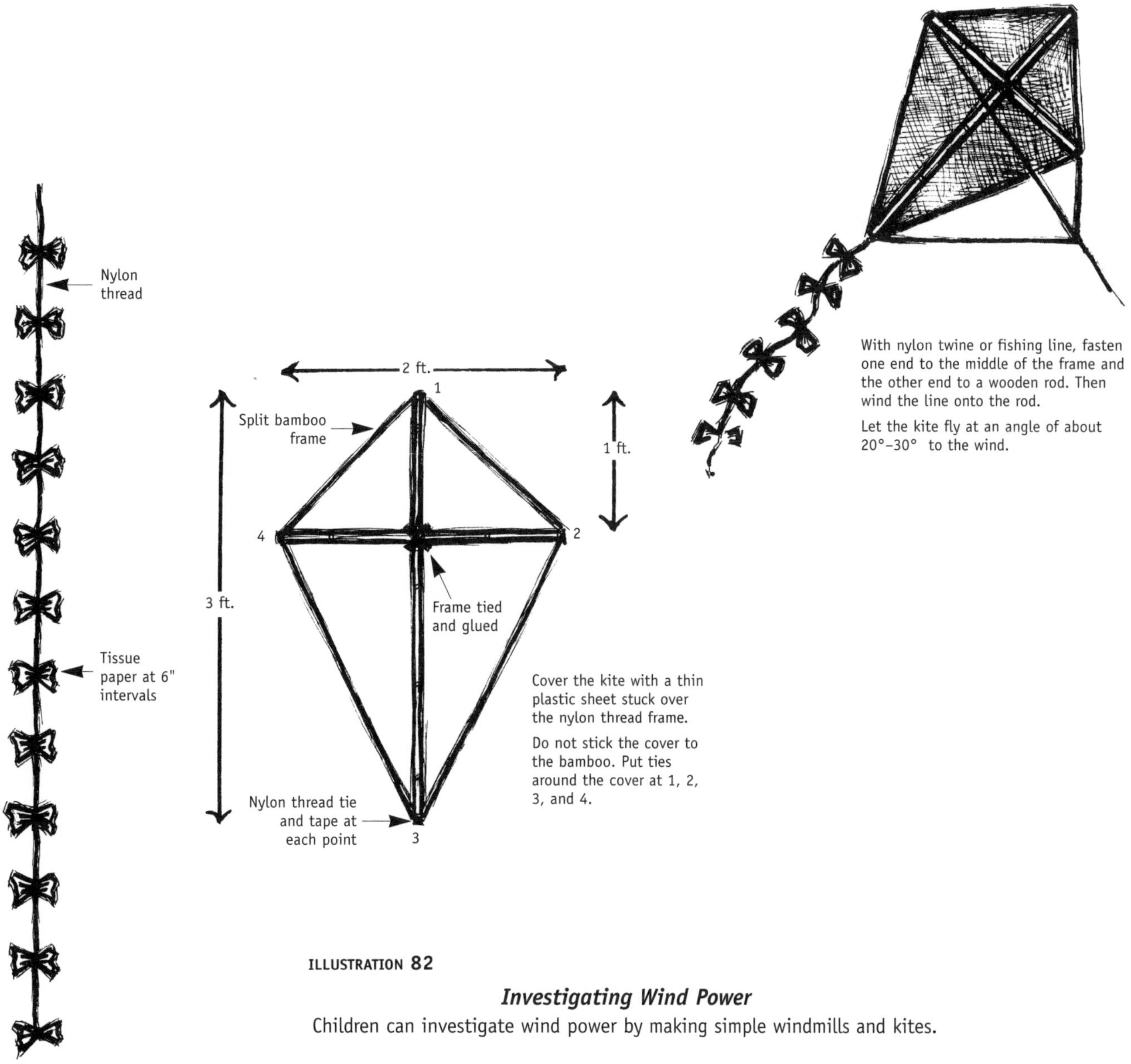

ILLUSTRATION 82

Investigating Wind Power

Children can investigate wind power by making simple windmills and kites.

Equilibrium and Strength of Structures—Bridges

►*Activity 49*

DEVELOPMENTAL LEVEL
4–6

GROUP SIZE
Small

KEY EXPERIENCES

- *Measuring, testing, and analyzing: assessing the properties and composition of materials*
- *Observing, predicting, and controlling change: understanding causality*
- *Designing, building, fabricating, and modifying structures or materials*
- *Reporting and interpreting data and results*

Materials available were deliberately limited to the following to encourage innovation on the part of the students: typing paper; glue; $\frac{1}{2}$" cellophane tape; sheets of very thin cardboard (postcard weight); newspaper; 1" nails for loads; matchboxes; straws; four sets of weights each containing $\frac{1}{4}$, $\frac{1}{2}$, 1, 2, and 7 pound weights; scissors; and rulers.

General Experiences the Teacher Had in Mind

• To stimulate children's thinking about the problem of bridging a gap

• To test some common bridge designs and, in so doing, to also test the strength of different shapes of structural material

Other Experiences the Teacher Hoped to Encourage

• To pose questions about measuring strengths by simple standardized means so that results can be compared

• To design bridges with two middle supports and with no middle support

• To test the strength of model bridges built to different designs and with different materials fabricated into shapes that give strength

• To encourage children to design bridges for specific purposes—to carry very light loads, to carry moderate loads of four passengers, to carry heavy loads of trucks and cars

• To survey the area around the school to compile a dossier of all the bridging methods that could be observed

Follow-Up Activities the Teacher Hoped to Stimulate

• To encourage children to make a collection of pictures of bridges in the local area. They could make the collection by photographing or drawing bridges, or by cutting pictures from newspapers and magazines. As the children studied the different designs, the teacher hoped the following questions would arise about each bridge: How wide is the gap to be bridged? How is the bridge made? What materials are used? What type of structure is it? How much traffic crosses it? How old is the bridge?

• To make bridges of different designs and test their relative strengths.

Activities That Actually Resulted

• The students identified various types of bridges in the local area from their collections of photographs, drawings, and newspaper cuttings. They captioned the pictures according to the design and construction materials used. They discussed the problems the bridge-builders face.

• Children made bridges of different designs using the simple materials provided (see Illustration 83). For example, students made bridges to span a 6" gap between two piles of books.

• Students tested the strength of different bridge designs. They made the following designs with 3" wide paper strips and tested their strength by determining how many nails each design could hold:

1. Single plank bridge of 1 sheet of paper

2. Single plank bridge of 3 sheets of paper stuck together to form a thicker plank

3. Single plank bridge of 8 sheets of paper stuck together to form a very thick plank

4. Simple beam bridge of 3 rolled paper strips (rolling the paper and gluing the edges to keep the rolled cylinder shape)

• The children made a table of the results of these experiments, wrote comments on the findings, and discussed the implications concerning the strengths of flat and cylindrical bridge beams. They decided which shapes were best for light loads, heavy loads, and very heavy loads.

• The students increased the gap between the books from 6" to 12" and investigated how this could be bridged. They tried to make: (1) a cantilever type bridge with two central supports, (2) a suspension bridge, and (3) an arched bridge. Using as much newspaper and glue as was necessary, the students tried to build a bridge over an 18" gap to take the weight of any child in the class. They kept exact records of all the materials used so that the results of the different groups could be compared.

Simple plank bridge

Strengthened plank bridge with arch support

Simple suspension bridge

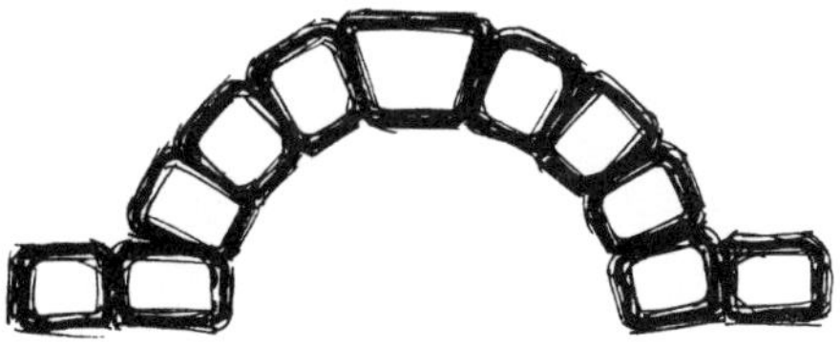

Keystone arch bridge

Simple truss bridge

ILLUSTRATION 83

Designing Bridges

Children can use a variety of simple materials to make bridges of different designs.

► *Appendix I*

Teaching Aids

This Teaching Aids appendix covers a range of topics that teachers will find useful as they prepare science education activities for children to carry out. Five areas are addressed:

• *Communication techniques for the classroom.* This section is divided into two parts. The first part provides the teacher with pointers on how to help children order and interpret information. The second part discusses how teachers can help children communicate and display the information that results from their science activities.

• *Materials and equipment.* This section emphasizes how teachers and children can use what is readily available to conduct science activities. Although the specific materials needed for each activity are described in the body of the text, this section encourages the use of commonplace materials to make discoveries about the world around us. A list of simple tools and equipment that teachers will find handy is provided.

• *Measurement in science.* There are two parts to the measurement section. The first part discusses measurement techniques and simple timing and weighing devices that are useful to have in the classroom. The second part describes the use of, and conversion to, metric measures—the standard measurement system of science.

• *Testing and analysis.* This section illustrates the process of testing and analyzing the properties of various animate and inanimate materials in the classroom.

• *Safety and science.* Safety must be an essential consideration in all aspects of education, perhaps most especially so in the area of science. Children will be working with unfamiliar materials, or with commonplace materials in unfamiliar ways. This section describes basic procedures and safety precautions that teachers and students should be aware of as they carry out the science activities.

► *Part 1*

Communication Techniques for the Classroom

Ordering and Interpreting Information

Making Surveys

Surveys are a form of collecting—collecting information. The usefulness of the activity will depend upon the interpretation and communication of the results by the collectors. There are many interesting subjects to survey and many ways to present the results. Following are some examples. The techniques described for communicating results in the early examples can also be applied to the suggestions in the later examples.

Collecting Personal Statistics From Members of the Class or Group

Some suggested collections include: ages, heights, weights, hand spans, shoe sizes, addresses for distance from the school, modes of transportation, hobbies, books students have read, pets, favorite colors, sweets, foods, names, and initials. The educational value of this work is enhanced greatly by the manner of presenting the results. These facts will be quantitative in one or more of their aspects; they are records of counting or some kind of measuring. They may be collected in no special order and may appear haphazard. Therefore, to be effectively communicated, that is, to see the significance of such results, they must be arranged and presented in ways that will show some pattern. This can be a regular sequence from the smallest to largest, or a trend, as in the case of the popularity of certain hobbies. Some useful ways of presenting information are given below. Teachers will note that there is a clear overlap with mathematics in this area of science activities.

Presenting Sets

When children have collected the information they desire and want to communicate it to others, they may provide suitable pictures and group these as pictures or symbols within an enclosed boundary. When two sets have some connection, they can be compared and the correspondences indicated by arrows, e.g., size of shoes and size of feet. Comparisons can be made more obvious if the sets are represented on graph paper. Place one element in each square, in columns, with the elements side by side. With this arrangement, matches can be seen at a glance.

Establishing an Order

There are many ways of ordering information—numerically, alphabetically, by visual arrangement. Once children understand the concept of *counting order,* they have a technique for sequencing that enables them to order by matching things to numbers. For example, the record of the numbers of birthdays occurring each month may be listed in this way. Another method of ordering is alphabetical. This can be used for surveys of names, comparing first names and second names in separate listings. Sometimes information is best presented as a rectangular array chart. This could be used for a survey of favorite colors or candies (see table below).

	George	Mary	Sue	John	William	Jane	Jack	Warren	Kay
Black									
Yellow	√	√		√	√	√	√		√
Blue		√				√		√	
Green	√		√			√			√
Red			√	√	√		√	√	√
White	√		√					√	
Brown		√		√	√		√		

When larger numbers are involved, a continuation of several individual surveys can be made to give numerical summaries.

Tabulating Results

Charts. When a large number of measurements have been taken, such as the heights of each child in the class, students can construct a chart to represent the results. The first job will be to put the results in order from smallest to tallest. Such a long list is not easy to study, but the results can be interpreted using markers; for example, by observing how many heights are above the chosen marker and how many are below. Results can also be grouped for clarity. For example, students can make a chart showing the ranges of heights and the numbers in that range (see Illustration A1). This could also be displayed on graph paper as a chart.

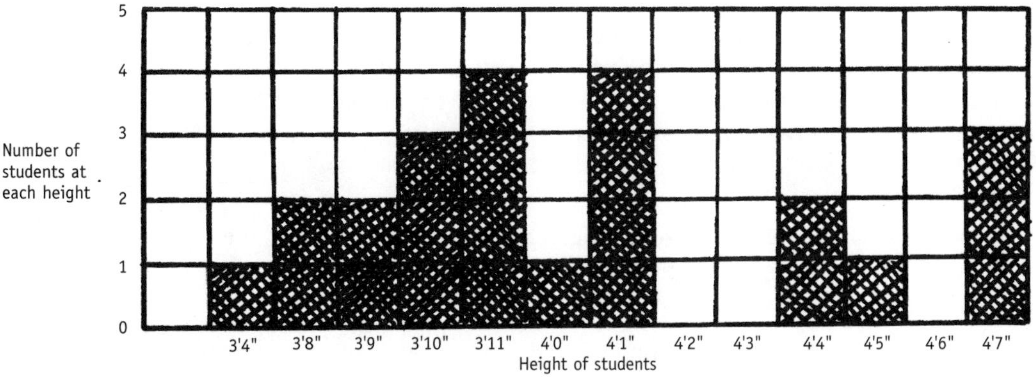

ILLUSTRATION A1

Chart Showing Height Range

Students take measurements and arrange the results in order to make a graph of heights in the classroom.

Pictograms. It is sometimes easier to represent information in pictorial form with symbolic figures such as ships, cars, stick figures, cats, dogs, and so on (see Illustration A2 on pg. 132). For younger children learning to count, letting one symbol represent each instance helps them to learn one-to-one correspondence. For older children, one picture or symbol can represent a number of facts; for example, each

ILLUSTRATION A2

Chart of Children's Pets

On this chart, one picture represents three pets.

book pictured can represent five books read. Using one to symbolize many is also a more sophisticated and efficient way of representing data, since it avoids the problem of having the space in the chart too crowded with symbols.

Pie graphs. A portioned or divided circle is a valuable way of showing how different pieces of information make up the whole picture. This type of representation is commonly called a pie chart (see Illustration A3). Children quickly learn how to mark out a clock face and divide the circle accordingly. There are many occasions when a class will find a pie chart the most telling way of exhibiting information, for example, the different means of transportation that children use to get to school. The limitation of the pie chart is that it does not lend itself to the comparison of two similar situations.

ILLUSTRATION A3

Pie Graph of How Children Get to School

A pie graph is a valuable way of showing how different pieces of information make up the whole picture.

Examples

The following examples will provide data that can be treated using the above ordering and interpretation techniques. Examples like these will be found throughout the books in this series.

Wildlife in an area. This information can be collected on a variety of topics. For example, data can be recorded on the total number of birds or the number of birds of different species seen at given times. Statistics could also be collected on the number of mammals seen, the number of insects observed in an area, or the number of spider webs. The statistics can relate to an area generally, such as the grounds outside the school, or to specific locations, such as a bird-feeding table.

Plant life in an area. Students can count and record various aspects of plant life. For example, surveys might include the total number of trees, the number of each of a certain type of small plant, weeds in a lawn, or seeds on seed heads of particular plants. More ambitious projects will involve inventing units of measurement for such tasks as estimating the number of leaves or apples on a tree, berries on a bush, or even flowers on a lawn or in a flower bed. Surveys of this type involve mathematical skills such as estimating and using one to represent many.

Materials used in buildings. Children, like most of us, accept their surroundings with little questioning until some aspect is brought to their attention. Buildings and building sites provide an opportunity for children to hone their observational skills and focus on structural phenomena they might otherwise pass by. Such settings are excellent places to conduct surveys and learn much about the process and content of science. Following are examples of some of the structural features of buildings that children can survey (see Illustration A4). [**Note:** Building sites can be dangerous places. Children should not visit them unaccompanied. All the work suggested here can be done by observation off site, i.e., from a safe distance or as a passer-by.]

• *Foundations.* All buildings have foundations. Most modern ones have concrete and brick foundations, but some older houses are set on stone pillars and large wooden beams. Students can seek out examples of all these in the area.

• *Walls and sides.* Most houses now are frame built; students can look for ongoing construction where the frame is still visible. They can record the pattern of the structure. They can observe how triangulation is used to provide strong shapes; using strips of stiff cardboard and brass paper fasteners to represent the shapes they see, they can test these shapes.

• *Brick work.* In some houses there is brick work. Students can look at the patterns made by bricklaying. Giving them their technical names is helpful. For example: bricks placed on their long sides are called *stretchers;* those with the short side facing are called *headers;* the layers of bricks are called *courses.* Students can represent what they see by making sketches of the patterns of brick work in a residential or commercial area.

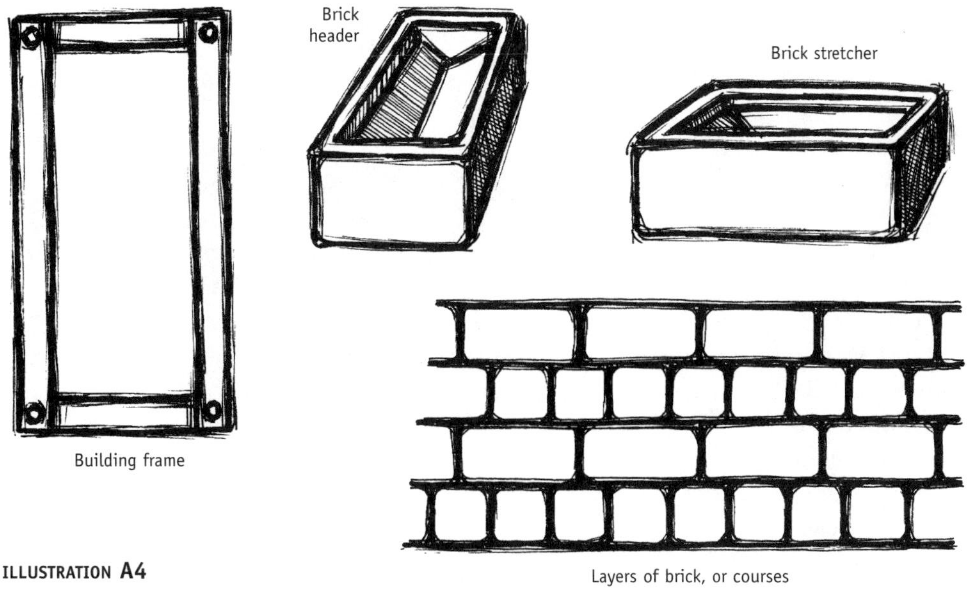

ILLUSTRATION **A4**

Materials Used in Buildings

Buildings and building sites provide children with an opportunity to observe many structural features and materials.

• *Roofs.* Most roofs have a covering of materials that are easy to put in place high on the sloping roof. Of course, they must be waterproof and easily kept in place. Students can make a survey of the roofing materials in the area. They can draw the patterns they see and observe how the ridge along the top of the roof is finished. Students can conduct a survey to answer such questions as: What are the most common coverings for roofs? What are the unusual ones? What different patterns do roof lines follow?

• *Paints and colors.* Students can make a survey of the colors used on the outside of local houses. They can develop a composite picture by investigating such questions as: What is the favorite color for window frames? Front doors? Balconies and porches? What colors are chosen most for painting the exterior walls of houses?

• *New materials.* Surveys can also highlight the variety of building materials used. For example, students might count and represent: How many houses have aluminum windows and doors? How many houses have plastic coverings on the window frames and doors? How many have a mixture of materials—brick, stone, wood—on their exterior?

Communicating and Displaying Information

The High/Scope Curriculum provides a means by which children's own chosen interests become activities that use their personal involvement to solve problems in the open manner of good science. The High/Scope *plan-do-review sequence* does more than merely unlock the gate to a successful way of working.

The "planning stage" provides an opportunity for teacher-child and child-child dialogue. This dialogue helps to shape the work, provides encouragement, and allows for guidelines and suggestions about procedures to be exchanged. It also creates a "public" awareness of what is going on. Dialogue in the planning stage begins the chain of events bound up in communication. It establishes that there are others interested in the questions addressed, how they will be investigated, and what the outcomes may be. It gives communicating the results a worthwhile and genuine purpose.

The "do" stage provides the power, the heightened interest, and the energy for the next stage as communication expands the ideas and activities engaged in by the students. Development during the doing phase sets the stage for the reviewing part of the sequence, when a description of the activities and their outcomes will be communicated. With something real to communicate—a description of a process, an accounting of what was learned—and a real and enthusiastic audience, the impetus to use effective means of communication is increased and the desire to do it well becomes a very important motivating force.

The "review" stage helps students to consolidate the knowledge they have gained and sets the stage for further activity. In recounting their experiences and observations, students are encouraged to organize their thoughts and convey to others what was meaningful about their activities. Because the reviewing stage is typically shorter than the doing stage, students must find ways to effectively summarize what they have done. Reviewing also helps students reflect on their experiences and consider what to do next. Are there still unanswered questions? Did the experiments suggest related avenues to explore? How can we communicate both the excitement of what we have learned and our enthusiasm for continuing the investigation?

Dialogue—verbally sharing procedures and results—is an important means of communication in science. Often overlooked, however, is the role that visually displaying results can play in communicating the scientific process and students' discoveries. In the rest of this section, options will be discussed for using visual display as the vehicle for communication in science. Just as it is important for all children to share their work verbally, so too it is important to provide opportunities for all children to display their work and to view the work of others. The emphasis should not be on adult-made polished displays that reflect the work of the teacher or a few selected students. Rather, displays should reflect the real work of all students as they grapple with issues of interest to them and create a picture of how the world functions.

Considerations of Space

Classroom facilities vary greatly, from cramped to spacious. School opportunities for displays are equally varied, from confinement to classrooms, or spaces in corridors, to larger scale opportunities in halls and open areas. The importance of the visual aspects of communication is often underestimated, especially in the cramped classroom. It is indisputable, though, that a great deal of what we learn is through the evidence of our eyes, rather than through our ears or other sensory organs alone. Quite apart from being informed, children (and adults) are excited, stimulated, and enriched by what they see. Material displayed should perform at least one of the three essential functions of display: to enhance the appearance of the area; to interest and inform some or all of the children; and to give the satisfaction of a real contribution to those involved in the work displayed.

Some teachers like to have two areas for display, one for finished work and one for work in progress. The first area can be used to showcase work that has run its course and reached a conclusion; it can present both the processes and the outcomes of the students' scientific investigations. The second area is where review-time work can be on temporary display, where half-finished charts can be pinned up for discussion; and where apparatus can be commented on. This display can create a sense of excitement as the changes each day reflect the ongoing discovery process. The finished space needs to be as large as can be afforded for science; the in-progress space can be smaller and might even rotate depending upon the area of the room where the work is being carried out. It is also a good idea to have a storage bin near the area where ongoing work can be safely and neatly looked after. Disorderly storage and general clutter in a room makes it difficult to focus on and observe the ongoing work; it also limits work efficiency. Although in a lively classroom, disorder is often present and can be a positive sign of active engagement, it is also one that should be managed. Cleanup time can take on added significance in this situation, as students determine how to maintain organization while at the same time permitting activity-based pursuits to continue.

Wall Displays

Whatever else a classroom lacks in terms of space, it will have walls, and these will afford a principal means of display. A trestle table, for example, can be erected when needed and placed against the wall. If space permits, one or more permanent tables for use in conjunction with wall displays are useful. Storage bins can be placed underneath the table(s) to conserve space (see Illustration A5 on pg. 136).

Pictorial work, charts and graphs, photographs, and diagrams all need mounting to create effective displays. A stock of old picture frames, without glass, is a quick and effective method for highlighting and giving a finished look to work without having to go to the trouble of cutting mounts. Double-sided cellophane tape will also hold work in place on wall displays. Finally, *good communication needs good labeling to carry its message.* Children can make these labels using a variety of techniques. For example, stencils, appliquéd letters, cutouts from magazines and newspapers, bold script, and varied fonts created on the computer—all are effective alternatives for creating eye-catching and informative labels.

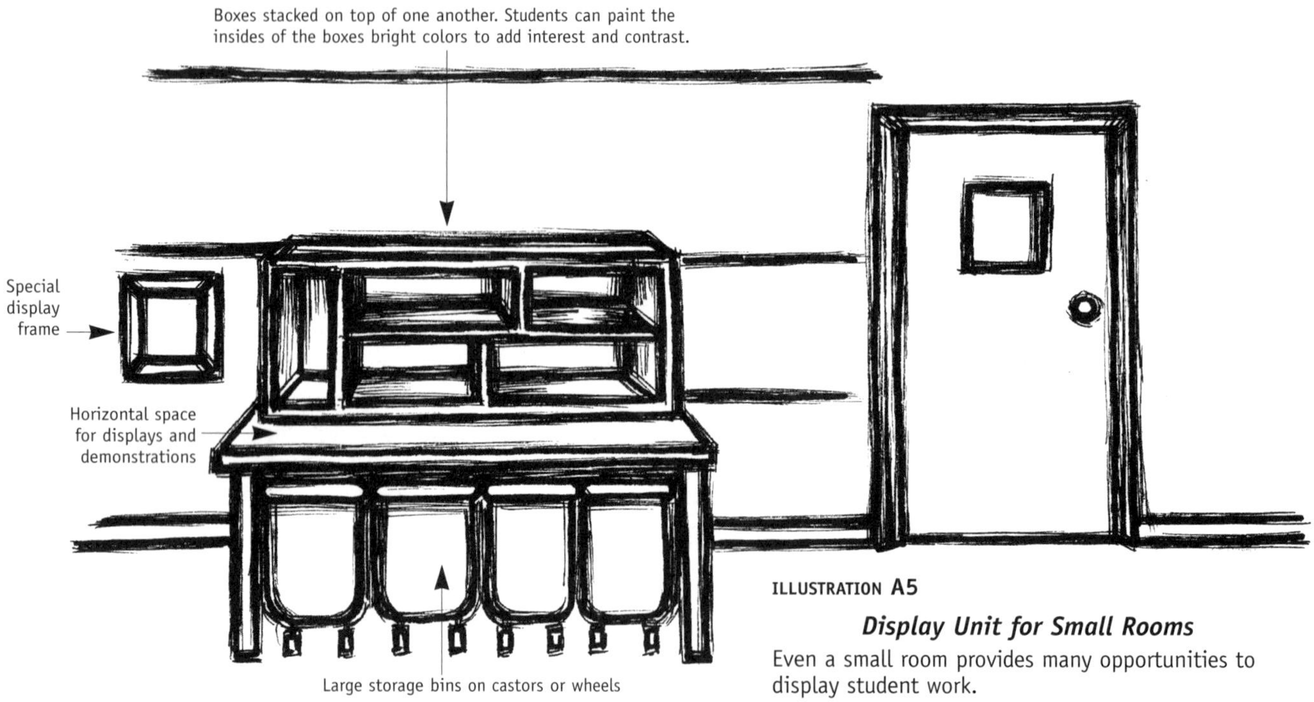

ILLUSTRATION A5

Display Unit for Small Rooms

Even a small room provides many opportunities to display student work.

Concertina Display Units

When wall space for display is limited, concertina (hinged and folded) display units can be made to increase the available surface area in the classroom. This method of display can also be used during special events, such as for parents and friends or children from other classes when extra display space is needed. Simply fix thick cardboard or hardboard sheets together so that they fold at the joins. Use wide packing tape to join the sheets, being sure to leave a gap between each sheet slightly wider than the material is thick. This allows for easy folding. The joints should be taped back and front. Smaller versions of this design can be made for tabletop displays. Make three or four sets of different sizes, for example, double- and triple-folded units. (See Illustration A6.)

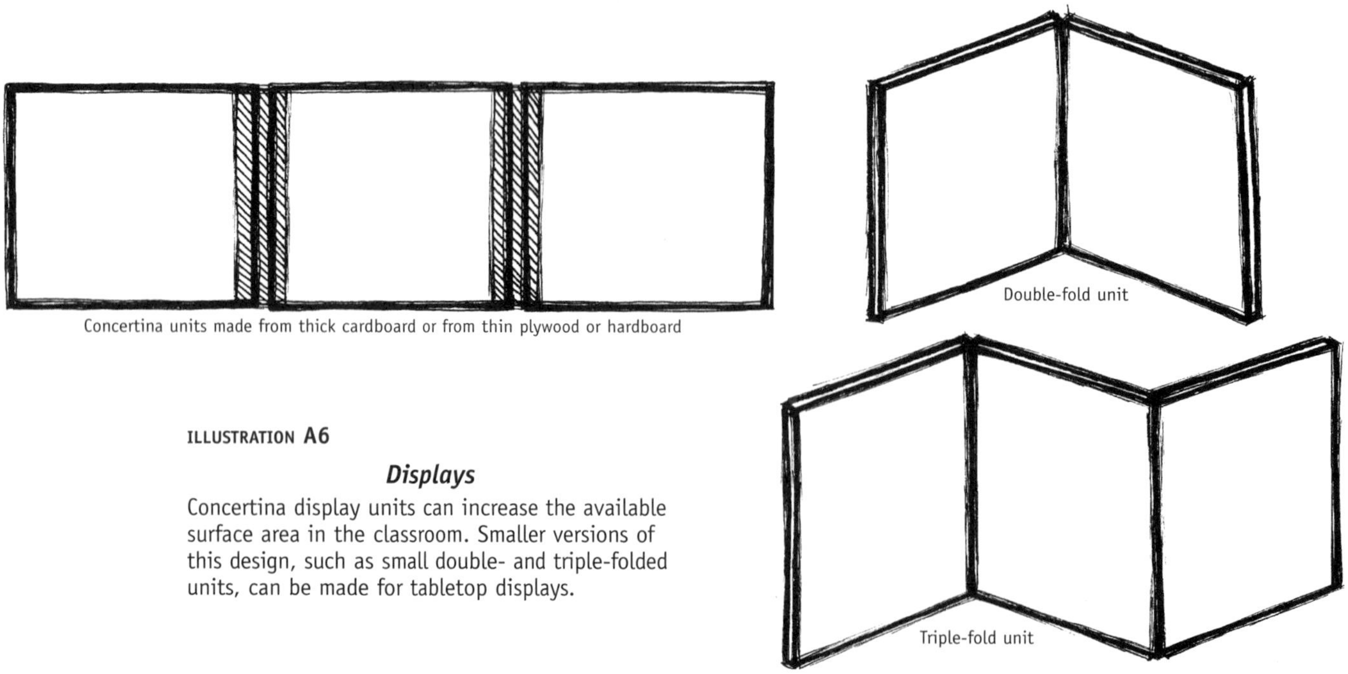

ILLUSTRATION A6

Displays

Concertina display units can increase the available surface area in the classroom. Smaller versions of this design, such as small double- and triple-folded units, can be made for tabletop displays.

Temporary Display Units: Brick and Board Shelves and Cubes

Sometimes an urgent need for additional shelf space occurs, especially if many children have to store their work temporarily at the same time. To accommodate this need at the end of a work session, shelves can be rapidly built on bricks or blocks, using planks (see Illustration A7). Do not try to support planks longer than 3 feet without extra bricks or blocks at 2-foot intervals. Once this arrangement has served its purpose, planks and blocks can be stacked away until they are needed again.

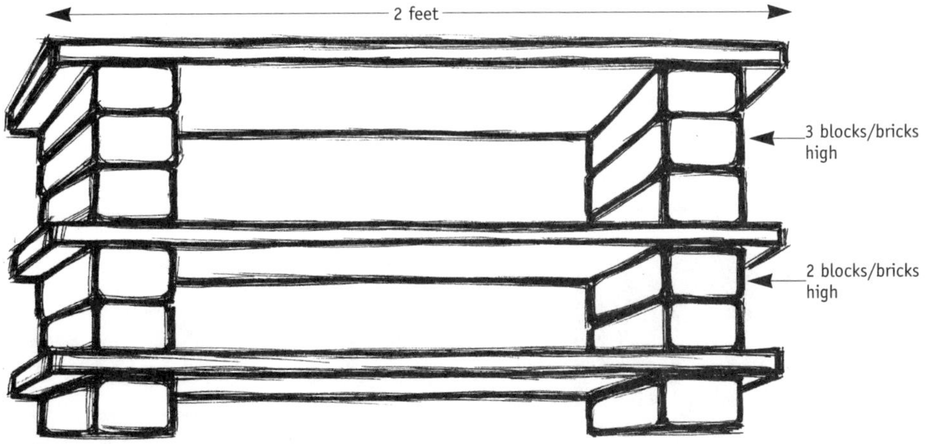

ILLUSTRATION **A7**

Shelves

Shelves can be rapidly constructed of boards supported by bricks or blocks. The space between shelves can be adjusted to accommodate the height of the objects displayed.

Other temporary display structures may be created. A shallow drawer painted white and with the handles removed makes a good display case for small collections. Adding a layer of sand, shells, pebbles, bones, or cones at the bottom can provide an effective background and emphasize the purpose behind the collection displayed on the surface. If you have a supply of cubical cardboard or plastic boxes about 12" by 15", these also make attractive display and storage units (see Illustration A8). They can be stacked and painted or covered with bright colors, both inside and out, to catch the eye.

ILLUSTRATION **A8**

Display Cubes

In addition to displaying objects inside the cubes, the way the cubes are piled up presents a design in itself.

Arranging the Display Space

Highlighting the work. Black mounts are effective for most written work (such as graphs and charts) because the light-color paper of the work shows up well against the dark background. Help children cut out their work and design the display; encourage them to leave ample space and avoid overcrowding. A few simple messages are often more telling than detailed explanations, which may be hard to see and read. Leave space for labels and other notes. A few arrows sometimes give a sense of direction. Before attaching the parts of the display, try laying everything out first to see how they fit. Make any necessary adjustments before completing the mounting. Fix the items with a touch of adhesive at each corner; pasting may cause wrinkles and problems in placing wet paper on the mounting sheet. Let the children design the sheet to tell its own story and reflect what they have done (see Illustration A9).

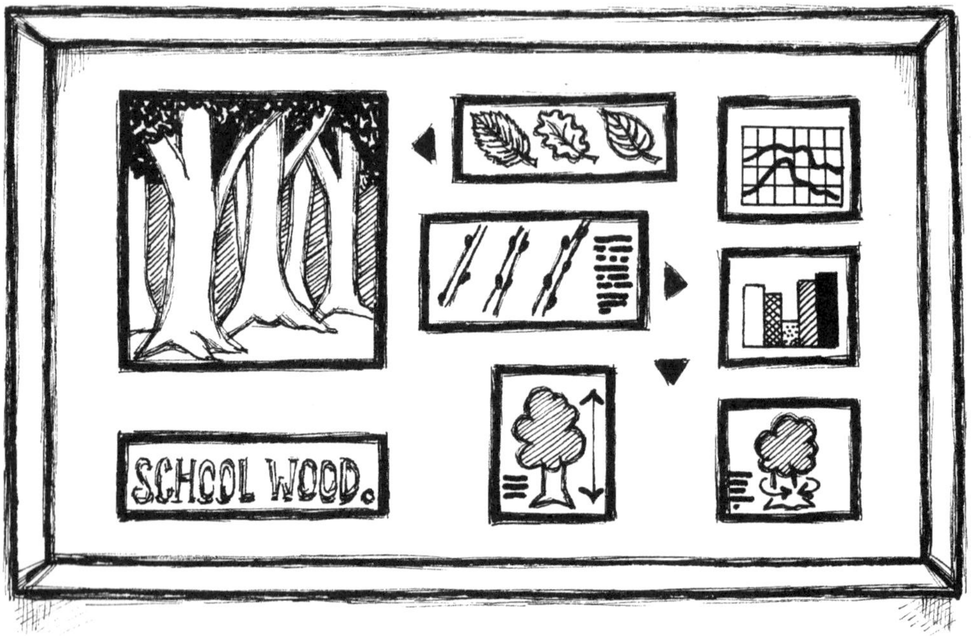

ILLUSTRATION **A9**

A Mounted Display Unit

Mounting the work on a background of contrasting color helps to highlight a display. Avoid overcrowding and keep labels and messages simple. Lay out everything to see how it fits before attaching the parts of the display.

Using multiple display strategies. A small display around the work of a single group is well-contained in ordinary classroom situations. However, when there is a considerable amount of material from a whole class, perhaps work distributed over several class periods, the problem is a different one. Not only will there be a great deal of material, but it may be of different kinds—some visual, some three dimensional, and some collections of objects.

Solving the problem of making the most of a limited classroom space for a large amount of material—or a major exhibition of science work—needs a plan. In planning, avoid putting all the material around the classroom walls. Try to arrange one display area that preserves the connections and continuity of the display. For example, this area could start in a corner of the room where the two walls provide a natural background for the display space. You can then clear an area in front of the walls to put up tables and screens, attracting attention to the display as a focal point in the room (see Illustration A10 on pg. 139).

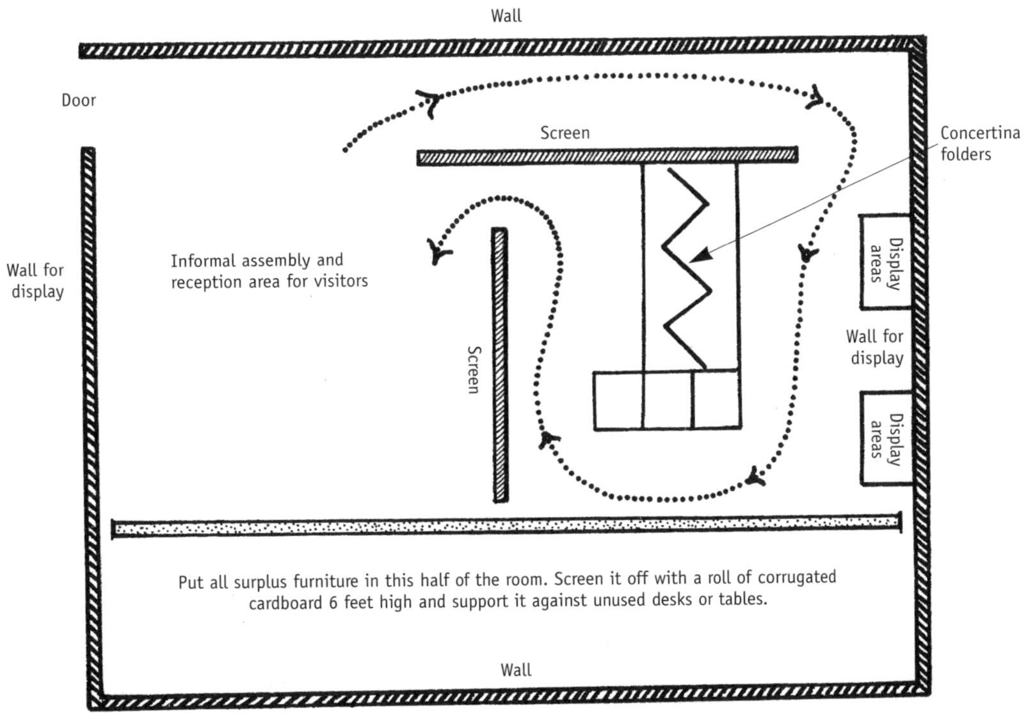

ILLUSTRATION A10

Using the Classroom as an Exhibition Space

In displaying a large amount of work, avoid putting all the materials around the classroom walls. Group the materials in areas to preserve their connections and to provide the display with continuity.

Student Involvement in Creating Displays

As much as possible, always include children in planning and arranging communications and displays. They will gain on many fronts: thinking about how to represent their work; exercising their visual judgment; reflecting on the lessons they learned and how to communicate them; and feeling a sense of worth as they see the display taking shape. If the teacher takes time and trouble to create opportunities for displaying student work, the children will themselves develop an appreciation for the importance of their scientific endeavors.

► Part 2
Materials and Equipment

The teacher will inevitably be a partner in the classroom in the action—as well as in the dialogue. Teachers are called upon to provide practical assistance with manipulative tasks and sometimes to help complete over-ambitious construction activities. It will be important to have on hand a few simple tools and to become proficient at using them. A very firm table or small workbench will make a great difference both to the ease of working and to competence and confidence in doing jobs. It will assist greatly if the basic materials and tools listed at the end of this section are readily available.

Think "Simple"

In many people's minds, science work is thought of in terms of test tubes, special equipment, and complicated electronics. This apparently specialized apparatus, however, need not be present in the elementary school. In fact, many of the world's great discoveries were made with apparatus based on everyday materials and on observations of commonplace phenomena. Nowhere is this more important than in early education. With young children, we need to expose the underlying science with minimal dependence on equipment. For children, science activities often lead to great discoveries, for they are first-time experiences for them. This "first-timeness" liberates an enthusiasm in children, a sense of wonder that becomes the spur for further activity and concentrated effort. Much of this excitement can be lost by a pedantic insistence upon the "right" things being used.

An Example

A good example of the advantages of simplicity is in the use of comparative measurements. For the youngest children, lengths of string are just as good as tape measures for assessing differences; they will be concerned only with which is longest or shortest, rather than with absolute dimensions (see Illustration A11). It will be at a later stage when they want to know exactly how much longer or shorter that measurement needs to be in more conventional terms. In the former case, the children using the string need the excitement of quickly seeing the result, not the frustration of reading the tape measure to the nearest small unit—that comes later when arguments need to be decided on the basis of greater accuracy. At this stage, the strings show the results very clearly and are better than tape measures.

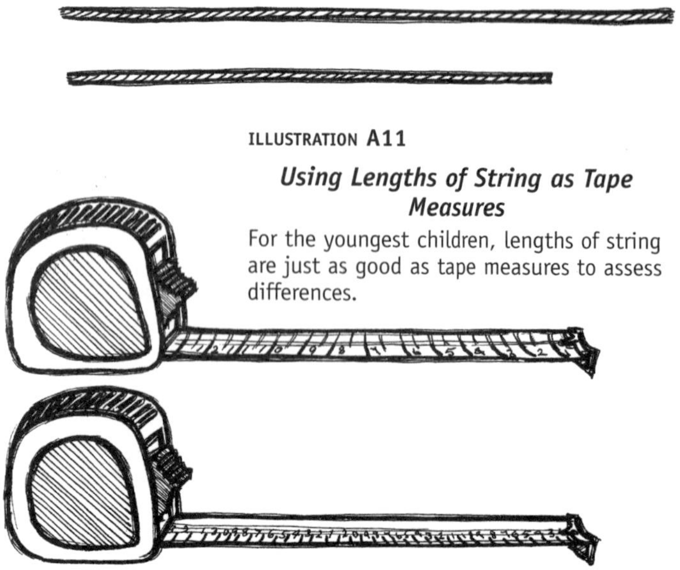

ILLUSTRATION **A11**

Using Lengths of String as Tape Measures

For the youngest children, lengths of string are just as good as tape measures to assess differences.

Begin With What Is Readily Available

In servicing practical activities, both children and teachers need to first ask: What is available? Next they can ask: How can I use these materials to help solve the problem? Often this act of thinking and improvising itself assists the problem-solving process, as it concentrates attention on essentials in the situation. Science is an empirical subject and is concerned with the practical, working out of ideas, especially at the primary school level. Here we are concerned more with starting points than end products. Thus, developing ideas about the use of simple materials may well open up student interest in a subject better than a formal introduction by the teacher. The creative manipulation of materials and the devising and setting up of experiments often opens the way for a realization of the need for more sophisticated apparatus. Again, children will come to look on materials as amenable to use in a variety of ways according to the needs of the situation. For instance, the common detergent bottle made of plastic can be a lighthouse in one context and a rain gauge in another (see Illustration A12).

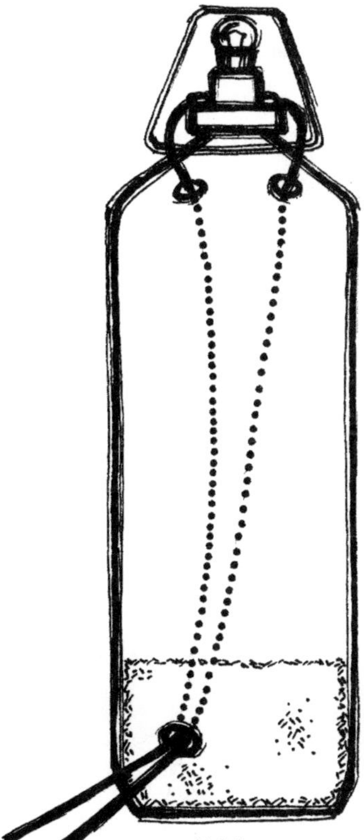

ILLUSTRATION A12

Uses for Plastic Detergent Bottles

Plastic bottles can be put to many uses in the study of science.

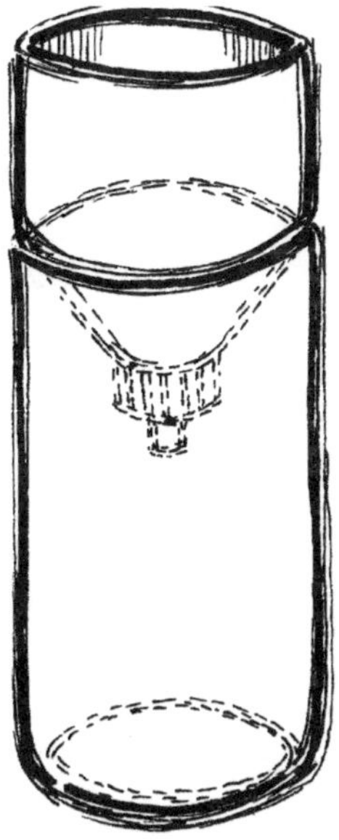

It can also be a musical instrument when peas or small nails are put inside as shakers. Sometimes work can be helped considerably by a few ready prepared items, which can overcome manipulative problems. A good example is the provision of ready-made electrical connection leads. These minimize the difficulties some children find in attaching wires to contacts. Crocodile clips at the ends of wires make excellent connectors and are easily made up by the teacher or a helper in advance of possible use (see Illustration A13).

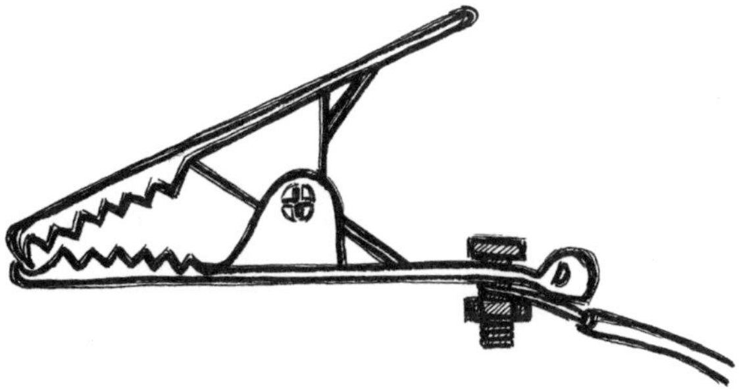

ILLUSTRATION A13

Crocodile Clip

Crocodile clips at the ends of wires make excellent connectors in the study of electricity.

Some supplies will need to be purchased, for substitutes are either hard to find or awkward to use. For example, one or two really powerful permanent magnets are essential, as is a varied collection of magnets children will collect. There are no substitutes either for a few, large, hand magnifiers. Again, children will collect smaller ones for themselves, and these will serve for some investigations. But for detailed observations, high-grade magnifiers are crucial if satisfactory results are to be obtained. The aim should always be to provide enabling materials and equipment that minimize the difficulties and keep the essentials of the problem clearly before the children.

Simple Tools for the Teacher's Use in Science

Below is a list of simple tools that teachers will want to have on hand. Their accessibility in the classroom allows students and teachers alike to improvise and to take advantage of spontaneous questions that arise in the course of scientific investigations.

- Hammer No. 0 or No. 1; Warrington type (not a heavy claw hammer)
- Brad awl size A $1\frac{1}{4}$". (This pierces holes by breaking the fibers; use before putting in screws.)
- 4" G clamp (or a clamp or vice)—this holds jobs firmly.
- 5" pincers
- Screwdrivers—large (10–12"); medium (4–6"); and small (2–3"); electrical, battery driven screwdrivers can also be handy for adult use.
- 5" universal pliers
- Junior hacksaw for cutting plastic and metal
- 8" tenon saw for cutting wood
- Wire stripper (bib stripper type)
- Hand drill with bits $\frac{1}{8}$", $\frac{3}{16}$", $\frac{1}{4}$" (not an electric drill)
- 6" triangular file
- Bench hook for cutting against
- Surform shaping tool (cuts wood, plastic, etc., like a file)
- Strong scissors

Equipment Generally Available in Schools and Classrooms

In addition to the tools that you will want to assemble, be aware of all the items you are likely to have available in the school and classroom that can be used for science activities. A list of commonly available equipment and materials follows:

- Writing paper—all kinds, including plain, lined, graph (squared), large for charts, drawing paper, colored papers
- Other paper—tracing paper, blotting paper, carbon paper, colored gummed back, tissue paper
- Paste—cold water, glue for general use, balsa cement
- Cardboard—thin for charts; thick and stiff for model making
- Scissors—round-ended safety scissors for younger children; pointed scissors for older children; one or two large pairs for cutting out shapes made of heavy materials

- Pins—large steel and large brass
- Thumbtacks—metal and metal covered in plastic
- Labels—glue-based and self-adhesive (including self-adhesive strips)
- Wall thermometer
- Cellophane tape—including wide, parcel-packaging tape
- Pencils, rulers, erasers
- String—different thicknesses, including twine and thread
- Clay—plasticine, modeling clay
- Paints—watercolors, either powdered or premixed
- Crayons—narrow for detail drawing and wide for labeling
- Paper clips—metal and plastic slip-on, brass fold-back eyelet type
- Rubber bands—assorted sizes (widths and lengths)
- Self-adhesive film—the type used for book covering
- Notebooks—spiral pads, memo pads
- Staplers—large and small
- Staple gun—tacker for teachers to use in mounting wall displays
- Hole punch—single, two-hole, and three-hole at standard widths
- Plastic containers—buckets and bowls
- Cleaning supplies—soap, detergent, towels

► *Part 3*

Measurement in Science

Measurement Techniques and Simple Devices

Timing and Timers and Time

While all classrooms need one or two "seconds" timers as part of their equipment, time measurement can also be done in broad terms, using other school-made devices. For example, some children will be conscious of the sunlight making its passage through different windows at different times of the day. What time is it? How long does it take? When does it seem to move fastest? These are all questions that can be answered with varying degrees of accuracy using child-made timing devices. The sun coming through the windows marks the passage of time in large intervals and may be a starting point for considering the passage of time in terms of the sun's movement.

Sundial (stick shadow). In an open space, have students set up a stick shadow and mark the shadow at regular intervals during a day, say, at 9, 10, 11, 12, 1, 2, and 3 o'clock. What happens to the length of the shadow? Students can make further observations at the set intervals and mark the length of the shadow on the ground. Place the times against the shadow marks (see Illustration A14).

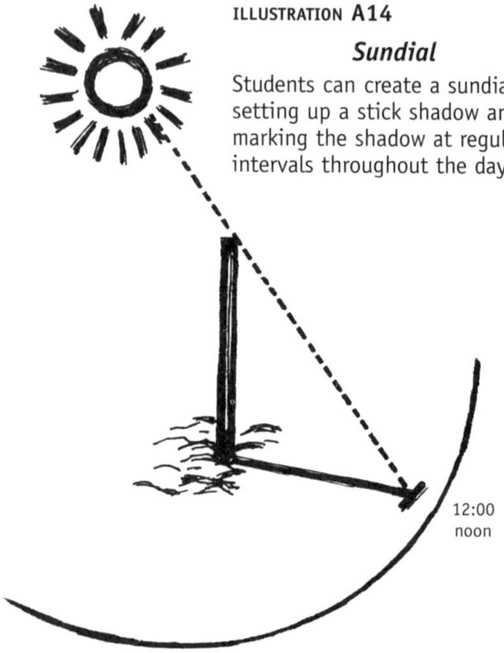

ILLUSTRATION **A14**

Sundial

Students can create a sundial by setting up a stick shadow and marking the shadow at regular intervals throughout the day.

Pendulum. Timing school activities will often require devices that indicate shorter units of time. There are several possibilities for creating such devices. The simplest is the pendulum, which can be a very exact way to measure the passage of time. Children can make a pendulum consisting of a piece of thin string with a small weight on the end. When put in a place where it can swing freely, a pendulum can measure seconds quite well (see Illustration A15 on pg. 145). The total length of the pendulum should be exactly 39 inches (1 meter). The accuracy depends on the length, even ⅛ inch longer or shorter makes a difference. Don't worry about the weight on the bottom or the width of the swing. It is the length that matters. Set up a pendulum and test it by answering these questions (use a timer or a watch or a clock with a second hand):

• When the length is exactly 39 inches, how many swings are there in a minute? (If the length is right, it will be 60.)

• Shorten the string by one inch. How many swings now?

• Lengthen the string by one inch to make it 40 inches. How many swings to the minute?

• Get the length back to exactly 39 inches and retime the pendulum. Let it have a big swing. Does it still do 60 swings to the minute? Let it have a short swing. How many now to the minute?

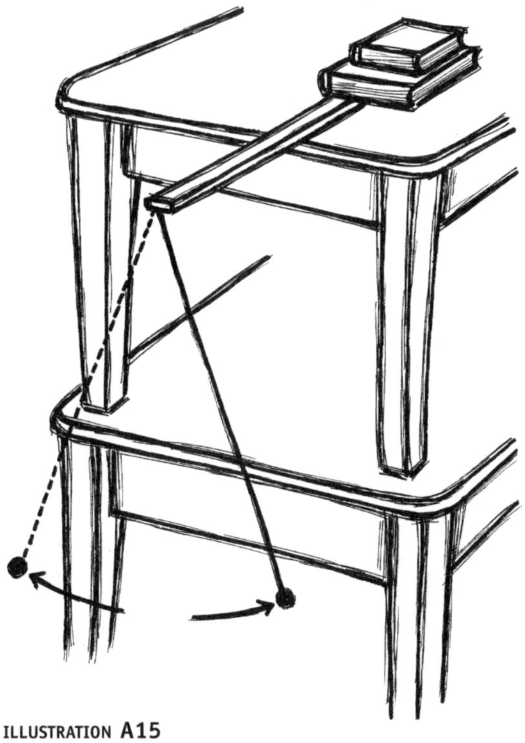

ILLUSTRATION **A15**

Constructing a Pendulum

Children can create a simple pendulum by attaching a piece of thin string with a weight attached to the end of a ruler.

Sand clocks. Sometimes a measurement device in-between the slow speed of the shadow stick and the fast speed of the pendulum is required. Students can make a sand clock and calibrate it. The secret of success with a sand clock is to have very fine, very dry sand. If none is available, the students can dry and sieve coarse sand for use through a nylon stocking sieve. Students can make a more accurate sand clock from two bottles as below. Use clear plastic bottles to avoid the danger of breakage (see Illustration A16).

Get two identical clear plastic bottles. Fill one bottle halfway with clean, fine dry sand. Cut a ring of cardboard to be an exact fit over the bottle tops without extending over the outside edges. Make a small, clean (clear) hole in the center of the cardboard. Put the cardboard on top of the bottle with sand in and the second bottle above. Have one student hold the bottles tightly together while another student fixes adhesive tape to keep them together. Invert the bottles and the sand will run from one to the other. Stick a paper scale on the outside of one bottle, then calibrate it using a watch as a timer. This will make a good timer. Students can experiment to get the size of the hole in the cardboard right.

ILLUSTRATION **A16**

Making Sand Clocks

To make a successful sand clock, sieve coarse sand through a nylon stocking funnel into a clear plastic bottle. Students can make a more accurate sand clock by using two plastic bottles.

Sieve

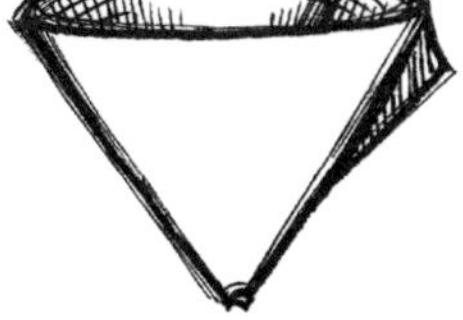

Nylon funnel

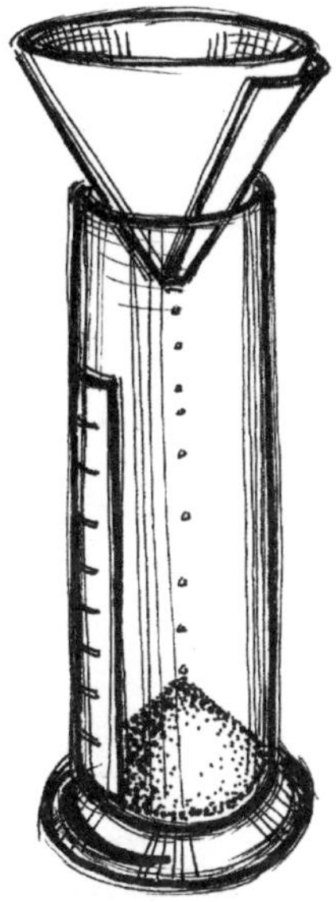

Plastic bottle

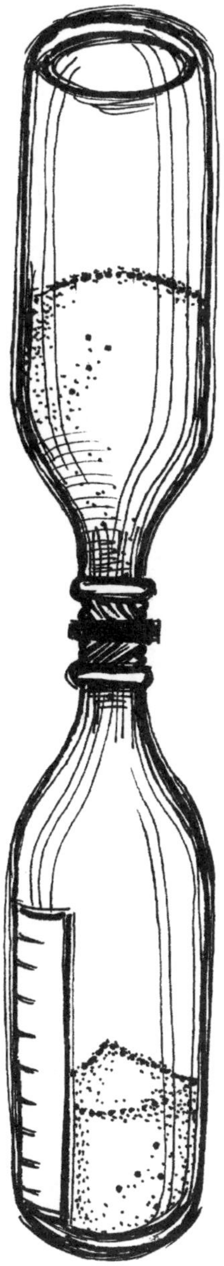

Water clocks. Water clocks have been used since ancient times. Some were very elaborate, while others were quite simple. The problem is to get a small-enough flow of water so that the clock works for a long-enough period without needing refilling. Below is a water clock that is easy for students to make. Get a plastic detergent container with a screw cap over a fine nozzle. Also, get a second, clear container for the first one to rest on; it could be a clear plastic bottle with the top cut off. This second container must hold more liquid than the first container. Cut off the bottom of the detergent (first) container. Plug the normal outlet hole with clay or plasticine. Make a very small hole (a pinhole) for the water to come out into the clear container. Calibrate the clear container with a paper strip (see Illustration A17).

Remove the screw-on stopper, leaving the exit hole and its parts intact and filling the shaped part with a plug of plasticine. As near the center as possible, make a very small hole for as little water as possible to flow out. The normal larger hole will make the clock "run out" of time too quickly.

Stand the water clock against a wall or another source of support when operating it; it will easily fall unless the base of the long container is weighted with plasticine.

Have students try variations on this design and solve these problems:

• What happens if you just use the original hole?

• What is the effect of larger holes? Smaller holes?

• Can you invent a clock with different rates of flow for different timings?

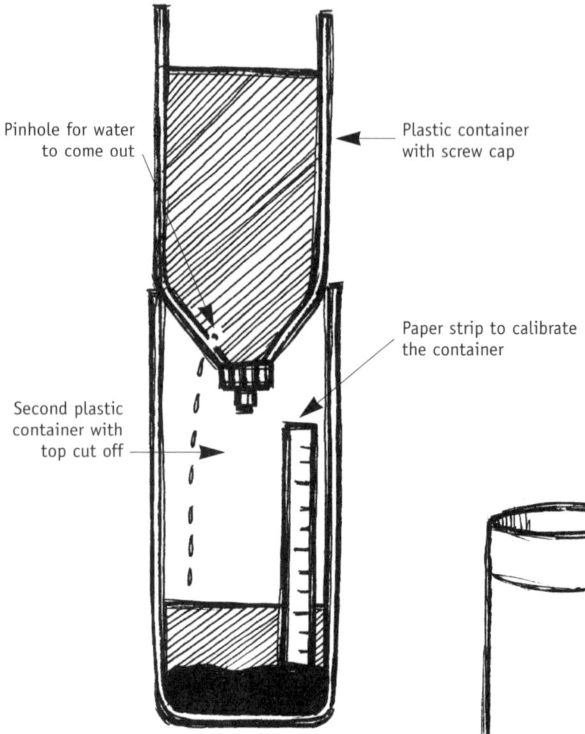

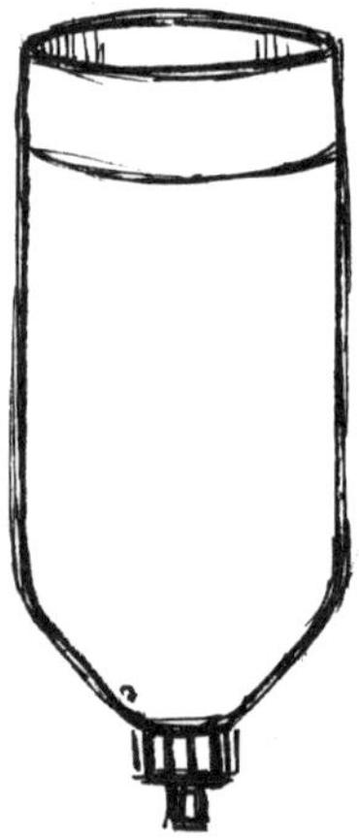

ILLUSTRATION A17

Making a Simple Water Clock

In making a water clock, it is important for the hole to be small enough so the clock works for a long time without needing refilling.

Weighing Devices

Weighing light objects. Quite often, simple weighing devices are needed. Children can easily improvise these items of equipment, especially when the measurements required are in terms of comparisons, not actual standard units.

For example, students can make yardstick balances with holes at each end for attaching pans or objects for weighing. Use a paper clip slide to trim the balance to the horizontal. Stretched springs or elastic bands also make useful weighing devices, and they can easily be calibrated against standard weights if required, although the accuracy needs regular checking as the elastic stretches with use. Students can use different thicknesses of elastic to make balances for different ranges. The elastic bands are easily purchased at sewing supply stores; students may also be able to bring in elastic scraps from sewing projects at home. (See Illustration A18 on pg. 147.)

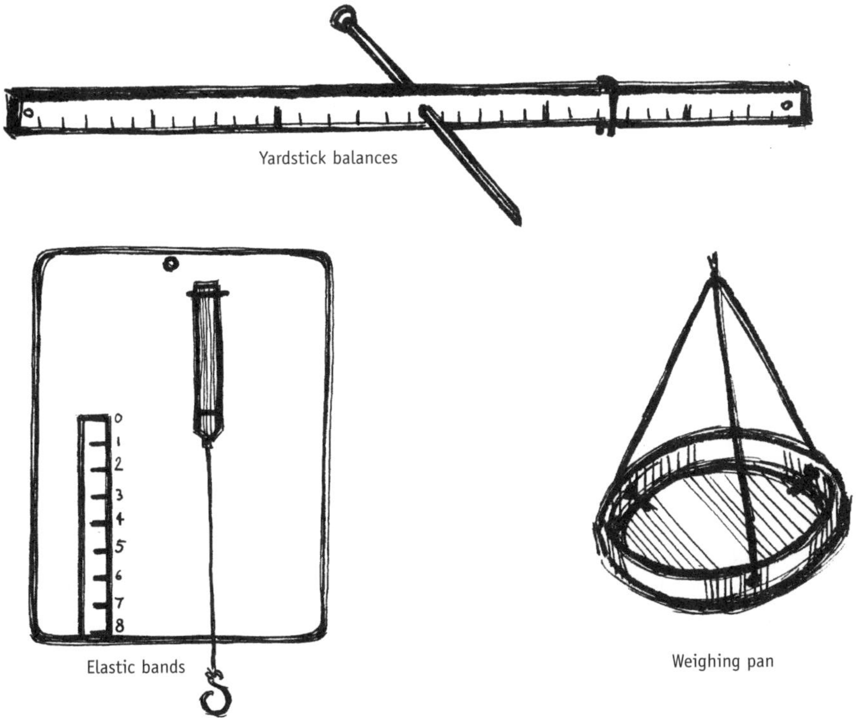

ILLUSTRATION A18

Weighing Devices

Simple weighing devices can be improvised when measurements are made for purposes of comparison and do not need to be in standard units.

Weighing heavy objects. Sometimes heavier and more awkward objects need to be weighed. Students can make a simple device from an old upholstery spring and two tin cans. First, get a medium-sized coil-type upholstery spring. Students can use various sizes of springs in this design, such as those obtained from chairs, car seats, and old mattresses. Then have students get a tin, with a top cut off cleanly (no sharp edges), into which the spring will fit entirely. Finally, have them find a smaller tin that will fit into the larger tin. Again the top should be cut off cleanly, and the edges of both tins should be smoothed with a file. The calibration can be made by covering the inner tin with paper or painting on the markings (see Illustration A19). This balance is not very good for small weights, but it will weigh liquids and heavier items. The students can calibrate it by using known standard weights.

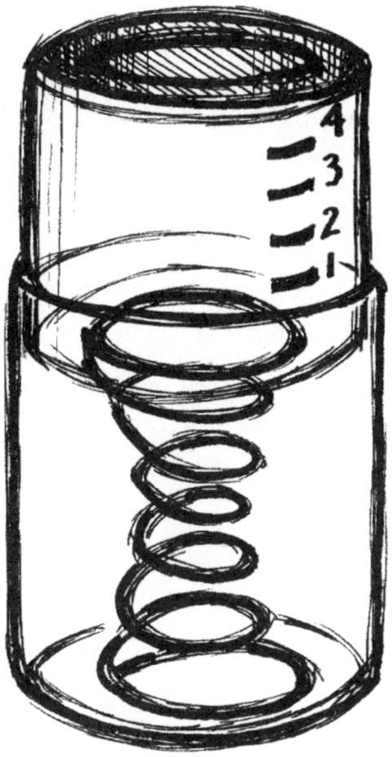

ILLUSTRATION A19

Upholstery Spring

Students can make a simple weighing device from an old upholstery spring and two tin cans. The device can be calibrated by covering the inner tin with paper or painting on the markings.

The Metric System: Communication in the Standard Measure of Science

The Improvised Conversion of Equipment to Metric Measures

With scientists universally using metric measures, schools will need to consider the wisdom of making some metric measures for themselves. This is an especially urgent need when working with younger children because they are still forming their concept of the real significance of measures. Some suggestions are given below for the improvisation of metric measures—first, to make equipment available quickly; and second, to provide schools with uses for existing material.

Metric Weights

A simple method for adjusting 2-lb. and 1-lb. weights from avoirdupois to metric units is to put the weight to be adjusted into a suitably sized cardboard box with a lid. Have students seal the lid on tightly with cellophane tape and pierce a hole in the corner of the box. They should then add fine dry sand until enough weight has been added to produce either 1 kilogram (for the 2-lb. weight) or 500 grams (for the 1-lb. weight). Then have students seal the small filler hole with tape and mark the appropriate weight on the box.

Where a reduction in weight is required (for example, when converting 8 ozs. to 200 grams; 4 ozs. to 100 grams; or ½ oz. to 10 grams), a different procedure is recommended before the weight is put in the box and treated as above. If it is a ring type of weight, the teacher or an older student can cut the metal ring through with a junior hacksaw, and this will probably make a reduction of weight below the quantity required. Box the weight and treat it as before (adding sand) to adjust the weight suitably. If the smaller weight is of a solid rather than a ring type, then cut a "V" shaped piece of metal from it with the junior hacksaw; if necessary, enlarge the "V" until the weight is reduced below that required. Box the weight and treat it as before—adding sand and labeling the box appropriately. One of the virtues of this boxing system is that it obliterates entirely any markings on the old weight and creates the new one in a form that is easily convenient for remarking.

There are other similar procedures that students can use to adjust metal weights and convert them from avoirdupois to metric measures. Instead of sand, weight adjustments can be made by affixing clay or cement to the top of the weight. Where a weight needs to be reduced, the teacher or older student can drill a suitably sized hole to reduce the weight below the desired level and adjust accordingly by adding material into the hole until it is of the required weight. Whatever the method of adjustment used, it will be important to obliterate the old markings by taping over them or covering them in some way and then remarking them. Furthermore, it will be necessary to check the final product carefully against some standard metric weight as a control. It must be stressed that the improvised weights are of an approximate order only, and they should be checked on a finer measuring scale than those on which they will normally be used.

The following table indicates the approximate adjustment that can be made to common avoirdupois measures to transform them into useful metric alternatives:

2 lbs.	plus	approximately 93 grams converts to 1 kilogram
1 lb.	plus	approximately 46 grams converts to 500 grams
8 ozs.	minus	26 grams converts to 200 grams
4 ozs.	minus	13 grams converts to 100 grams
½ oz.	minus	4 grams converts to 10 grams

Scales and Spring Balances

Many domestic scales can be recalibrated by simply covering the old calibrations with plain paper and then remarking against standard weights. It is sometimes possible to simplify the number of calibrations and make the scale more useful for school purposes in this way. The larger type of parcel balances can easily be recalibrated by producing a new ring to stick over the existing one. Some may be available commercially, and these might be bought cheaply and recalibrated.

Most spring balances of the extension-type have a dual scale on them already. If this is so, it is easy for students to cover the avoirdupois side with either paper or tape. Spring balances that have only a single calibration in avoirdupois units can be converted quite easily with a plain scale affixed for calibration against standard metric weights.

Capacity Measures

Measures of capacity can be made from existing vessels. The following seem the most useful in conducting science activities:

- 2 pints will convert to a 1 liter measure by **adding** .054 liter
- 1 pint will convert to 500 milliliters by **adding** .017 liter

If a small measure is wanted (for example, a 10-milliliter measure), students will find that some bottle tops will serve excellently for this purpose. All these improvisations will call for a recalibration of the vessel. Students should use waterproof adhesive tape for this purpose. Semi-transparent plastic vessels can be marked by: (a) scratching a notch on the outside to the required height; (b) filling the vessel with a dark coloring material; and (c) marking the vessel evenly all round at the level of the liquid with waterproof ink.

Rulers

An easy method for recalibrating rulers is for students to apply ready-made calibrated tape to the ruler. One limitation of tape is its tendency to stretch, and it is very difficult to recalibrate longer measuring sticks without a considerable amount of "creep" on the tape. Tapes are likely to peel off if the rules are not well-cleaned before taping. Where longer rules are to be cut to a new length in metric units, students should cut them to a dead length, that is, without stop ends. This will make for a greater accuracy of use by the children, and it will be easier to affix tape or make fresh markings. If foot-long rulers are to be cut, they can be conveniently converted into one 20-centimeter length and one 10-centimeter length. These lengths will obviously have their uses. Yardsticks can also be used; however, there is a temptation to reduce them to 25 centimeter lengths, whereas most teachers feel it is far better for the child to get used to using measures that go up in even multiples of 10, that is, 10 centimeters, 20 centimeters, and so on. Emulsion paint is the most suitable for obliterating markings, as it is quick drying and covers well with one coat. However, incised markings will always show through. For the greatest permanency, students can cover the paint with a clear polyurethane varnish.

► *Part 4*
Testing and Analysis

Students can perform many simple tests and examine the properties of materials with simple procedures.

Constituent Mixtures

Sorting objects according to their attributes is an activity commonly undertaken in High/Scope classrooms. The physical analysis of mixtures of materials is a science activity that will extend this type of learning. Below are some examples of the kinds of constituent mixtures that students can explore.

Mixed Fruits

What types of different fruits make up the packages of mixed dried fruits commonly used in the kitchen? How many of each kind are in a package? Children must first identify the different fruits and put aside a specimen of each. Next, working in groups of three or four, children can start separating the different constituents. They can give them temporary identities for the purposes of the work, perhaps numbering or naming them arbitrarily. They can then answer questions such as the following: How many different types of fruit are there? How many fruits of each type are in the package? Are there equal numbers of each type in the mixture? What sort of fruit is most used in the mixture? What sort is used least? How do the fruits differ from each other in terms of size, color, shape, texture, taste, etc.? What are the real names for the fruits? Are the fruits whole or in parts? What parts of fruits are in the package (for example, there may be peel in some mixtures)?

The results can be set out both in chart or tabular form and as numerical statements. Examples of each of the identified fruits can be displayed together with its name, with pictures of the fruit in its natural state, and with information about its growth and nutrition.

Mixed Seeds

A procedure similar to that used for analyzing packages of mixed fruits can be applied to the packages of mixed seeds used to feed birds. An added benefit is that the analysis may require some additional investigation; while common seeds such as corn and sunflower seeds are in the mixture, teachers and students may find that less common seeds are also included (for example, thistle seed and various woodland plant seeds). Students may analyze a variety of mixtures. For example, mixed corn feed is relatively simple to separate and identify. Others mixtures may have more unusual elements. Students can generate the factors on which they want to compare the seeds in the mixture. In addition to obvious variables such as size, color, and shape, students may also notice other differences. For example, do the seeds have coverings? Are certain types of seeds more variable in appearance than others?

Mixed Candies

Packages of mixed candies are another obvious choice for this type of sorting activity. In addition to selling prepackaged mixtures, many stores offer bulk candy bins from which one can create a customized mixture of sweets. Students and teachers can choose their own combinations, deliberately varying the candies along a number of dimensions. As with the dried fruit, one attraction of this type of analysis is that you can eat the materials after you have compiled the results!

Ferrous Objects in a Room

How can all the ferrous (iron) objects in a room be found? First, children will need to experiment with magnets to establish that magnets only pick up, or stick to, ferrous materials. During this experimenting, children will be able to answer the following questions based on their experiences: Do magnets pick up anything without iron in them? Do magnets work through coverings such as paint? Paper? Plastic? Cloth? Other metals, such as brass or chrome plating?

To provide opportunities for all these investigations, teachers should have items and materials that exhibit all of the properties mentioned above. These items, which can be collected from everyday sources, include the following: iron hooks or screws covered with a thin layer of brass; solid brass hardware; plastic-covered curtain wire; uncovered curtain wire; metal strips covered with paper; metal strips covered with cloth; and pieces of cloth, pieces of wood, cardboard, paper, and plastic. There should also be painted iron items, aluminum pieces and copper wire, and metal and plastic paper clips.

When children have established to their own satisfaction the power of the magnet to detect ferrous items, they can begin examining any objects in the room that they suspect are ferrous. Children can work as individuals or in small groups. To record their results, children could make a plan of the room (or several plans, one for each area of the room) and label the different objects they test. They can also record their results on various charts and tables that they devise.

The Strength of Different Shapes

How strong are different shapes of building materials made from single strips of paper? Students can set up a testing bridge situation, as illustrated below. Make beams of different shapes (round, triangular) with rolled or folded paper, rest the beams on brick piers at either end, and place small boxes containing various weights of nails on the beams to test their strength (see Illustration A20).

Round beams. Have students cut three strips of paper, each 11" × 2", and roll each strip round a pencil to form a tube. This tube is the "beam" to be tested. Use cellophane tape about two inches from each end to retain the shape of the tube. Take the pencil out of the paper tube. Use two bricks at either end as piers, placed 4" apart, and place the three beams parallel to one another and ½" apart across the piers. Fill a small box or boxes with increasing numbers of nails to see how much weight the beams can support. Record the results. Next, have students place the piers 2" apart. Test this arrangement with loads of nails and have the students record the results. What effect does the spacing between the piers have on the ability of the beams to support the weight of the nails?

Triangular beams. Take three strips of paper cut to the same size as above (11" × 2") and fold each lengthwise into four equal parts. Open out the folded strip and refold it to make a triangular shape (see Illustration A20 on pg. 152). Keep the shape in place with narrow cellophane tape strips 2" from each end. This now makes a triangular beam to test. Place the three beams ½" apart on the test piers, set 4" apart, and test the strength of the beams as before; repeat this procedure with the supporting piers 2" apart and record the results. Have students compare the four test results in which the shape of the beam and the distance between the supporting piers have been varied. Which arrangement is the strongest? Which is the weakest?

Extensions. Students can extend the experiments by increasing and decreasing the distances between the two supporting piers. They can also try other beam shapes, such as flat strips or squared beams. Another variation would be to try different thicknesses of paper for the beam shapes.

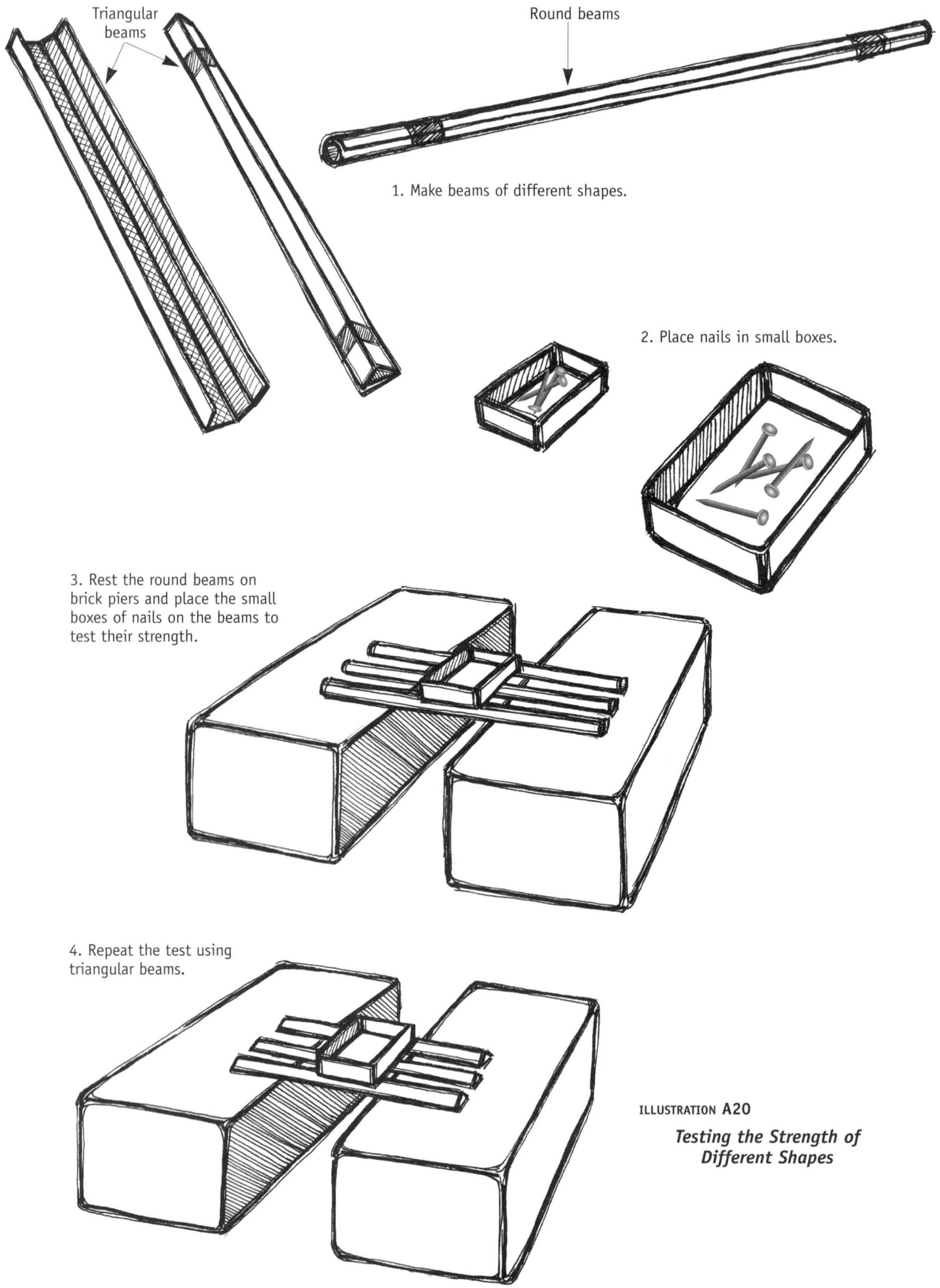

ILLUSTRATION A20

Testing the Strength of Different Shapes

Waterproof Properties of Different Materials

Waterproof quality is an important feature of many materials, especially when used for clothing and shelter. Testing materials can be an interesting activity for children who have already observed how their own clothes have either become wet or have resisted the rain.

Collect various materials of approximately the same thickness. Include, for example, cotton, nylon, wool, plastic sheeting, paper, and leather. Cut 4" (10 cm) squares of each material for testing. Place the test pieces on a large sheet of white blotting paper or other fairly absorbent paper. Make a colored solution with diluted ink, food coloring, or water soluble dye. Using a dropper (a pen filler, an eye dropper, a dropper bottle, or a drop falling from a paintbrush), have students put 10 drops of the color solution on each piece to be tested (see Illustration A21). Allow a set time, for example 3 to 5 minutes, to elapse. Then have the students make the following inspections:

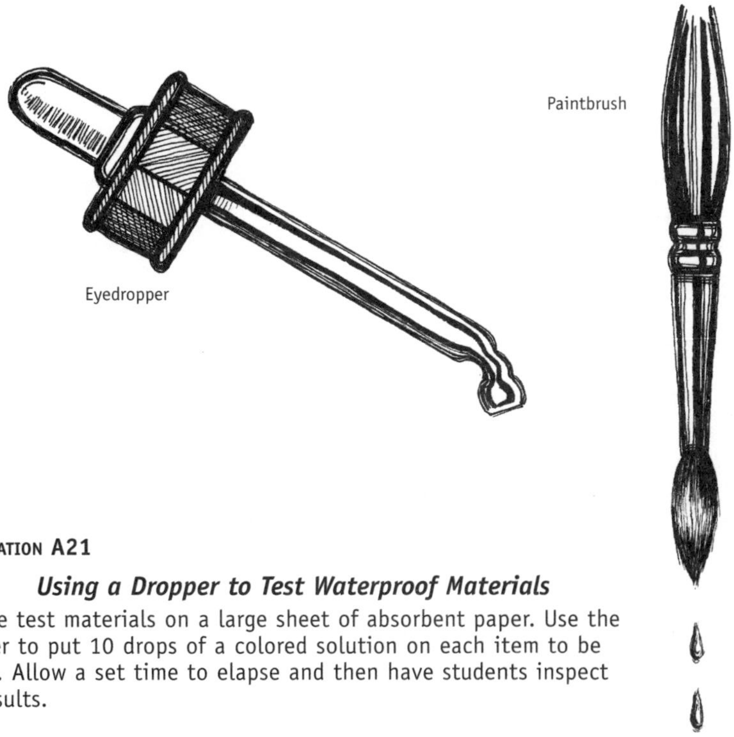

ILLUSTRATION A21

Using a Dropper to Test Waterproof Materials

Put the test materials on a large sheet of absorbent paper. Use the dropper to put 10 drops of a colored solution on each item to be tested. Allow a set time to elapse and then have students inspect the results.

• Inspect the blotting paper to see any markings left by the water soaking through the material. Have students note the evidence using a scale; for example: 0 = no penetration; 1 = some penetration; 2 = much penetration. Older students may develop a more elaborate scale.

• Inspect the material itself to see over what area the water had been absorbed. Have students note the evidence on a scale similar to the one(s) they devised above.

• Feel the material to see how wet the marked areas feel. Have students note the evidence on the scale; for example: 0 = not wet; 1 = wet only on the surface; 2 = damp throughout; 3 = wet throughout. Again students can devise their own scales for observing and recording the results.

As another way of representing the results, have students place the materials tested in their order of water resistance (from least to most, or vice versa). Have them discuss which material would be best for a raincoat. Which would let the most wet through? Are there times when you want a material to not be water resistant? What materials would serve those purposes?

Students can also investigate the reverse process of drying. Have them soak all the specimens that retain water and then hang them up on a line to dry in the same order as their waterproofness. At regular intervals, students can check the materials for dryness and record the results. Students can test for dryness using several criteria:

- Feel—Test the materials by gently rubbing them on the hand or cheek.
- Appearance—Do the materials look dry? Are they dry on just one side or on both sides?
- Smear test—Do the materials leave a moist smear when rubbed on a window?

After the results are recorded, have students place the specimens in order of speed of drying. How does this order compare to the order of waterproofness? Which materials would be most suitable for a coat? Are there situations where you would *not* want something to dry quickly? Which materials would be suitable for those purposes?

The question of how to waterproof material is a good extension of this investigation. For example, pose the question: How could you waterproof cotton cloth? Provide a supply of 4" (10 cm) squares of cotton cloth; you can cut up old shirts or handkerchiefs for this activity. (**Note:** Nylon fabric or synthetic materials generally are not useful for these experiments.) Through a dialogue approach with the children, have them examine and discuss the waterproofing properties of different coatings, such as oil, wax, fat, paint, and plastic stuck to the fabric. Display the results in chart form.

Seeds and Water

Mung bean seeds germinate quickly and are good for investigating the sprouting and growth of seeds. The seeds are inexpensive and are easily obtained through seed catalogs and garden stores. Local produce sellers may also help you locate packages of seeds. Here are some questions the students can consider:

- Will the seeds germinate on their own if one or two are left in the package?
- When are seeds usually planted outdoors? Why? Would seeds germinate more rapidly near the central heating system? What would happen to seeds put into the refrigerator?
- Do seeds need warmth only? Do seeds need moisture to germinate? Will they grow under water?
- Do seeds planted in soil all grow at the same rate?
- Is there a right way up to plant seeds? What happens if some are planted one way up and others the reverse way?

(**Note:** Try these experiments with large seeds such as broad beans as well as the smaller mung beans.)

Have students set up experiments with the seeds set in various ways: on moist cloth, on dry cloth, left on an open saucer; in moist soil, in dry soil, left on an open saucer; and in moist sand, in dry sand, left on an open saucer

Students can either work individually or in groups to carry out these experiments. See that the conditions are well-controlled, so that the dry soil and sand is really dry, and the moist soil is kept moist with exactly the same amount of water in each sample. In the case of the soil and the sand, see that the seeds are set at the same depths. Put the groups of experiments in a place where they will get the same amount of light and not be disturbed, but can be observed easily by the students. The results can be communicated in a variety of ways, through charts, diagrams, tape recordings of procedures, and a display of actual specimens.

If an interest in seeds develops among the children, there are several longer term experiments they can set up. It is worth remembering that in school, longer term science studies can go on in parallel with shorter term interests and activities. Here are some activities to try to answer students' questions about where plants come from and under what conditions they grow:

• Have students bring into the classroom a shovel full of top soil from any part of the area that apparently has no plants growing on it. Set this soil in a dish, keep it warm and moist, and see if anything grows.

• After a walk on open ground where the natural vegetation grows thickly, have students collect all the mud from their shoes. Put the mud in a dish, keep it warm and moist, and see if anything grows.

• If the school has an open site with garden space around it, have students clear and dig over a square yard of ground until it appears cleared of plants. Have them observe what happens as time goes on and record the results.

► *Part 5*

Safety and Science

The study of science is exciting, but it also holds potential hazards for students as well as for any wildlife that students may be examining. Below are some basic procedures and criteria to follow to ensure that science education at the elementary level is carried out safely.

Adult Supervision

It should be assumed that anything done in school, even with adult supervision, may be attempted out of school without any adult available. Adults should inform children of these potential risks and explain the dangers. It is also helpful for teachers to inform parents about the kinds of science activities being conducted in the classroom. This will not only help parents anticipate some of the activities that children might want to try on their own, but will also give them the opportunity to become involved and supervise their children as they investigate and extend their learning at home.

Sources of Heat

Sources of heat should be limited to the following:

- Hot air from a heating system in the classroom
- Heat from a conventional domestic radiator
- Warm water from a temperature-controlled tap (not from an electric kettle)
- Heat from the sun

Note that the above list precludes the use of the following:

- Open flames of any kind
- Electrical heaters and fans
- Gas burners and spirit lamps

Electrical Energy

Electrical energy should always be from battery powered sources. Electricity from a main electrical outlet should NOT be used in any work, even via a low-voltage supply. Where essential equipment such as computers are connected to main outlets, the plugs should be of a safeguarded pattern and never handled by the children. Where rechargeable cells are used, the charging process should be done privately by the teacher in the absence of the pupils. Plugging in batteries to charge them is not a task for children at school.

Tools

When tools are used in school they should be restricted to simple, nonpower ones, such as hammers, pincers, pliers, hand-operated screwdrivers (not battery driven for this age group), bradawls, gimlets. Drills are best avoided, and where possible predrilled materials should be available. When construction work is undertaken it should always be on a firm surface. If cutting is essential the materials cut should be of a "soft wood" or hardboard and cut with a junior hacksaw. A vice or clamp to hold material to be cut is essential. Cutting of hand-held material should be prohibited. Knives are not suitable for children to use in these contexts. Suitable scissors should be available for cutting, round-tipped for younger children and pointed for older children. Whenever questions about safety arise, the best solution is for the teacher to supply partly prepared material, leaving the final construction decisions to the children by means within their safe capabilities.

Living Material

If living material is used, it should be handled sensitively. Plants should be carefully treated, and only common species should be removed for use in school. It is best to grow plants in school from wild plant seed or seeds purchased specifically for that purpose. Investigations involving molds and fungi and dead material generally are best avoided. The likelihood of infection is too great to overlook. When animals are kept, they should be held under as near-natural conditions as possible. In the case of mammals, it will usually be best for them to be temporary visitors to the classroom; the care of mammals in schools, other than laboratories, is not easy. Small animals such as ants, snails, worms, butterflies, and moths should be also be housed in conditions as near their natural habitats as possible. When their life in school is at an end, they should be returned to their natural surroundings and a teaching point should be made of this procedure.

Kitchen Foods and Chemicals

Keep in mind that not all the substances found in the kitchen are safe. Safe items include soap, salt, sugar, washing soda, food coloring, lemon juice, vinegar, flour, olive oil, and dried foods. Unsafe items include bleach, oven cleaner, mineral spirits, kerosene, metal polish, and ammonia. Safety in the kitchen also means that items handled and used for experimentation should not be eaten. Keep extra supplies of these edible materials on hand; make sure that children understand when their investigations involve *eating* the materials and when they entail *handling* the materials.

Environmental Safety

There are a few basic rules to observe concerning outdoor work. These rules are for the benefit of the children as well as for the wildlife they will be studying:

• *Wear appropriate footwear.* Children's footwear should allow their feet to stay dry and should minimize the risks of slipping and falling.

• *Do not work alone outdoors.* Children should always work in pairs or groups and not take off to observe or collect materials on their own. If the location involves waterside activities, this will be an especially important rule.

• *Stay on the ground.* Tree climbing, rock climbing, and the like are not activities for school-inspired work for young children.

• *Avoid handling animals.* Remember that animals are best observed, not handled. Handling often injures the animal, and sometimes the animal can injure the handler. When children are taken on farm visits, they need to be prepared well beforehand about how to approach animals.

There is an increasing need to create an environmental awareness in children, one that includes a respect for all living things and the environment in which they live. Science education provides an opportunity for children to learn valuable lessons that will affect their attitudes and behavior for the rest of their lives.

Appendix II

The Development of Problem-Solving Skills

The Definition of Problem Solving

Problem solving is deliberate discovery making, or discovery by intent. A problem is a situation in which there are apparently more unknown elements than known elements. The solution depends on discovering how to either expose more known elements or deal directly with the unknown factors. The problem solver then reconstructs the balance of knowledge in the situation to favor the known over the unknown elements.

Problem Solving: The Way Into Science

Discovery methods are the basis of active learning in education, and this is certainly true in science. In fact, science education is all about problem solving. For students, successful problem solving is a liberating and motivating educational tool. For teachers to use these powerful forces, it helps to know something of the nature of problems and the process of problem solving.

Levels of Complexity in Problem Solving

The problem-solving process depends in part on the level of complexity of the problem. This process may be thought of as having four levels, listed below. In this hierarchical arrangement, levels II and III correspond to what most people accept as the definition of a problem. Level IV most closely resembles the disciplined and rigorous true scientific procedure.

- *Level I: The intuitive response.* The solver immediately recognizes the nature of the problem and its solution.

- *Level II: The procedural response.* The solver knows the rules or procedures for obtaining a solution.

- *Level III: The improvisation or trial-and-error approach.* The solver knows neither the solution nor the rules for obtaining it, but must improvise procedures to create the rules and obtain a solution.

- *Level IV: The methodological approach.* The solver has to reformulate the problem to make it manageable, to make the question answerable. Having reformulated it, the solver tests the validity of the new definition. Then the solver improvises rules and procedures to produce a solution.

It is important for teachers to understand and appreciate these levels so that they may better recognize where children, and they themselves, stand in relation to this process. Within each classroom, students' problem-solving operations will be at differing levels of complexity; the same student may operate at different levels in different contexts. At the primary grade level, most children will be at levels I and II; few, if any, will be at level III. By contrast, the complexity of academic and interpersonal problems that teachers deal with most of the time means that they are typically operating at levels III and IV.

Stages in the Problem-Solving Process

There are many types of problems and many possible models for solving them. To make this process comprehensible and workable for teachers, the process of solving a problem is divided into six identifiable stages:

- *Stage 1.* The solver recognizes that there is a problem with some element(s) that can be identified and labeled.

• *Stage 2.* The definable element(s) are examined. Other information is collected (for example, from memory, records, past experiences, observation of the environment, etc.). The information is placed in context and related to the parameters of the problem.

• *Stage 3.* The total information now available is analyzed and structured into possible plans for the solution(s).

• *Stage 4.* The plan considered most promising as a solution is selected from the possibilities for trial.

• *Stage 5.* The selected plan is used to address the problem.

• *Stage 6.* The effectiveness of the plan is assessed. If a satisfactory solution is achieved, the problem is regarded as having been resolved. If not, another one of the solutions is tried and/or the problem is further redefined and the cycle is repeated.

Qualities Required of the Problem Solver

The steps involved in problem solving are only one aspect of this complicated process. Equally important is the human dimension. In order to succeed in this process of problem solving, an individual needs to possess a variety of capacities. The problem solver should be able to:

• Perceive that a problem exists and be able to define it sufficiently and clearly so that it retains its essential characteristics

• Accept that he/she wants to and can solve the problem

• Bring to mind relevant information (concepts, experiences, observations), using memory and data-gathering skills, and assess whether the current information is sufficient for a solution

• Search actively for additional relevant information that may be useful in enlarging the knowledge base available in seeking a solution

• Establish links between components of the knowledge base (concepts, materials, facts) and the problem formulated so that the knowledge can be applied toward finding a solution

• Be brave enough to take a risk with a solution and face failure

• Be able to adopt a feasible and creative, but clear-sighted, approach to generating new solutions when previous attempts fail

• Make decisions based on the most likely solution and carry through in implementing them

• Overcome failure when a selected solution proves unsuccessful

• Monitor, criticize, and revise solutions and methods of attacking a problem

• Add new information to the store of rules when a preferred solution is successful or an improvement is effective

• Develop an increasing ability to work through processes carefully and systematically

• Make continuous attempts to match effort to initial goals, particularly in the face of negative results

• Possess these qualities, or show evidence of being able to develop them: curiosity and an inquiring mind; persistence and perseverance; and flexibility

• Begin to develop these mature attributes: independence of thinking; open-mindedness; and confidence when handling new and unknown ideas and situations

Index

M

N

O

P

Q

T

V

W

Y

About the Author

DISTINGUISHED BRITISH AUTHOR AND EDUCATOR

Frank F. Blackwell

has contributed to science education in a wide range of professional roles. Having earned an M.A. degree in Curriculum Studies, Blackwell began his career as a classroom teacher and headmaster at the early childhood, primary, and secondary levels. He became involved in the development of children's science curricula during the 1960s as a Nuffield Foundation Research Fellow in Science Education, serving on the team that developed the Nuffield Junior Science Project series. His contributions to science education extend to radio and television, where he has served as a scriptwriter, consultant, and researcher for science programming. For some 12 years, he was an Inspector of Schools in the London area. During this time, he also served as a university lecturer in teacher education and was seconded as director of a five-year national project in developing the use of new technologies in education in the early years. Blackwell then moved to the Netherlands to assume the post of Chief of Division with the Bernard Van Leer Foundation. After five years in this post he became Senior Advisor to the President of the High/Scope Educational Research Foundation. In addition to authoring this Elementary Science Activity Series, Blackwell is co-author of another High/Scope Press publication, *Elementary Curriculum: Science*, as well as Series Consultant for all the Elementary Curriculum Guides published by High/Scope Press.